Climber's Guide to

DEVIL'S LAKE

Climber's Guide to
DEVIL'S LAKE

THIRD EDITION

Sven Olof Swartling and Pete Mayer

Photographs by Eric Andre

Introduction by George J. Pokorny

THE UNIVERSITY OF WISCONSIN PRESS

The University of Wisconsin Press
1930 Monroe Street, 3rd Floor
Madison, Wisconsin 53711–2059

www.wisc.edu/wisconsinpress/

3 Henrietta Street
London WC2E 8LU, England

5   4   3   2   1

Printed in the United States of America

Library of Congress Cataloging-in-Publication Data
Swartling, Sven Olof.
    Climber's guide to Devil's Lake / Sven Olof Swartling and
Pete Mayer. — 3rd ed.
        p.   cm.
    Includes bibliographical references and index.
    ISBN 978-0-299-22854-5 (pbk. : alk. paper)
    1. Rock climbing—Wisconsin—Devil's Lake—Guidebooks.
2. Devil's Lake (Wis.)—Guidebooks. I. Mayer, Pete. II. Title.
    GV199.42.W62D488   2008
    796.522′30975576—dc22

                                         2008013450

CONTENTS

West Bluff Climbs

South Bluff Climbs

ILLUSTRATIONS

West of the Quarry Rocks

The Guillotine

East Rampart

WARNING

Rock climbing is a dangerous activity. You and your companions must employ good judgment to minimize the risks posed by climbing.

This guidebook directs you to known climbing routes, but it cannot provide for your safety if you choose to climb them. Other books are available on rock-climbing instruction, including safe climbing techniques, but no book is a substitute for qualified firsthand instruction.

No attempt has been made to identify hazards on the routes described within this guidebook. The ratings provided are an attempt to characterize the difficulty of a climb, not the danger. Climbers must assess the risk for themselves and assume responsibility. By choosing to climb, you agree to release the authors, publisher, and distributors from liability for any injury, including death, that might result.

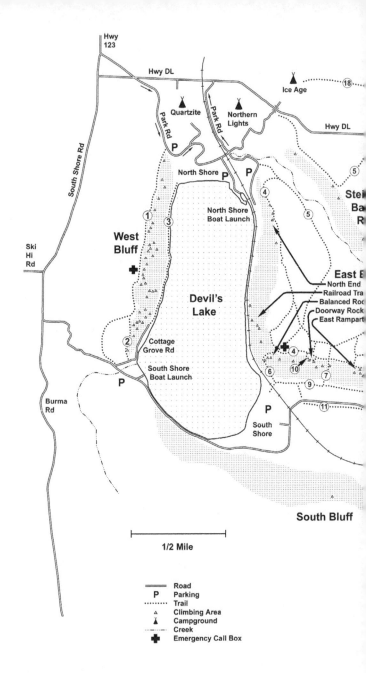

Devil's Lake State Park

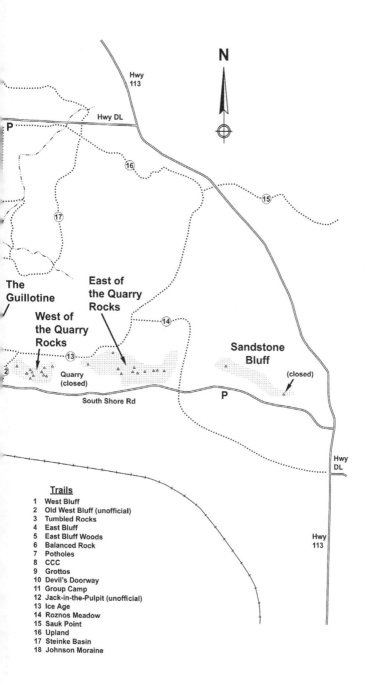

N

Hwy 113

Hwy DL

P

16

17

The Guillotine

East of the Quarry Rocks

West of the Quarry Rocks

15

14

13

Quarry (closed)

Sandstone Bluff

(closed)

South Shore Rd

P

Hwy DL

Hwy 113

<u>Trails</u>
1   West Bluff
2   Old West Bluff (unofficial)
3   Tumbled Rocks
4   East Bluff
5   East Bluff Woods
6   Balanced Rock
7   Potholes
8   CCC
9   Grottos
10 Devil's Doorway
11 Group Camp
12 Jack-in-the-Pulpit (unofficial)
13 Ice Age
14 Roznos Meadow
15 Sauk Point
16 Upland
17 Steinke Basin
18 Johnson Moraine

INTRODUCTION TO THE THIRD EDITION

George J. Pokorny

Since the initial printing of this guidebook in 1979, sport climbing, rock climbing, and mountain climbing have become increasingly popular. Additionally, the popularity of climbing walls has introduced a larger number of individuals to this activity and drawn them to outdoor climbing areas such as Devil's Lake. Although this guidebook has been corrected since the first edition and later printings, the format has changed little. This new edition has a considerable number of changes and additions. Additions include a diagram for the North Slope, a diagram and route descriptions for the South Bluff, diagrams and route descriptions for four new climbing areas in Steinke Basin, and other new climbs that have been reported to the authors. These additions result in over 100 new routes. Photographs of many of the climbing areas with representative routes indicated and GPS coordinates and elevations for most climbing areas have also been added. Another major change is the relocation of approach information to the beginning of each climbing area.

In the early days of climbing at Devil's Lake, during the 1920s and 1930s, there was little need for a formal guide to list available climbs. The small number of climbers had a few favorite climbs and did a lot of exploring without documentation. Information about climbs was spread by word of mouth, and few records were kept. With the organization of area climbing clubs in 1940, principally the Chicago Mountaineering Club (CMC) and the Iowa Mountaineers, more climbers came to the lake, and the need for reliable and detailed information about climbing routes became necessary. With the ever-increasing numbers of people being attracted to the sport, it became essential to bring to their attention routes that might otherwise be ignored and thus, it was hoped, spread the climbers over a larger area.

One of the earliest attempts to list climbs at Devil's Lake was a manuscript typed in 1941 titled *Rock Climbing in the Chicago*

Area by Jack Fralick. Unpublished, it listed over twenty routes on the East and West Bluffs and identified first ascents by members of the CMC (it's unclear if unaffiliated climbers made first ascents of the difficult routes, but it's unlikely that they did). Another guide, compiled by William Plumley in 1941 and also titled *Rock Climbing in the Chicago Area,* was a set of 8 × 10 inch black-and-white photos of climbing at Devil's Lake and elsewhere. It contained annotated material both historical and descriptive in nature.

With the growing organization of climbers in the early 1950s, the concept of a comprehensive rock-climbing guide to the entire Devil's Lake area was suggested. From time to time descriptions of climbing routes appeared in the CMC newsletters. In 1965 the CMC published a privately printed, limited edition guidebook to Devil's Lake, Bill Primak's *Guide to the Practice Climbing Areas of the Chicago Mountaineering Club, Devil's Lake Section.* This guide summarized the club's activities in the early 1950s and covered all climbing areas located in the park. Routes were described in terms of their problems rather than by a formal classification system. Much attention was given to older and traditional routes preferred for their similarity to problems a climber might encounter in the mountains. Primak was guided by the philosophy of the CMC at that time: "Climbing at the lake was not an end in itself, but rather a training ground for climbing to be done in the mountains."

In 1970 the University of Wisconsin Hoofers published *Climbers and Hikers Guide to Devil's Lake* by David Smith, Roger Zimmerman, and Errol Morris. This guide contained an exhaustive description of the popular climbing area on the East Bluff above the old Civilian Conservation Corps (CCC) camp. Unfortunately, only a few other East Bluff climbs and areas were described. The book is a fine example of the prevailing guidebook writing of the period.

In 1979 the first edition of the present book was published. It described most of the known climbs at the time and contained much information from the previous publications. In addition to diagramming and describing the climbs, the book provided the usual fare of natural history information as well as a hiking trail guide. The book had some shortcomings, the principal objection being the closed NCCS "F" grading system.

In 1985 Leo Hermacinski published *Extremist's Guide to Devil's Lake New Climbs*. This small guidebook listed several routes put up since the publication of the CMC guidebook. It does not embrace the entire lake area but concentrates on the East Bluff and Sandstone Area. Most of the climbs listed are in the 5.8 to 5.12 range. A revised edition of the *Extremist's Guide* was prepared but not published. Both of Hermacinski's guides include historic information on first ascents and first leads as well as other commentary.

The second edition of this book, published in 1995, changed the climbing ratings to the Yosemite Decimal System and added a significant number of climbing routes, including information on areas east and west of the old quarry and the New and Old Sandstone Areas. All of these areas are located on land purchased by Devil's Lake State Park since the first edition was published.

This third revised edition of *Climber's Guide to Devil's Lake* has been long in preparation and remains the definitive guidebook to all of the Devil's Lake climbing areas. It is the result of the time and effort of many individuals. All information from previous guides is included by permission.

PREFACE

Devil's Lake, in south-central Wisconsin near Baraboo, provides extraordinary climbing opportunities for the rock climber, sport climber, and mountaineer. The hard quartzite cliffs are a geologic anomaly in a region better known for its unusual sandstone formations. The rock terrain is hard, with sharp fractures, cracks, ledges, slabs, chimneys, and a variety of rock forms that make this the best rock-climbing area in the Midwest. Historically, Devil's Lake has provided enjoyment for hikers and walkers since the mid-1800s, and, doubtless, scrambling over the boulderfields and lower cliffs was also popular. It was not until 1927, however, that true Alpine-style rock climbing was introduced to Devil's Lake by Joe and Paul Stettner. Using the traditional climbing techniques of their native Bavarian mountains, the brothers trained countless numbers of midwesterners to the then unique sport of roped rock climbing.

In 1940 the Chicago Mountaineering Club was established, and the lake bluffs became the preeminent training area for the club's members. With scheduled monthly climbing weekends at Devil's Lake, the CMC trained additional midwesterners in the sport and prepared them for climbing in the mountains. The decade of the 1960s was marked by continuous raising of the standards, accomplished mostly by college students. John Gill made some exceedingly difficult climbs in 1960–61, and it was three to four years before anyone approaching his skill came along. Between 1960 and 1966 some fine routes were developed by climbers from the University of Chicago, with the best routes put up by Richard Goldstone and Steve Derenzo. In 1965–68 the Wisconsin Hoofers (the University of Wisconsin outing club) completed several difficult routes on the East Rampart that had not been previously climbed. Some of the climbers of that period were Dave and Jim Erickson, Sheldon Smith, Scott Stewart, Errol Morris, and Pete Cleveland. In recent years the popularity of rock climbing has brought enormous numbers of climbers to the lake from climbers' clubs, sport gyms with climbing walls, and unaffiliated individuals. The list of exceptional people climbing at the upper levels is large and growing, and since the 1980s the standard of climbing is well beyond what had previously been climbed. Climbers such as Eric Zschiesche, with his ascent of Rubber Man (5.13a) and solo of Zipper (B2), and Dave Groth, with his ascent of Ice (5.13b), reflect the high standard of lake ascents since the 1980s.

Devil's Lake State Park continues to suffer from overcrowding. Each year brings more hikers to the trails in addition to rock climbers. It is hoped that this guidebook will help to distribute climbers to areas of the lake that have been overlooked and underclimbed in the past.

Many individuals drawn to Devil's Lake were introduced to climbing in physical education classes, in sporting clubs with climbing walls, and by private instruction at Devil's Lake and elsewhere. The newcomers trained on climbing walls find that outdoor climbing at Devil's Lake differs from an indoor wall. Even talented indoor climbers soon discover that climbing outdoors in the elements can be profoundly different. The natural handholds and footholds are not always obvious, and friction at Devil's Lake, unlike that on an artificial wall, is minimal, to say the least. This does not detract from the beauty of climbing at the lake, which is a unique and satisfying experience.

We hope that the descriptions and grading of the climbs will enable climbers to select climbs that match their skill and ability and permit them to climb safely. Every effort has been made to include as many climbs as possible and grade them correctly in this guide. There may still be routes to be discovered, and we would be grateful if those who make discoveries or find errors would contact the authors or communicate with the Chicago Mountaineering Club.

ACKNOWLEDGMENTS

This guidebook edition builds upon two previous editions, the first of which was coauthored by William Widule. We are grateful for his contribution and for the assistance we have received from climbers and others over the years.

In preparation of this edition we appreciate the assistance of Bill Dietrich, who prepared much of the initial documentation for new climbs in Steinke Basin. We are especially grateful to Pete Cleveland for his valuable input on routes and ratings, Dave Groth for sharing his knowledge of the East Rampart, and Jay Knower of mountainproject.com. We would also like to thank Eric Andre and John DeBauche for recording GPS waypoints throughout the park.

Finally, we would like to thank Sue Swartling for her contributions and support over the years and Joy Mayer for her support during the writing of this edition.

Climber's Guide to
DEVIL'S LAKE

A GEOLOGIC AND NATURAL HISTORY OF THE BARABOO HILLS, WISCONSIN

Patricia K. Armstrong

Devil's Lake, Wisconsin, is one of the most beautiful and unusual areas in the Midwest. Precambrian seas formed the rock of the Baraboo Range, while Pleistocene glaciers shaped the topography and created the lake and its botanical environment. Devil's Lake itself (approximately 1 mile long and 0.6 mile wide) lies in a north–south gap cut by preglacial rivers through 500-foot-high bluffs. Cliffs and talus border the lake on three sides. The old river valley trends eastward away from the lake at its south end. Terminal moraines from the last glaciation block the valley east and north of the lake.

The Formation of the Baraboo Quartzite

The story of the Baraboo quartzite began 1.5 billion years ago in the Huronian period of the Precambrian era beneath a quiet sea. Incredible amounts of nearly pure quartz sand were deposited and accumulated at the bottom of this sea until the weight began to press the sediments together into sandstone. Iron oxide and silica (quartz SiO_2) in solution filled in the spaces and cemented the sand grains together. The pink, red, or purple color resulted from the incorporation of small amounts of iron and manganese. The original formation is thought to have been several miles thick, but weathering through the ages has reduced it to its present 4,000–5,000 feet.

Although most quartzite comes from sandstone that has been heated and pressed to fuse the sand grains together, microscopic study of the structure of the Baraboo quartzite reveals that it solidified slowly, without crystal distortion or high temperature mineral growth. This means that it is essentially sedimentary instead of metamorphic quartzite. Structures such as ripple marks, bedding planes, cross-current stratification, and pebble layers are perfectly preserved. Ripple marks are especially plentiful around Turk's Head on the West Bluff, and pebble layers can be found east of Devil's Doorway on the East Bluff. Areas in the original sea containing silt were lithified into

3

phyllite, which can be seen as thin, slaty rock, sandwiched between quartzite along the CCC Trail to The Guillotine.

Sandstone is dull and porous and breaks around its cemented sand grains, making rounded holds and sandy ledges. Quartzite, although identical to sandstone in chemical composition, is much harder and breaks across its cemented sand grains, producing a smooth, shiny surface and sharp edges. Thus, the cliffs at Devil's Lake are much better for climbing than the sandstone cliffs southeast at Gibraltar Rock. On the wall north of Leaning Tower and the cliffs to the east the cement between the sand grains has weathered away, leaving the rock more like sandstone than quartzite, with slightly different climbing conditions.

The Building of the Baraboo Range

About 1.45 billion years ago tectonic forces bent, cracked, and folded the huge thickness of Baraboo quartzite into a mountain chain that took the shape of an oval celery dish 10 miles wide and 25 miles long. It trends west–southwest from Interstate 39/90/94 to a few miles west of Rock Springs, with the village of Baraboo approximately in the middle. The north rim is lower in elevation, with nearly vertical bedding planes visible at the Upper and Lower Narrows of the Baraboo River. The south rim, in which Devil's Lake lies, is higher in elevation and slopes north at 20–25 degrees. This can be seen when looking across the lake at either the East or the West Bluff.

The quartzite was extremely brittle and fractured as it was bent, causing both horizontal and vertical cracks. Some slippage along these cracks occurred, as evidenced by pearl-like surfaces on the quartzite. Good examples of polished surfaces are at The Flatiron and a slanted rock in the Balanced Rock Trail that is now almost entirely covered by a flat rock and concrete. Some of the smaller cracks were subsequently filled in by silica solution and show today as white quartz-filled veins. A few wider ones have angular pieces of quartzite (breccia) mixed with the quartz. Examples are visible along the Potholes Trail on the East Bluff.

Tropical Islands in the Cambrian Sea

The next geologic event is one of the most interesting. About 600 million years ago the Baraboo Range, having undergone weathering for nearly a billion years, was submerged in a Cambrian sea. At this time the quartzite mountain roots (called monadnocks) stood 200–600 feet above the water as a tropical atoll. A white to tan sand mixed with quartzite blocks, boulders, and gravel eroded from the land and was deposited around these islands.

Studies of the orientation of cross-stratifications in the sandstone and in boulder/gravel accumulations around the islands, supported by paleomagnetic evidence, has led some scientists to postulate that the lagoon and atoll were located in a trade wind zone 10 degrees south of the Cambrian equator.

Fine examples of the cross-bedded Cambrian sandstone with quartzite boulders and gravel can be seen up the Koshawago Spring Valley (southwest of the lake) and at Parfrey's Glen (5 miles east of the lake). Near the north end of the East Bluff, in the vicinity of Elephant Cave, are other examples of conglomerate and sandstone formations. Elephant Rock itself bears evidence of wave polishing received when it rested on the shores of the Cambrian sea.

The Missing Record and Mysterious Rivers

Other sandstones, limestones, and dolomites were deposited around the quartzite islands until the Ordovician period some 430 million years ago. These can be seen at Gibraltar Rock and other places south and west of the Baraboo Range. From then until the advance of the Pleistocene glaciers 1 million years ago little is known. If other deposits were laid down, they have since been removed and nothing can be learned about them.

Sometime before the first advance of the glaciers, tremendous rivers cut through the quartzite, making the gaps now filled by the Baraboo River (Upper and Lower Narrows) and Devil's Lake itself. A well drilled at the south shore in 1990 apparently hit bedrock at 419 feet, making the old river channel where Devil's Lake lies approximately 1,000 feet below the present bluff tops.

Water-polished gravels called the Windrow Formation, believed to be Cretaceous (150 million years old), have been found above 1,460 feet in elevation on the bluffs. These gravels can be seen near the top of the Potholes Trail on the East Bluff. The potholes themselves are an enigma. They had to be formed at the base of a waterfall, yet they now stand near the top of the bluff. There are also huge boulders bearing potholes in the woods on top of the East Bluff.

The Pleistocene Glaciers

Several times between a million years ago and the present glaciers advanced and retreated over the face of the Midwest. In a majority of cases the most recent stage, called the Wood-fordian or Cary stage (13,000–16,000 years ago), blotted out all indications of preceding glaciation. The terminal moraine from this glacier averages 20–60 feet high and 300 feet wide. It snakes its way across Wisconsin and covers half of the Baraboo Range. Portions of this terminal moraine are seen as prominent forest-covered ridges at the north end of Devil's Lake and across the valley east of the south end of the lake. Devil's Lake lies between them, just outside the glaciated area.

Scientists long ago recognized a narrow island of topography in northwestern Illinois, southwestern Wisconsin, northeastern Iowa, and southeastern Minnesota as being very different from the rest of the Midwest. It was long thought to be nonglaciated and was called the Driftless Area. Today some scientists think that the Driftless Area was glaciated by earlier slow-moving glaciers that left little evidence of their passing. Small round kettle ponds west of Baraboo, mixed gravel and sand, till-like deposits near Leland, and large boulders out of place, like the pothole rocks on top of the East Bluff, may indicate that glaciers were in the Driftless Area before the Woodfordian era.

In any case, from 12,500 to 30,000 years ago the climate around Devil's Lake was like that in the high Arctic today. Temperatures dropped below freezing several times during the day and night. Water trapped in the cracks and joint planes of the quartzite repeatedly froze and thawed. This frost plucking/ice wedging caused huge blocks to topple from the cliffs, making the talus below. Cleopatra's Needle, Turk's Head, Tomahawk Rock, Balanced Rock, and Devil's Doorway were produced in this manner.

The last glacier advanced over the Baraboo Hills about 13,000 years ago and stood stationary around Devil's Lake for 600 years. It filled in the ancient river valley with 2 billion cubic feet of debris. Some of it slumped down into the preexisting boulderfields to form the cool depressions along the Grottos Trail. Runoff from the melting ice brought the sand for the swimming beaches and filled the gap between the bluffs and moraines with the waters of Devil's Lake.

Finally, the glaciers disappeared, and the ancient river (which used to run through the Lower Narrows and Devil's Lake Gap) was diverted elsewhere. Devil's Lake today is several hundred feet above the Wisconsin River. It is 45 feet deep, is fed by springs and two small creeks, and has no surface outlet. The water is clean and cold and lost by seepage and evaporation. Its beautiful setting, surrounded by pink cliffs and boulder-fields, makes many habitats for plants and animals and an attractive place for outdoor sports of all kinds.

Plants and Animals

The uniqueness of the Devil's Lake area owes much to its geo-logic past. Without the quartzite bluffs and boulderfields, gla-cial lakes, outwash plains, and moraines there would be less varied habitats for plant and animal life. The area not covered by the most recent glaciation acted as a refugium where plants and animals could live while the rest of the area was under ice. These relic communities from the past spread out and met other plant communities reinvading the newly bared glacial landscape from the north and south. About 950 species of vas-cular plants grow in the park, approximately 40 percent of all the species of vascular plants in the whole state.

On top of the bluffs are upland forests composed primarily of oaks with an understory of red maple. There are also a few hickories and basswoods. On dry southern exposures juniper and rare plants from the south (like prickly pear cactus) can be found. Hill or goat prairies have tall prairie grasses, creamy baptisia, lead-plant, bush clover, shooting star, yellow star grass, bird's foot violet, and other plants typical of the grasslands to the south and west of Wisconsin.

The cliffs and boulderfields are home to white pine, paper birch, mountain ash, Virginia creeper and poison ivy vines, red elderberry, alum root, pale corydalis, cup plant, many species of ferns, and hundreds of different mosses and lichens. Narrow glens and canyons hold the most exotic plants, such as hem-locks, yellow birch, blue beech, twisted-stalk, Canada may-flower, dwarf ginseng, trailing arbutus, and shining club moss. Cold grottos at the base of the boulderfield have rare northern plants like mountain maple, beaked hazel, shin leaf, oak fern, palm tree moss, and rose moss. Nearby lowlands have kettle ponds, wet meadows, sand prairies, and tamarack-sphagnum bogs.

Because of the rich assortment of habitats and plants, there are a great number of animals too. Approximately 110 species of birds nest here, and more than 100 additional species can be seen in migration. The rare peregrine falcon used to nest at the lake. Of particular interest are turkey vultures, pileated woodpeckers, whippoorwills, and winter wrens. Occasionally, bald eagles and ospreys fly over the bluffs.

The largest mammal in Devil's Lake State Park is the white-tailed deer. Gray and red foxes also reside but are rarely seen. Many small mammals, such as raccoons, woodchucks, squirrels, and chipmunks, are common visitors to the campgrounds. There are forty kinds of mammals altogether.

Ten species of snakes dwell within the park, including the beautiful yellow phase of the timber rattlesnake. This snake is not common, however, and is very secretive and rarely seen. There are also eight types of frogs, one type of toad, four types of turtles, and five types of salamanders. In the lake itself are northerns, walleyes, rainbow and brown trout, small- and largemouth bass, perch, and several types of panfish.

Vulnerable areas where rare and unusual plants or animals live need to be protected from trampling and overuse. Most people do not recognize rare plants, and indiscriminate hiking and snowmobiling, cutting firewood, and vandalizing rocks have been very harmful. Efforts should be made to restrict human activities in areas of special scientific interest (like Parfrey's Glen, the Grottos, and the South Bluff). Only in this way can their unique flora, fauna, and geologic attractions be saved for future generations to enjoy.

Humans and the Baraboo Hills

At the time that the last glacier was melting from the Baraboo Hills, Paleo-Indians were using rock shelters west of the lake. Five hundred generations of Native Americans knew Devil's Lake before the coming of the Europeans. The effigy mound builders built their bird, lynx, and bear mounds around the lake some eight hundred years ago. In more recent times several Indian tribes, notably the Ho-Chunk, gave their names and interpretations to the lake.

The Ho-Chunk camped at the lake until 1900 and described the forces that shaped it as a battle between thunderbirds and water spirits. Another legend tells of a great meteorite that produced the Devil's Lake Gap and cliffs. The Ho-Chunk name for the lake was Ta-wa-cun-chuk-dah or Da-wa-kah-char-gra, meaning Sacred Lake, Holy Lake, or Spirit Lake. Other Indians called it Minni-wau-kan, meaning Bad Spirit Lake or Mystery Lake. Mysterious musical hammering sounds were supposedly the source of the intrigue.

While doing research on the lichens and mosses of Devil's Lake, I noticed that when the early morning sun warmed the boulderfields or when the evening shadows crept across the rocks, strange melodious "plonks" occurred on the average of one to two per minute in one small area. These heat expansion/cool contraction sounds, when heard across the distance of the lake and supported by echoes and sounds from other areas, could be the reason for the Indian names.

French voyageurs and missionaries came south from the Great Lakes and north from the Fox River valley in the 1630s. Settlers began to arrive in the 1830s. Because of the sandiness of the glacial outwash in this area and the rockiness of the Baraboo Range, much of the land was unsuited for farming and thus remained somewhat wild through the years.

The popularity of Devil's Lake as a vacation retreat dates to the mid-1800s. From 1866 to the early 1900s the Minniwauken House (later Cliff House) served thousands of tourists at the north end of the lake. After the railroad was completed in 1873 up to eighteen passenger trains a day went by the lake, nine each way. Side-wheel steamers plied the waters. Kirkland, at the south end of the lake, had more rustic cabins and picnic grounds for the public.

Quarrying operations and proliferating resorts led many local people to seek state park status for Devil's Lake. After a long battle the lake became Wisconsin's third state park in 1911. The original purchase was $128,000 for 1,100 acres. (In 1919 the quarry operations were finally removed from the park.)

During the 1930s a Civilian Conservation Corps camp was built a mile east of the lake at the south end. It consisted of fifteen buildings and had its own water and sewage systems. Two hundred young men age eighteen to twenty-five arrived at the camp in 1935 and did various jobs throughout the area.

They built trails, signs, picnic tables, buildings, and roads. They removed dangerous or infectious plants. They learned about the plants and the park and conducted tours on the bluffs. The CCC program ended in 1941, but the camp served to house employees of a nearby ammunition plant from 1942 to 1945. All the buildings are gone now.

Today Devil's Lake State Park's 9,000 acres host over a million visitors a year. An active naturalist program of hikes and slide shows helps them understand the natural history of the park and the necessity to protect it from the pressures of tourism. In 1971 the park became part of the Ice Age National Scientific Reserve. Users of the Midwest's most popular park must be willing to sacrifice their own selfish comforts for the preservation of this unique and beautiful area.

GUIDEBOOK USER'S INFORMATION

General Overview

This guidebook describes rock-climbing routes in Devil's Lake State Park near Baraboo, Wisconsin. The bluffs consist largely of typical alpine talus about 400 feet high, made of rocks ranging in size from small boulders to some as large as a room. Most climbing is done on the broken-up summit cliffs above the talus. In some areas rock outcroppings also appear on the lower slopes, for example along the railroad tracks on the east shore of the lake. Climbing areas are spread out on the bluffs surrounding the lake and along South Shore Road east of the lake. Over 100 named climbing areas are included, covering more than 1,700 climbing routes.

Climbing areas on the east side of the lake, commonly referred to as the East Bluff, are divided into smaller groups. The descriptions start with Sandstone Bluff at the far eastern end of the bluff near Highway 113 and continue west along South Shore Road, north along the lake, then northeast of the lake (Steinke Basin). Each group is further divided into individual climbing areas.

Climbing areas on the west side of the lake, commonly referred to as the West Bluff, are also divided into smaller groups. Descriptions start with Stettner Rocks in the south and continue north. Each group is further divided into individual climbing areas.

The small climbing area on the South Bluff (southeast of the lake) is also included.

This guidebook provides maps, diagrams, approach and route descriptions, elevations, GPS waypoints, and photographs to help you locate the individual climbing areas. We feel this information will help you locate each climbing area, especially where no trails exist. We also feel that minimizing the duration of your hike in will reduce the impact on the environment.

Diagrams have been provided for most of the climbing areas. Numbers on the diagrams denote the location of described climbs. In areas where climbs are located close to one another, multiple climbs are listed under a single number. Shaded portions on the diagrams indicate areas at a higher elevation. Magnetic north is indicated by an arrow.

During the early climbing years at Devil's Lake many first ascents were not recorded. Because of this great uncertainty regarding the real first ascent, descriptions omit mention of the first ascent or first lead of a route.

Waypoints and Map Coordinates

The map coordinates included for each climbing area can be used with GPS receivers by entering the coordinates as waypoints. Map and compass users will also find this information useful for navigating within the park. Waypoints are provided in two formats, and a complete list is provided at the end of the book.

Most GPS users are familiar with the latitude/longitude coordinates commonly used for recording GPS waypoints. Coordinates are also provided using the UTM (Universal Transverse Mercator) System, which is more valuable for map and compass users.

A GPS user should simply make sure the GPS receiver is set to the WGS 84 (or NAD 83) datum and then enter the waypoints as latitude/longitude or UTM coordinates. It is typically as simple as selecting WGS 84 from the setup screen. See the GPS receiver's instruction manual for more information.

Map and compass users should understand how to decode a UTM coordinate. The first number of a coordinate is the zone. The entire park (and a large chunk of the Midwest) is within UTM zone 16. The zone is sometimes followed by a letter called the zone designator, which is T for all locations within the park. The second number is the easting, and it may be followed by the letter E. The easting number is in meters, and it gets bigger as you go from west to east within the zone. The last number is the northing, and it is often followed by the letter N. The northing is the distance north of the equator in meters. The easting and northing are the key pieces of information; they are always given in this order. For example, the full UTM coordinate for Cleo Amphitheater is UTM 16T 278303E 4810809N. It has an easting value of 278,303 meters and a northing value of 4,810,809 meters.

The real value of the UTM coordinate system shows when navigating from one coordinate to another. The difference in the easting numbers indicates how far (in meters) you need to hike to the east or west. The difference in the northing number tells how far you need to travel north or south. With the information in this guide you can easily figure out the distance between two climbing areas. For example, to navigate from The Frigate (UTM 16T 278281E 4810726N) to Cleo Amphitheater (UTM 16T 278303E 4810809N), you must walk 22 meters east and 83 meters north. To go to a higher easting number you go east. To go to a lower easting number you go west. The same principle holds true for the northing number. To go to a higher northing number you travel north. To go to a lower northing number you head south.

Elevations

Elevations given in this guidebook are an approximate average of the base elevations of significant climbs within an area. Some climbing areas also list an approximate elevation for the top of the routes. Please note that some climbing areas do not have continuous climbs from bottom to top.

Altimeters that rely on barometric pressure, such as those used during the writing of this book, are easily influenced by the weather. For best results, calibrate your altimeter at a known elevation before heading to a new climbing area. It is possible for changing weather to cause an altimeter to be off by 200 feet or more. When the weather improves during the day (rising barometer), your altimeter may read lower than reality. When clouds move in or rain threatens (falling barometer), your altimeter will tend to read higher than it should. Some GPS receivers with built-in altimeters will automatically try to correct for changes in barometric pressure by using the signals received from space. The result is not terribly accurate due to trees and bluffs that block and reflect too much of the signal, so you may decide to disable this feature to prevent your altimeter from wandering on days when the barometer is steady.

To calibrate your altimeter set the elevation to 970 feet when standing on portions of the South Shore Road that closely follow the lake, on the Tumbled Rocks Trail, or in the picnic areas at either end of the lake. Set the elevation to 1,065 feet in the

CCC parking lot or to 1,210 feet at the Steinke Basin parking lot. These numbers should get you to within plus or minus 25 feet of your desired location unless the weather is changing. NOTE: The elevations listed in this book were corrected using simultaneously recorded barometer readings to provide for the best possible accuracy.

Climbing Ratings

The Yosemite Decimal System (YDS) with a "+" added within grade 5.9 is used throughout this guidebook. In addition, B1, B2, and B3 are used to rate a few short climbs or boulder problems.

Rating Examples

The following climbs are generally taken to be indicative of their class and are frequently used as benchmarks for rating other climbs.

Although all attempts were made to be as uniform as possible in assigning ratings, differences in individual build, technique, and preference make some climbs seem harder or easier than their ratings.

1	The CCC Trail	5.10a	Congratulations
2 & 3	East Bluff talus slope	5.10b	Cheatah
4	Lost Face access gully	5.10c	Jack the Ripper
5.0	Easy Street	5.10d	Flake Route
5.1	The Little Thing	5.11a	Black Rib
5.2	Anemia	5.11b	Callipigeanous Direct
5.3	Boy Scout	5.11c	Hourglass
5.4	Beginner's Delight	5.11d	No Trump
5.5	The Bone	5.12a	Double Clutch
5.6	Brinton's Crack	5.12b	New Light Waves
5.7	Vacillation	5.12c	Steak Sauce
5.8	Roger's Roof	5.12d	Phlogiston
5.9	Upper Diagonal	5.13a	Modern Art
5.9+	Chiaroscuro	5.13b	Ice

Climbing Ethics

More than any other sport, rock climbing needs an ethical code with respect to the environment. Unlike most other forms of recreation, the very essence of rock climbing depends on the natural scene, a nonrenewable resource. The popularity of rock climbing is causing a tremendous human impact on the cliffs and the surrounding land at Devil's Lake.

The future of climbing is dependent on a minimum-impact approach. The ecological systems have only a brief growing season between melting of the last snows and the onset of long harsh winters. Rock formations broken by the deliberate or thoughtless action of unmindful climbers cannot mend themselves or recover. They are a rather fragile, easily marred, and nonhealing climbing medium. Federal and state agencies as well as private organizations and owners are increasingly concerned about the protection of this environment. In some areas limitations on use have been imposed. Continuous access to the rock walls at Devil's Lake and elsewhere will depend upon the care with which they are treated.

Therefore, climbers are urged to consider the cumulative effects of climbing activities and follow a code of ethics that will preserve rock-climbing areas and leave them accessible to future generations. Self-restraint and discretion must be employed by every individual in order to preserve the climbing areas and the sport. It is difficult to suggest a set of rules or principles to govern the conduct of people who love freedom and who climb because it makes them feel free. Inasmuch as no specific code of rock-climbing ethics exists, it is recommended that the guidelines given here be followed as a minimum approach to good environmental conduct.

1. *Climb clean.* Do not use protection devices such as pitons and bolts. These will permanently deface the rock and degrade the route for subsequent climbers. Nuts and mechanical camming devices have replaced pitons at Devil's Lake because, in addition to affording adequate protection, they leave the rock intact. On a few routes an occasional "fixed" piton may be encountered. These pitons were left in place to protect the rock and should not be removed.

2. *Use chalk sparingly if at all.* Like other climbing aids, the use of chalk is controversial. The usual argument is that it leaves the cliffs unsightly, spoiling the beauty and visual impact. In addition, it marks holds for the next climber, spoiling the climb for others. Finally, heavy use of chalk is a form of pollution that rains do not wash away for some period of time. If chalk must be used, it should be used sparsely and only on the most severe pitches.

3. *Protect the flora.* The area beneath a climbing route or a belay stance above the climb is frequently off the trail and may be near flowers or a grassy patch. If the climbing party is large, the impact of many footprints may be too much for the delicate microenvironment to bear. This situation is difficult to resolve. If at all possible, try to refrain from overuse of such areas or stay on the rocks near the start of the climb while awaiting your turn to climb. Also, when hiking or approaching a climb, climbers should stay on existing trails as much as possible to minimize the abuse of delicate plant life. Another abuse perpetrated by climbers is the "gardening" of ledges or holds, frequently removing entire plant colonies from the cliff face. This practice is difficult to defend. It is hoped that awareness of the problem will lead to a certain amount of restraint.

4. *Protect the trees.* Continuous use of trees for belay and rappel anchors can damage and even kill them.

5. *Don't litter.* Climbers who carry food and beverages with them should carry all resulting trash and garbage back to suitable trash containers. Additionally, the concerned climber will pack out litter left behind by the thoughtless person who will always be with us, no matter how high the general level of consciousness becomes.

6. *Be considerate of fellow climbers.* Respect for other climbers should be expressed in a sportsmanlike manner. Don't hog climbs. It is very inconsiderate to drop several ropes on nearby climbs and then climb one route at a time. This may "reserve" climbs for your party, but it prevents others from climbing in the same area. As Devil's Lake becomes more crowded, climbers must learn to share the limited routes with others.

7. *Observe Devil's Lake park regulations.* The climbing areas described in this guidebook are entirely within Devil's Lake State Park. Therefore, climbers should be familiar with park regulations as outlined in the visitor's guide available at park headquarters. Park users have a responsibility to become familiar with these regulations and abide by them.

Safety

Your enjoyment of climbing at Devil's Lake will be greater if you follow a few simple safety rules:

1. *Do not climb alone.* Novices should climb with experienced climbers or join a club to learn and practice good technique.

2. *Climb with proper equipment.* Roped climbing at Devil's Lake requires a 120–150-foot climbing rope. For top-roping climbs a 200-foot rope, a set of nuts or cams, and several long pieces of webbing (10–30 feet) are recommended.

3. *When top roping, put in a minimum of three separate anchors.* When climbing on ropes you have not set up, make sure the rope is correctly set up. Check anchors and slings frequently for dislodgment and wear.

4. *Develop a "feel" for the friction on Devil's Lake quartzite.* Remember that wet rocks, particularly when lichen covered, are virtually frictionless.

5. *Be aware that you may encounter wasps and rattlesnakes.* Although wasps can be present at any time of the year (except during the winter months), they are most prevalent in the fall. Rattlesnakes are found in the park and occasionally encountered in less climbed areas.

6. *Do not dislodge rocks.* If rocks are accidentally dislodged and fall, warn those below by calling "rock." Try to discourage thoughtless persons from throwing rocks. Wear a helmet!

7. *Learn to recognize poison ivy.* This plant grows in abundance near some trails and climbing areas.

8. *Know where to go for help in an emergency.* Carry a cell phone, but remember that reception may be unavailable in portions of the park. Emergency call boxes are located on the West Bluff above Prospect Point Rampart (near the Great Chimney) and on the East Bluff at the intersection of the East Bluff Trail and the Balanced Rock Trail. Phones may also be available at some trailheads.

EAST BLUFF CLIMBS

EAST BLUFF

The East Bluff, by popular convention, is the entire bluff extending south along the east shore of the lake, turning east at Balanced Rock and extending 2.5 miles east to Highway 113.

Three maintained trails reach up the talus to the top of the bluff: Balanced Rock Trail, Potholes Trail, and CCC Trail. A fourth maintained trail, East Bluff Trail, starts at the north end of Devil's Lake and follows the crest of the bluff. An unofficial Jack-in-the-Pulpit Trail begins near the group campground road east of the CCC parking area and ends at the Ice Age Trail/Upland Trail. Farther east near the Sandstone Bluff, the Roznos Meadow Trail reaches up the wooded slope ending at the Ice Age Trail/Upland Trail. This trail does not pass near any climbing areas. There are also climbers' trails leading up to the Old and New Sandstone Areas. Of course, it is possible to reach any part of the bluff by going up boulderfields or the wooded slopes.

Parking is available at the South Shore picnic area and 0.5 mile east, at the beginning of the CCC Trail. Parking is also available below the Old Sandstone Area, at the North Shore picnic area, and at a parking area along Highway DL for climbs in Steinke Basin.

Major Rock Groups of the East Bluff

Near the east end of the East Bluff, 2.5 miles east of Devil's Lake, is the Sandstone Bluff, a summit band 0.4 mile long. Moving west, the next group of outcroppings is East of the Quarry Rocks, which consists of small outcroppings scattered across the upper half of the bluff. West of the quarry is West of the Quarry Rocks, a group of relatively small outcroppings covering the entire height of the bluff.

NOTE: *The quarry itself is closed to public use.*

East of the upper portion of the CCC Trail is a group of outcroppings called The Guillotine. West of The Guillotine is East Rampart, an almost continuous band of summit buttresses with the highest concentration of climbs. It is the most popular climbing area.

After a break in the summit band, the cliff resumes west of Potholes Trail with the largest and most expansive cliff area, Doorway Rocks, which includes the spectacular Devil's Doorway. Continuing westward the outcroppings are discontinuous until Balanced Rock Wall, named after a large boulder perched near the edge. The bluff then turns abruptly north and follows the shoreline.

The north leg of the East Bluff has a pronounced diagonal decline to the north. It is made up of several distinct bands. Horse Rampart, Birthday Rocks, and Railroad Amphitheater are interesting areas in the lower, southern rock band. At the north end of the lake are a few small outcroppings: Monolith Blocks, Tomahawk Rocks, and Elephant Rocks. East of the north end of the lake off Highway DL is Steinke Basin Rocks, which consists of four low rock outcroppings.

In general there is little difference between climbing on any of the bluffs with the exception of the sandstone areas. The greater concentration of longer, difficult climbs and the well-developed trail system on the East Bluff between the CCC Trail and Balanced Rock Trail tend to draw more climbers.

SANDSTONE BLUFF

The Sandstone Bluff is at the eastern end of the East Bluff near Highway 113. It consists of a summit band approximately 2,000 feet long. The sandstone is generally of good quality, unusual for southern Wisconsin. In many places quartzite pebbles are embedded in the sandstone.

The Old Sandstone Area at the western end of the summit band is the most prominent, with climbs up to 75 feet high. The New Sandstone Area at the eastern end has short, difficult, overhanging climbs. It is currently closed to climbing. The section of bluff extending between the Old Sandstone Area and the New Sandstone Area is interrupted by a great number of ledges and gullies and offers no climbing. The south-facing slopes in this area are home to many varieties of thorny plants, so cross-country travel between the two climbing areas is not recommended.

Old Sandstone Area (Diagram 1 E)

APPROACH: A small parking area is located 1.25 miles east of the CCC parking area on a small rise along the south side of South Shore Road. An unmarked trail starts across from the parking area and leads to the west end of Old Sandstone Area. The Roznos Meadow Trail crosses South Shore Road 350 feet west of the trail leading to Old Sandstone Area.

Waypoint 1: Parking for Old Sandstone Area
    UTM 16T 282415E 4810064N
Waypoint 2: Old Sandstone Area
    UTM 16T 282530E 4810238N
Base Elevation: 1,104 feet

ROUTES:
1   MAMMALARY MAGIC, 5.10a. An enjoyable slab route with one large quartzite pebble and several smaller ones embedded in the sandstone. Many variations are possible.

Sandstone Bluff. Photo: Sven Olof Swartling.

2 WOBBLY DIHEDRAL, 5.9. Slightly left-leaning, overhanging dihedral.

3 HAS BEEN, 5.10c. A long, narrow face between Wobbly Dihedral (route 2) and Chez's Chimney (route 4). The focus of the route is a large quartzite pebble on the face.

4 CHEZ'S CHIMNEY, 5.4. Obvious chimney.

Old Sandstone Area

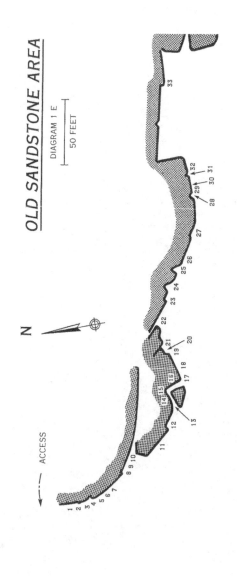

OLD SANDSTONE AREA

DIAGRAM 1 E

50 FEET

N

ACCESS

Routes 5–7 have the same start. The roof referred to is 30 feet up.

5 TEAM ARTURO, 5.10b. Climb to the left side of the roof. Move up and left using the crescent-shaped crack. Continue straight up, staying left of the pebbles.
Variation, ARTURO DIRECT, 5.10b. Crack 5 feet right of Chez's Chimney (route 4). Joins Team Arturo at the upper crack.

6 ALLIGATOR WALL, 5.9. Climb to the left side of the roof. At roof level, step up and right over the roof. Continue up and slightly left on the embedded quartzite pebbles.

7 DANCING MADLY BACKWARDS, 5.10b. Climb to the left side of the roof, then traverse right to the end of the roof. Step up and left over the roof onto some pebbles. Continue up and slightly left to a difficult finish.
Variation, 5.11c. Start directly below the right end of the roof.

8 CURVING CRACK, 5.8. Crack curving slightly right. The hardest move is at the top.

9 DECEPTIVE, 5.10c/d. Start 4 feet right of Curving Crack (route 8) on small, sharp flakes. Climb up and slightly right to a rest spot, then straight up. Finish just right of Curving Crack.

10 OUT THERE, 5.9. Start near dirty chimney/crack. Climb straight up to small overhang at 20 feet. Continue up and right past several flakes. Finish at tree.

11 FREAKY FACE, 5.8–5.10d. A steep, clean face with several variations.

12 5.7. Crack in inside corner. When the crack ends 10 feet below the top, continue on rounded corner to top.

13 SEPSEN WALL, 5.12a/b. Climb through obvious notch in overhang. Continue up and slightly left on wall above.

14 UBERSCHMITT, 5.12a. Start in inside corner. Pull up over right end of big overhang. Continue on wall above.

15 TARANTULA, 5.10b. Same start as Uberschmitt (route 14). Use underclings to exit left around the roof, then climb to the big overhang. Finger traverse right to join Gargantua (route 16).

16 GARGANTUA, 5.10b. Climb crack in nice-looking roof to an easier crack leading almost to the top. Finish on short upper face.

Curving Crack (Diagram 1 E, route 8). Climber: David Harrison.
Photo: Sven Olof Swartling.

Variation, 5.9. Avoid the roof. Same start as Baker Street (route 17), then traverse left above the roof and join Gargantua crack.

17 BAKER STREET, 5.10d. Follow thin, curving crack up and slightly left. Continue on face with small, sharp holds. Don't get too close to Gargantua (route 16).

18 PACIFIC OCEAN WALL, 5.11d. Ascend left side of wave. A hard pull leads to more difficult climbing in the thin groove above.
WAVE MECHANICS, 5.12c. Climb overhanging wave starting 5 feet right of Pacific Ocean Wall.

19 SEVEN SEAS, 5.11b. Climb right side of wave. A lunge to a jug hold on the corner (wave crest) is needed. Avoid the tree.

20 AMERICAN BEAUTY CRACK, 5.8. Slightly overhanging, off-width crack.

21 EVERLEIGH CLUB CRACK, 5.8. Finger-sized layback crack left of gully.

22 5.9. Start climb in dihedral. Exit left and finish on wall above.

23 5.7. Crack.

24 5.8. Crack.

25 PTOOEY, 5.8. An interesting and awkward crack in the inside corner that tends to spit the climber out rather quickly.

26 THREE CHOICES, 5.8–5.10a. Start from top of boulder. Climb 15 feet to diagonal ledge. From the ledge there are three ways to continue.
5.10a. Follow ledge up and left to corner, then straight up to top.
5.9. Climb straight up face.
5.8. Climb face a few feet to the right.

27 HALF CRACK, 5.7. Climb halfway up crack, then over flakes straight to top.
Variation, 5.6. Follow crack to top.

28 BASS TREE, 5.3. Wide crack.

29 TEN-ISH SHOES, 5.10a. Climb corner a few feet right of Bass Tree (route 28).

30 EIGHT PLUS, 5.8. Climb flaky central section of face to small overhang. Pass overhang on the left.

31 BROKEN FOOT, 5.5. Wide diagonal crack.

32 DOWN UNDER, 5.9. Start 2–3 feet right of Broken Foot (route 31). Climb straight up past a couple of small overhangs using underclings.

33 SHIN BONE, 5.10b. You'll have bleeding shins if you slip. Climb as close to the corner as possible.

New Sandstone Area (No Diagram)

NOTE: *New Sandstone Area is closed to climbing at the time of this writing.*

APPROACH: From the small parking area described for Old Sandstone Area, continue 0.4 mile east along South Shore Road (approximately 0.25 mile west of Highway 113). Walk north-northwest up the slope or locate a faint climbers' trail leading up and west to the overhanging rock outcropping. The hanging dihedral at the left (west) end is named Donkey Dihedral (route 2). There is a low-level traverse starting left of Donkey Dihedral ending right of Thin Tips (route 7). The climbs are described from west to east.

Waypoint 3: On road below New Sandstone Area
　　UTM 16T 283049E 4809891N
Waypoint 4: New Sandstone Area
　　UTM 16T 283018E 4810009N
Base Elevation: 1,050 feet
Top Elevation: 1,086 feet

ROUTES:

1 LASER BEAM, 5.11b. Thin, right-curving groove in smooth wall. Finish in jam crack.

2 DONKEY DIHEDRAL, 5.12b/c. Located 31 feet right of Laser Beam (route 1). Climb through the first overhang on good holds. Continue with crotch-splitting stems to reach easier climbing to top.

3 SHAKING HANDS WITH THE CHIMP, 5.13a. Located 30 feet east (right) of Donkey Dihedral (route 2). Climb up and left to an arête, then up the arête for 10 feet to a long stretch across a blank slab to an overhanging groove. (Enjoy the swing if you come off.) Continue up groove to roof and finally up crack to top.

4 KINGSBURY NON-ALCOHOLIC ARÊTE, 5.12b. Climb arête left of Kingsbury Cruise (route 5).

5 KINGSBURY CRUISE, 5.11a. Climb overhanging crack to bulge (crux), then up to final roof. Finish directly over roof.

6 WET PAPER BAG, 5.10c. Located 8 feet right of Kingsbury Cruise (route 5). Layback up to an overhanging crack. Exit right at roof.

7 THIN TIPS, B1. Bulge 7 feet right of Wet Paper Bag (route 6).

East of the Quarry Rocks. Photo: Sven Olof Swartling.

EAST OF THE QUARRY ROCKS

East of the Quarry Rocks extends approximately 1,200 feet east of the old quarry. Rock outcroppings are found along most of this section of bluff. They fall into several bands, with one band considerably more prominent than the others. The main band is interrupted twice by partially open slopes about 100 feet wide, conveniently dividing the rocks into three major subsections: Far East, Middle East, and Near East. There is also a separate Summit Band.

NOTE: *No climbs are in the old quarry. All the quarried area, including the quarry floor, is closed to all public use.*

Far East

The easiest way to locate climbing areas in Far East is to walk up to Siamese Buttress from South Shore Road, 0.9 mile east of the CCC parking area, then traverse west. Refer to the elevation drawing of East of the Quarry Rocks, East Section, for the relative location of the buttresses.

Siamese Buttress consists of two narrow buttresses separated by a steep couloir.

Prayer Wall is the most prominent rock outcropping in Far East. The southeast-facing vertical wall has several excellent climbs.

Rattlesnake Ridge has short climbs on its east flank.

Bandshell Ridge is named for the semicircular rock outcropping below the major outcropping. The lower outcropping is composed of closely layered, highly fractured rock and therefore is not climbed. Climbing is concentrated on a pair of buttresses 35 feet high with a chimney complex tucked between them. This chimney complex, The Gullet, is the distinctive feature of the area.

Siamese Buttress (Diagram 2 E)

APPROACH: Ascend the east bluff (see above) to reach the base of the buttress.

ALADDIN'S CASTLE   BASTILLE ROCK

FEBRUARY WALL   CONDOR CORNER   RATTLESNAKE RIDGE

U-HAUL OVERHANGS   MOUSEHOLE BUTTRESS   PRAYER WALL

BANDSHELL RIDGE   SIAMESE BUTTRESS

EAST OF THE QUARRY ROCKS

EAST SECTION

TO DEVIL'S LAKE

NEAR EAST   MIDDLE EAST   FAR EAST

ROAD TO HWY 113 →

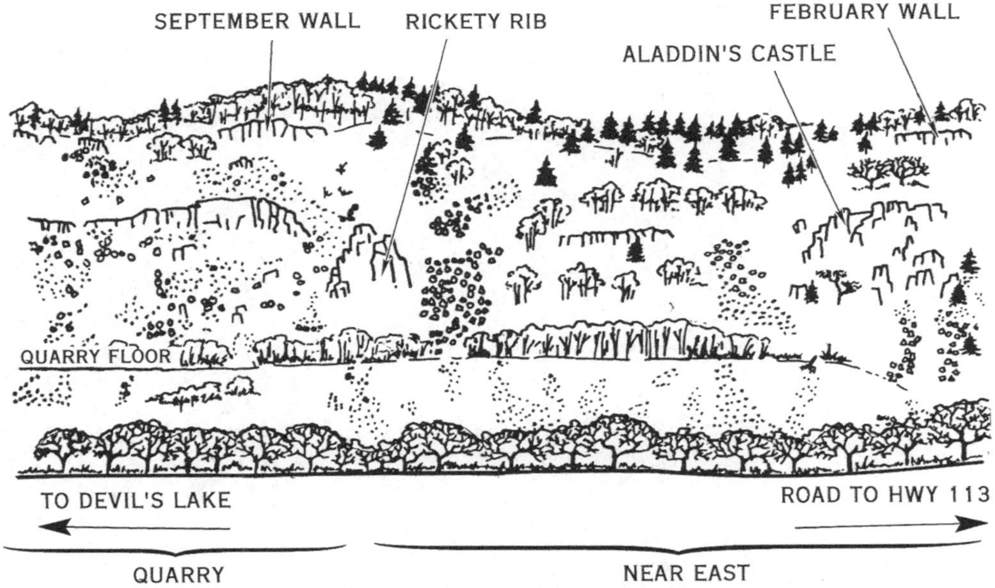

FEBRUARY WALL

ALADDIN'S CASTLE

SEPTEMBER WALL

RICKETY RIB

ROAD TO HWY 113

NEAR EAST

QUARRY FLOOR

TO DEVIL'S LAKE

QUARRY

EAST OF THE QUARRY ROCKS

WEST SECTION

Waypoint 5: On road below Siamese Buttress
    UTM 16T 281978E 4810055N
Waypoint 6: Siamese Buttress
    UTM 16T 282006E 4810195N
Base Elevation: 1,037 feet
Top Elevation: 1,097 feet

ROUTES:
   1 EAST SIAM, 5.4. Start from ledge, climb overhang, and
      finish on face above.
   2 HALFWAY, 5.5. Climb subbuttress starting partway up
      gully.

Siamese Buttress

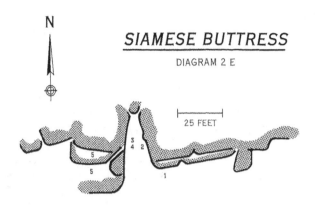

SIAMESE BUTTRESS

DIAGRAM 2 E

25 FEET

3 WEST SIAM, 5.6. Start at the southeast corner of the buttress, right and below the southeast platform. Climb groove to shattered rib, then to overhang, which is passed on the left.

4 SVEN GOLLY, 5.9. Start on the southeast platform 15 feet above the base of the buttress. Climb east side of the prominent southeast corner, staying left of groove in West Siam (route 3).

5 THREE STEP, 5.8. Climb the center of the face with two wide ledges.

Bad News Gully (No Diagram)

Bad News Gully is located 75 feet west of Siamese Buttress and forms its western boundary. The name reflects its character—narrow, very steep, and dirty. There are a few short climbs halfway up the gully on the west side and a couple of interesting longer climbs higher up. West of the gully there is a rather complex section of short slabs and walls.

Prayer Wall (Diagram 3 E)

Approach: From Siamese Buttress, traverse 225 feet west, pass Bad News Gully, and ascend 100 feet to the base of Prayer Wall.

Waypoint 7: Prayer Wall
  UTM 16T 281945E 4810197N
Base Elevation: 1,100 feet
Top Elevation: 1,161 feet

1. THE ROOK, 5.8. Climb the narrow face left of This Is A Six? (route 2). There are some long reaches on small, sharp holds. It is easier than it looks.

2. THIS IS A SIX? 5.6. Jam crack that is harder than it looks.

3. SICKLE, 5.10b/c. Start 7 feet right of This Is A Six? (route 2). Climb face and shallow cracks to left end of a curved slot. From slot, follow crack straight to top.

Prayer Wall. Photo: Pete Mayer.

4 BISHOP, 5.7. This climb follows the long, left-slanting crack. It is an attractive route with continuous 5.7 climbing.
Variation, 5.11b. Start a few feet left of Bishop crack. Climb the face and join the crack at 20 feet.

5 PRAYER WHEEL, 5.11b/c. Start just left of inside corner/slab and climb straight up to a triangular pocket at 15 feet. Continue on wall above to top of summit block. Avoid using the right edge holds halfway up.

6 THE PAWN, 5.4. Climb inside corner and slab. At 20 feet, switch to crack on the left wall. Finish right of summit block.

7 5.6. Climb overhang on upper wall just right of grungy-looking chimney.

8 BUDDHA, 5.8. There are two starts to reach the middle ledge with one large block; climb crack in middle of bulge or start at right corner. Continue in center of upper wall.

9 MAGELLANIC CLOUD, 5.11d. Climb lower face, 6 feet left of Close Call (route 10). Thin cracks lead to better holds. Joins Buddha (route 8) at ledge.

10 CLOSE CALL, 5.6. Well-defined inside corner.

11 PRAYER FLAG, 5.7. Crack in southwest face, right of inside corner. Joins Close Call (route 10) halfway up.

12 NO VACANCY, 5.8. Starts 25 feet above base platform. Climb crack past overhang, finish in groove above right side of overhang.

PRAYER WALL

DIAGRAM 3 E

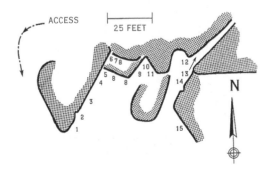

13 VACANT, 5.10a. Starts 25 feet above base platform. Climb center and upper right side of narrow face. Avoid using right corner near top.
Variation, 5.11b. Same start, then climb left side of upper face.

14 5.9. Start from block in gully and climb 20-foot face left of broken chimney.

15 5.4. A 30-foot face route ending halfway up buttress.

Rattlesnake Ridge (Diagram 4 E)

APPROACH: From the lowest western point of Prayer Wall, traverse 100 feet west to Rattlesnake Ridge.

Waypoint 8: Rattlesnake Ridge
   UTM 16T 281918E 4810195N
Base Elevation: 1,106 feet
Top Elevation: 1,145 feet

ROUTES:
1 THE RATTLE, 5.5. Climb face past a 3-foot-square flake 10 feet up on the right.
Variation, 5.8. Climb over flake or stay left. Use caution, the flake is loose!

2 RIGHT NOSE, 5.5. Climb, staying close to corner.

3 LEFT NOSE, 5.6. Climb just left of corner.

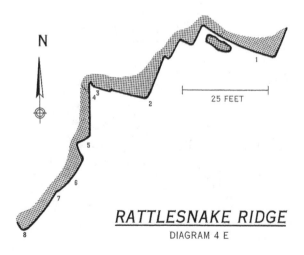

N

25 FEET

RATTLESNAKE RIDGE
DIAGRAM 4 E

4 TIMBER SNAKE, 5.9. A thin joint 4 feet left of an obvious V-chimney.

5 SNAKE SKIN, 5.6. Start in niche, climb wide crack that slants slightly right.

6 5.8. Start in center of wall, climb up and right to a crack, then back left to top.

7 5.6. Wide crack in the left part of the wall.

8 5.6. Corner.

Rattlesnake Ridge

Bandshell Ridge (Diagram 5 E)

APPROACH: From the lowest blocks of Rattlesnake Ridge, traverse diagonally up and west 175 feet to Bandshell Ridge.

Waypoint 9: Bandshell Ridge
   UTM 16T 281841E 4810190N
Base Elevation: 1,107 feet
Top Elevation: 1,138 feet

Bandshell Ridge

ROUTES:

1   5.9. Start on ledge. Climb left side of wall.

2   LARGO, 5.8. South corner of west buttress. A long reach is helpful.

3   ENCORE, 5.8. Climb southeast face and crack straight up to the top of the buttress. This is another long-reach route.

4   FINE TUNING, 5.8. Climb 15 feet to a 6-foot right-slanting crack. Use bucket hold in crack for one move, then climb straight up to top.
Variation, 5.7. At 15 feet, follow right-slanting crack.

5   MINUET, 5.4. Climb blocky crack and wall.

6   THE GULLET, 5.5. Climb the 5-foot-wide gap by stemming. Some people prefer to face in, while others prefer to face out.

7   TUBA, 5.11b. Overhang inside gullet.

8   5.6. East wall of gullet.

9   ARM OVERTURE, 5.7. Jam crack 8 feet right of The Gullet (route 6).

10   5.6. Crack 5 feet right of Arm Overture (route 9).

11   5.5. Climb into small niche. Continue on southwest corner of buttress.

12   FIRST MOVEMENT, 5.6. Start near small hickory tree, climb straight up to top.

13   TORN JOINT, 5.10d/11a. Climb center of face, aiming for a vertical crack near the top.
Variation, 5.9+. Same start, but traverse right and up using a couple of holds near right corner. Then traverse left to center of face and finish in vertical crack near top.

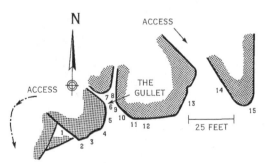

BANDSHELL RIDGE

DIAGRAM 5 E

14 5.5. Broken southwest face and crack.
15 5.4. South corner.

Middle East

Mousehole Buttress is located on the lower level of Middle East. The buttress has a few 60-foot routes interrupted by a large bench.

Condor Corner is located on the upper level of Middle East, three-quarters of the way up the bluff. The oversized corner of this 40-foot wall is its most striking feature.

Bastille Rock is located almost directly below Condor Corner and is not a particularly eye-appealing outcropping. The central (highest) part has a few 35-foot climbs.

Mousehole Buttress (Diagram 6 E)

APPROACH: From Bandshell Ridge, traverse west 100 feet across a small boulderfield to Mousehole Buttress.

Waypoint 10: Mousehole Buttress
  UTM 16T 281779E 4810173N
Base Elevation: 1,070 feet
Top Elevation: 1,141 feet

ROUTES:
  1 MOUSEHOLE, 5.5. Start in short chimney, climb crack leading out of chimney.
  2 JERRY, 5.7. Climb corner to bench. Continue in wide crack, finish on upper corner.

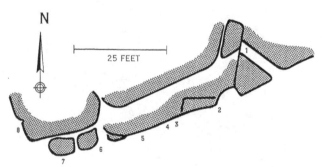

MOUSEHOLE BUTTRESS

DIAGRAM 6 E

3 TOM, 5.7. Thin crack 4 feet right of Mouse Crack (route 4).

4 MOUSE CRACK, 5.7. Climb crack in lower wall to bench with juniper tree. Start at flake on upper wall, pass overhang on right or left.

5 TRAP, 5.11a. Face 4 feet left of Mouse Crack (route 4).

6 EAST PILLAR, 5.5. Climb east corner, finish on slab above.

7 WEST PILLAR, 5.6. Climb south face of pillar, finish on slab above.

8 5.5. Climb crack, or just right of crack, 12 feet left of West Pillar (route 7).

Mousehole Buttress

Condor Corner (Diagram 7 E)

APPROACH: From the top of Mousehole Buttress, traverse 125 feet diagonally up and west to the base of Condor Corner. This area can also be reached from the Ice Age Trail/Upland Trail along the top of the bluff. Descend a faint ridge 150 feet east of February Wall to the top of Condor Corner.

Waypoint 11: Condor Corner
    UTM 16T 281751E 4810217N
Base Elevation: 1,164 feet
Top Elevation: 1,213 feet

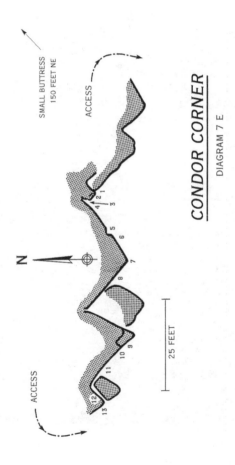

Condor Corner

Routes:

1 5.4. Climb lower wall into a subsidiary inside corner. Several easy climbs are possible farther right.

2 SALT PETER, 5.8. Climb hanging pillar and crack 2–4 feet right of Condor Corner (route 3).

3 CONDOR CORNER, 5.5. Impressive inside corner/chimney.

4 SHOOTING STAR, 5.11d. Crack system in center of face. Near the top use bucket hold below the left crack to move up and right. Climb the overhanging crack and face above; avoid using right corner. This route ends at the high point of the buttress.
Variation, 5.11a. From bucket hold, climb the left crack.

5 THE JOKER, 5.6. Climb past block-filled niche to platform. Finish on upper right corner.

Routes 6–8 end on the ledge 15 feet below the high point of the buttress.

6 PETE'S NEMESIS, 5.9. Thin crack 3 feet left of The Joker (route 5). Avoid using holds near The Joker.

7 COSMIC, 5.10d. Corner. Getting off the ground is the crux.

8 GOT YOU, 5.8. Short jam or layback crack. A harder variation uses only the crack for holds.

9 5.5. Crack and upper corner.

10 5.8. Crack just left of route 9.

11 5.7. Crack.

12 5.7. Face. Avoid using the tower behind and your behind.

13 5.8. Face just left of corner behind a small pine tree.

Buttress Northeast of Condor Corner (No Diagram)

APPROACH: This small buttress is located 150 feet northeast of Condor Corner.

Routes:

14 5.5. Crack in south-southwest face.

15 5.6. South corner. Climb through open book halfway up.

Bastille Rock (Diagram 8 E)

APPROACH: From the base of Mousehole Buttress, traverse west 100 feet or descend 100 feet from Condor Corner.

Waypoint 12: Bastille Rock
    UTM 16T 281738E 4810182N
Base Elevation: 1,088 feet
Top Elevation: 1,137 feet

ROUTES:
 1 LOUIS V, 5.5. Corner.
 2 LOUIS VI, 5.6. Face and crack.

Bastille Rock

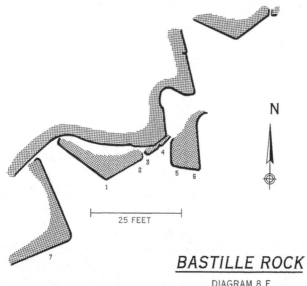

BASTILLE ROCK

DIAGRAM 8 E

3 FENESTRATION, 5.6. Start in short chimney. Climb to substantial ledge about midlevel. On upper wall climb into a small, deep V-notch near top.

4 GINNY CREEPER, 5.6. Start 5 feet right of Fenestration (route 3). Climb lower crack to inside corner, then right to corner ledge. Continue up just right of overhang. *Variation,* 5.8. Climb overhang direct.

5 WARDEN I, 5.8. Slightly overhanging corner.

6 WARDEN II, 5.10a. Short overhang problem.

7 DEALER'S CHOICE, 5.2–5.4. Low wall 20 feet left of Louis V (route 1).

Near East

The easiest way to locate climbing areas in Near East is to walk up from South Shore Road, 0.7 mile east of the CCC parking area. Ascend the bluff following the east edge of the scree slope formed by the quarry operation. When level with the quarry floor, two rock outcroppings can be seen halfway up the bluff in spring and late fall.

Aladdin's Castle is the upper western outcropping of Near East. It can be seen in early spring or late fall when level with the eastern end of the quarry floor. A 40-foot inside corner is its prominent feature.

U-Haul Overhangs is the lower eastern outcropping of Near East. The climbs are on two small formations, 80 feet apart at roughly the same level. The western formation is 30 feet high and slightly overhung, with two distinctive cracks 3 feet apart. There is a large boulder below the right crack.

Rickety Rib is an impressive 40-foot buttress well hidden in the trees near the eastern edge of the quarry. This small area with lots of loose rock is difficult to reach since the quarry floor is closed to public use. There is no climbing description for this area.

Aladdin's Castle (Diagram 9 E)

APPROACH: *From below*—From the east end of the quarry floor, walk 350 feet straight up the bluff (north) to Aladdin's Castle. (*Avoid the quarry floor, which is closed to public use.*) *From above*—From the base of February Wall, walk straight down (south) to Aladdin's Castle.

Waypoint 13: On road below Aladdin's Castle
UTM 16T 281676E 4810028N
Waypoint 14: Aladdin's Castle
UTM 16T 281616E 4810206N
Base Elevation: 1,175 feet
Top Elevation: 1,256 feet

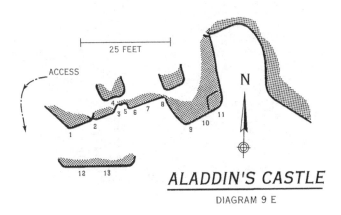

ALADDIN'S CASTLE

DIAGRAM 9 E

ROUTES:

1 SECOND WISH, 5.7. Corner with small overhang at 12 feet.

2 FLYING CARPET, 5.7. Crack with two small V-niches. Careful, you may go for a ride.

3 5.4. Start in V-chimney, continue in inside corner to large platform.

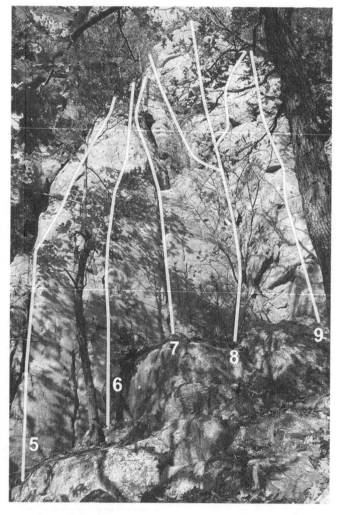

Aladdin's Castle

4 SZHAZAM, 5.8. From the platform, climb short, tricky face to top of lower (western) high point. Do not use left corner.

5 THE LAMP, 5.5. Chimney/crack route starting near route 3. Climb up and right. Finish right of lower high point.

6 WISH GRANTED, 5.7. Start in cracks on lower face 3 feet right of The Lamp (route 5). Continue on rib to small pine tree.

7 FIRST MAKE A WISH, 5.8. Quarter-inch crack that can be identified by a pinch hold 10 feet up. Don't take this line lightly. The difficulty is not apparent at first glance.

8 THREE WISHES, 5.6. Start in inside corner below higher (eastern) high point. About 20 feet up, there are three ways to continue:

5.6. Chimney left of eastern high point.

5.10c. Rounded overhanging corner.

5.5. Steep ramp leading up and right.

9 GENIE, 5.10a. Rounded corner leading to ledge below eastern high point.

10 FIRST WISH, 5.10b. Face right of Genie (route 9). Avoid using right corner.

Variation, 5.10d. Climb face without using the two large holds near the corner.

11 5.6. Start in short crack, continue on corner above.

12–13 THIRD WISH, 5.6–5.7. Two short crack routes on lower wall.

The rock outcroppings east of Aladdin's Castle have a few short climbs.

U-Haul Overhangs (Diagram 10 E)

APPROACH: Refer to Near East description for directions to the east end of the quarry floor. From there traverse diagonally up (northeast) 200 feet to reach the base of the rock outcroppings. U-Haul Overhangs is about 300 feet west of Bastille Rock. (*Avoid the quarry floor, which is closed to public use.*)

Waypoint 15: U-Haul Overhangs
   UTM 16T 281641E 4810163N
Base Elevation: 1,102 feet
Top Elevation: 1,143 feet

Routes:

1 FREE MILEAGE, 5.7. Start at lowest point of south wall between the boulder and the corner. At 15 feet move right and continue on east wall.

2 BUDGET, 5.6. Crack with good jam holds. Easy in spite of being overhung. More challenging if you avoid using the boulder at the start.

3 HURTS, 5.8. Continuously overhanging crack with good holds most of the way.
   Variation, 5.10a. Climb left of Hurts without using the crack.

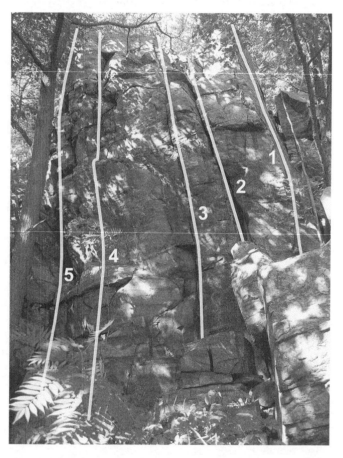

U-Haul Overhangs. Photo: Pete Mayer.

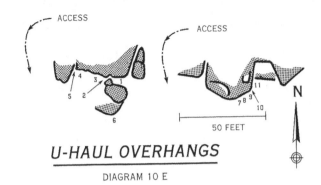

U-HAUL OVERHANGS

DIAGRAM 10 E

4 AVIS, 5.8. Wall just right of corner. At ledge 20 feet up, continue to top on corner or move right to crack.

5 RENT-A-WRECK, 5.5. Chimney/crack at west end of wall.

6 5.7. Short climb on lower east wall.

7 5.6. Center crack and inside corner on left side of pillar.

8 NOSE, NOSE, ANYTHING GOES, 5.8. Climb face straight up below hanging corner. Continue on corner to top.

9 WE TRY HARDER, 5.8. Start on east corner. At 10 feet step left onto lip of overhang. Finish on face above.

10 . . . AND HARDER, 5.10c. Same start as We Try Harder (route 9). At 10 feet step right and finish on corner and crack right of corner.

11 BANANA PEEL, 5.10a. Climb up and right on sloping ramp to upper overhang. Pass overhang on the left and follow corner to top.

Summit Band

The Summit Band consists of two low walls located near the top of the bluff, September Wall and February Wall. September Wall, well above the eastern edge of the quarry, can be seen from below, though it is practically hidden by trees.

September Wall (Diagram 11 E)

APPROACH: The Summit Band is best reached from the Ice Age Trail/Upland Trail, which follows the top of the bluff. Follow the CCC Trail from the CCC parking area to the top of the bluff. Above D'Arcy's Wall, walk 250 feet north through the woods to the East Bluff Woods Trail/Ice Age Trail. Follow the trail east for 350 feet to where the Upland Trail joins and the East Bluff Woods Trail turns north. Continue east on the Ice Age Trail/Upland Trail for 2,000 feet to a clearing at the top of the bluff and the Western Cwm boulderfield. Walk east another 1,000 feet to a short, left-turning, uphill section. Just before this small hill, leave the trail and follow a faint trail 200 feet south (right) to September Wall.

A shorter route to the Ice Age Trail/Upland Trail is the un-official Jack-in-the-Pulpit Trail. It joins the Ice Age Trail/Upland Trail near an obvious low point between the East Rampart and West of the Quarry Rocks. This faint trail starts across the road and 10 feet east of the group campground exit, (roughly 500 feet east of the CCC parking area) and goes north into the woods. Where the slope begins a large fallen tree lies directly on the trail. Traverse east around the tree and pick up the original track. Where the slope appears to ease the trail splits; follow the rocky gully (dry streambed) up and right. Near the top the trail becomes level and very indistinct. Continue northeast about 300 feet to the Ice Age Trail/Upland Trail. Turn right (east) and walk 1,200 feet to a clearing at the top of the bluff and the Western Cwm boulderfield. Continue as above.

Waypoint 16: On Ice Age Trail/Upland Trail above September Wall
UTM 16T 281346E 4810300N
Waypoint 17: September Wall
UTM 16T 281361E 4810239N
Base Elevation: 1,358 feet
Top Elevation: 1,397 feet

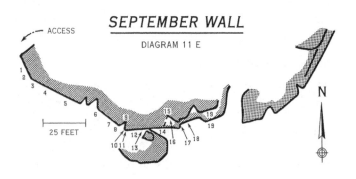

SEPTEMBER WALL

DIAGRAM 11 E

ACCESS

25 FEET

N

Routes:

1 HICKORY LEFT, 5.10a. Thin crack.

2 HICKORY RIGHT, 5.9. Start in shallow inside corner. Finish slightly left of nose.

3 5.8. Face 4–5 feet right of Hickory Right (route 2). Balance up on small ramp a few feet above the ground. Continue up and slightly right to top.

4 EQUINOX, 5.5. Right-slanting crack.
   Variation, 5.8. Climb just right of the crack. Avoid holds in or on the edge of the crack.

5 LABOR DAY, 5.7. Climb face to crack starting 8 feet up. Follow crack to top.
   Variation, 5.8. Start 5 feet left of crack, then move right back to crack.
   FIRST MONDAY, 5.9. Start 4 feet right of Labor Day (route 5), climb face with an interesting undercling hold near top.

6 IN STEP, 5.8. Start under overhang. Climb past overhang on the right. Continue just right of corner to top. Do not use holds on corner.
   LONG WEEKEND, 5.8. Face left of In Step. Avoid using right corner.

7 FALL IS NEAR, 5.7. Interesting crack.

8 PHIL'S NOSE, 5.10a. Corner.

9 5.4. Deep inside corner.

10 LADY AND THE TRAMP, 5.11b. Start on narrow face left of End of September (route 11). At 10 feet, move left around the corner to an overhanging crack.

11 END OF SEPTEMBER, 5.9. Start left of corner. At 10 feet move right around corner, then continue on face straight to top. A long reach is required.

12 5.10d. Start in center of face between End of September (route 11) and The Fang (route 13). Climb up and slightly left. End at top of End of September.

13 THE FANG, 5.9. Left-curving jam crack.

14 5.7. Climb to top of hanging inside corner. Continue in diagonal crack.

15 5.5. Inside corner.

16 QUEEN OF HEARTS, 5.10b. Nice face route on thin holds.

17 THE CHOPPER, 5.8. Climb inside corner to platform below overhang. Follow crack up and slightly left to top.

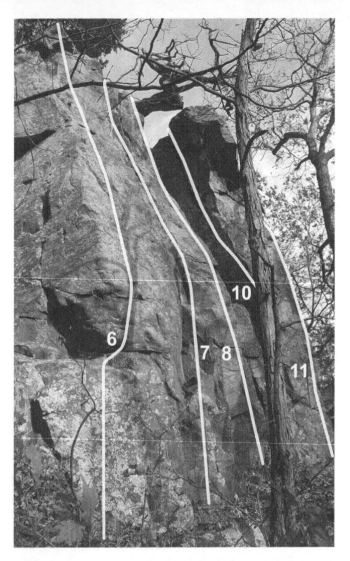

September Wall

Variation, 5.7. Move right at overhang and climb over wobbly block.

18 SON OF CHOPPER, 5.10d. Start on the first ledge 12 feet up. Climb face and corner to wobbly block. This route is 4–6 feet right of The Chopper (route 17).

19 BEHIND THE PINE, 5.7. Climb crack in lower flaky face to ledge, move left, and step up on a small foothold behind pine tree to instant exposure. Continue straight up on face.

February Wall (Diagram 12 E)

Approach: Refer to Approach for September Wall. February Wall is located 800 feet east of the faint trail leading to September Wall. Turn south (right) just before a short, left-turning, uphill section and walk approximately 25 feet to the top of February Wall.

Waypoint 18: February Wall
   UTM 16T 281576E 4810335N
Base Elevation: 1,396 feet
Top Elevation: 1,424 feet

Routes:
   1 FEBRUARY 29, 5.8. Start on corner just left of shallow inside corner. Climb corner and finish on ledge just left of top overhang.
   Variation, 5.8. Climb corner right of shallow inside corner. Finish on same ledge.
   2 FEBRUARY 28, 5.10b. A straighter line. Climb middle of face, finish in notch of overhang.
   3 DOUBLE FIN, 5.8. Start in thin crack just left of Flying Fish (route 4). Follow zigzag cracks to top.

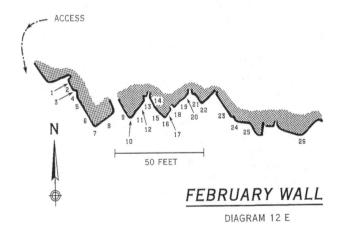

FEBRUARY WALL

DIAGRAM 12 E

4 FLYING FISH, 5.8. Wide crack system whose offset cracks are harder than they look.

5 FISH FACE, 5.8. Face 4 feet right of Flying Fish (route 4). Climb face straight to top.

6 STRIDE RIGHT, 5.9. Nice face route. Same start as Fish Face (route 5). Climb up and slightly right to small overhang, then straight to top.

7 LEAP YEAR, 5.7. Start just left of corner and climb straight to top, passing overhang on the left.
Variation, 5.7. Same start. At 10 feet, step right onto lip of overhang and follow corner to top.
Variation, 5.8. Climb overhanging corner directly.

8 5.5. Crack.

9 5.6. Crack system and shallow inside corner.

10 TURNCOAT, 5.10a. Corner with a few small holds.

11 5.7. Start 3 feet right of corner, finish on ledge below top.

12 5.5. Face.

13 5.4. Chimney.

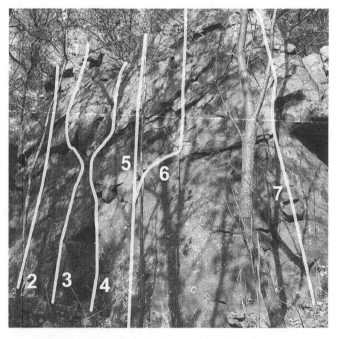

February Wall

14 MINOR TECHNICALITY, B1. Climb face just left of Bread and Jam (route 15) on very thin holds. Finish in crack.

15 BREAD AND JAM, 5.7. Climb diagonal crack without using right corner.

16 5.4. Corner.

17 5.4. Crack that joins corner at top.

18–20 5.4. Three cracks.

21 5.5. Face.

22 5.6. Corner.

23 5.4. Crack.

24 5.6. Start on corner 4 feet right of crack. Finish in groove.

25 PHOOEY, 5.8. Inside corner with overhanging crack at top.

26 5.4. Corner.

West of the Quarry Rocks. Photo: Sven Olof Swartling.

WEST OF THE QUARRY ROCKS

West of the Quarry Rocks extends approximately 1,000 feet west of the old quarry. The rock outcroppings are separated by three large boulderfields, dividing them into West Ridge, Vulture Lookout, and West Terraces.

Two of the boulderfields start at road level and connect at the very bottom of the bluff in a line of trees. The eastern boulderfield reaches up through the middle between West Ridge and West Terraces and provides relatively easy access to the top of the bluff. The western boulderfield reaches up around the west side of West Terraces.

The third boulderfield, the Western Cwm, is located on the upper third of the bluff, above and west of the old quarry. It separates the upper part of West Ridge (Red Nose Wall) from Vulture Lookout.

The rock outcropping above the west part of the quarry that is visible from the road offers no climbing. A small outcropping on the upper part of the bluff, between West Ridge and West Terraces, has a few climbs.

West Ridge *(Diagram 13 E)*

The West Ridge consists of Crashing Rock Wall, Lost Temple Rock, Farewell to Arms, and Red Nose Wall. These four separate rock outcroppings form a broken ridge up most of the bluff.

Crashing Rock Wall is a low rock outcropping hidden by trees and named for the numerous loose rocks that fell in the early climbing days.

Lost Temple Rock is above and slightly east of Crashing Rock Wall, near the edge of the quarry. The entrance to the climbing area is through a narrow notch that was lost once or twice.

Farewell to Arms is named for the condition of your arms after climbing several of the routes.

Red Nose Wall is named for its geologic features. The color of the rock is redder than other areas at the lake. The northeast end of the upper wall resembles a nose in profile.

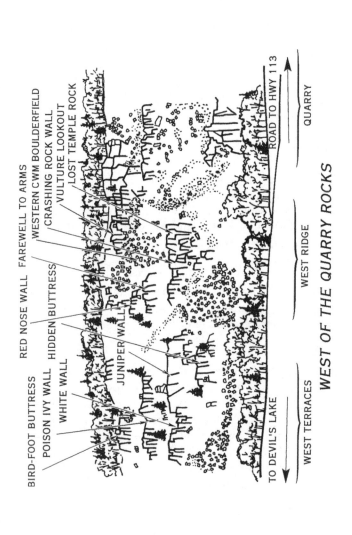

BIRD-FOOT BUTTRESS RED NOSE WALL FAREWELL TO ARMS
WESTERN CWM BOULDERFIELD
POISON IVY WALL CRASHING ROCK WALL
HIDDEN BUTTRESS VULTURE LOOKOUT
WHITE WALL LOST TEMPLE ROCK
JUNIPER WALL

TO DEVIL'S LAKE   WEST TERRACES   WEST RIDGE   QUARRY   ROAD TO HWY 113

WEST OF THE QUARRY ROCKS

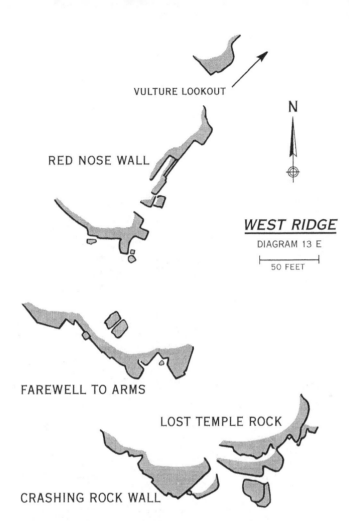

VULTURE LOOKOUT

N

RED NOSE WALL

WEST RIDGE

DIAGRAM 13 E

50 FEET

FAREWELL TO ARMS

LOST TEMPLE ROCK

CRASHING ROCK WALL

Crashing Rock Wall (Diagram 14 E)

APPROACH: Refer to Diagram 13 E, West Ridge. *From below—* From the CCC parking area, walk east on the South Shore Road approximately 1,000 feet to where the road begins to descend the moraine slope. Turn northeast (left) and walk through the woods to a boulderfield. Continue up along the east edge of the boulderfield until a low, unnamed rock outcropping can be seen above. Crashing Rock Wall is above this low rock outcropping behind some trees. *From above—*Descend from the Western

Cwm boulderfield on the Ice Age Trail/Upland Trail. Refer to Approach for Vulture Lookout and Diagram 13 E, West Ridge.

Waypoint 19: On road below Crashing Rock Wall
    UTM 16T 280950E 4810017N
Waypoint 20: Crashing Rock Wall
    UTM 16T 280985E 4810145N
Base Elevation: 1,185 feet
Top Elevation: 1,230 feet

Crashing Rock Wall

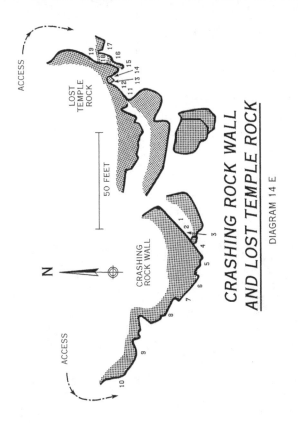

CRASHING ROCK WALL AND LOST TEMPLE ROCK

DIAGRAM 14 E

ROUTES:

Routes 1–3 start from a ledge.

1 THE EASEL, 5.9. Face route.

2 5.4. Crack system passes a small pine in center of wall.

3 5.4. Crack system with birch bushes.

4 THE BLACKBOARD, 5.10b. Smooth face below high point of buttress.

5 5.3. Climb just west of the corner. This is a longer route than most climbs in the area. Beware of loose rock on upper part of route.

6 5.5. Crack system with several variations.

7 5.5. Crack system with several variations.

8 5.8. Climb face, then continue up overhang.

9 5.7. Corner.

10 5.7. Climb crack up and right to groove.

Lost Temple Rock (Diagram 14 E)

Approach: Refer to Approach for Crashing Rock Wall and Diagram 13 E, West Ridge.

Waypoint 21: Lost Temple Rock
   UTM 16T 281008E 4810139N
Base Elevation: 1,190 feet
Top Elevation: 1,254 feet

ROUTES:

11 FURIOUS FUNNEL, 5.8. Climb lower wall to ledge at 15 feet. Continue up from left end of ledge into the funnel, a

Lost Temple Rock

short chimney formed by a projecting block. Climb the funnel, staying right of block. Continue climbing just left of and as close as possible to upper corner.

12 5.7. Start in short crack near center of amphitheater and climb to same ledge as Furious Funnel (route 11). Continue up steep gully with loose rock to top.

13 NEMESIS, 5.8. Start on left side of corner pedestal. Continue straight up steep face. Finish on ledge to right and above pointed overhang.

14 LOST TEMPLE CORNER, 5.6. Start on right side of corner pedestal. Continue in prominent inside corner. From obvious resting ledge, follow crack to top.

15 FAITH, HOPE, AND TENSION, 5.8. Southeast corner. Start 4 feet right of corner, traverse left to corner as soon as possible. Follow corner to top.
Variation, 5.10c. Start left of corner with a jump move.

16 THE DOOM, 5.10b. Start up slight groove and climb over the right end of overhang to ledge.
Variation, FATE, 5.11a/b. Same start, but pass lower overhang on the left.

17 5.5. Climb short inside corner with deep crack to ledge.

18 5.6. Start from ledge, climb crack left of offset in wall.

19 5.6. Start from ledge, climb crack right of offset in wall.

Farewell to Arms (Diagram 15 E)

Approach: Refer to Approach for Crashing Rock Wall and Diagram 13 E, West Ridge.

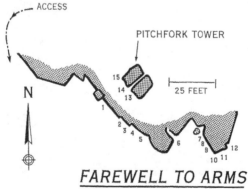

FAREWELL TO ARMS

DIAGRAM 15 E

Waypoint 22: Farewell to Arms
  UTM 16T 280971E 4810166N
Base Elevation: 1,283 feet
Top Elevation: 1,325 feet

ROUTES:

1 ANNE'S 8, 5.6. Crack leading to large pine tree at top.
2 FAREWELL TO ARMS, 5.8. Start in shallow inside corner/crack. Continue in crack above overhang.
3 SKIN GRAFT, 5.11b. Climb thin crack just left of corner.
4 COUNT YOUR FINGERS, 5.8. Inside corner crack with a very, very sharp edge.
5 5.7. Start 5 feet right of Count Your Fingers (route 4). Finish in crack above.
6 5.4. Corner and overhang.
7 5.5. Chimney. Pass top block on the right.

Farewell to Arms

8 NO ONE BUT ME, 5.11c. A tight crack 3 feet left of route 9.

9 5.7. Jam crack.

10 KEYSTONE, 5.10b. Corner.

11 THIS IS HARD! 5.11b. Crack in center of face.

12 5.5. Chimney/crack.
      Variation, 5.7. Climb rounded corner right of chimney/crack.

Pitchfork Tower (Diagram 15 E)

This small tower is named for the pitchfork that used to be stuck in the chimney.

APPROACH: Refer to Approach for Crashing Rock Wall and Diagram 13 E, West Ridge.

Waypoint 23: Pitchfork Tower
    UTM 16T 280971E 4810173N
Base Elevation: 1,325 feet
Top Elevation: 1,355 feet

ROUTES:

13 5.4. Chimney.

14 5.6. Same start as route 13. At 8 feet step out of chimney and climb left corner and face to top.

15 PITCHFORK, 5.10d. Overhanging southwest corner.

Red Nose Wall (Diagram 16 E)

APPROACH: Refer to Approach for Crashing Rock Wall (to approach from below) or Approach for Vulture Lookout (to approach from above) and Diagram 13 E, West Ridge.

Waypoint 24: Red Nose Wall
    UTM 16T 280993E 4810208N
Base Elevation: 1,376 feet
Top Elevation: 1,427 feet

ROUTES:

1 DIRTY JIM'S CRACK, 5.7. Awkward inside corner.

2 WHITE WASP, 5.11a. Start below overhang on corner. Climb overhang. Continue in inside corner, just right of corner.

3 THE REVOLT OF THE NERDS, 5.6. Start in inside corner, continue in crack above.

4 ELIMINATION, 5.6. Crack.

5 5.10a. Narrow face between Elimination (route 4) and A Girl Named Sue (route 6).

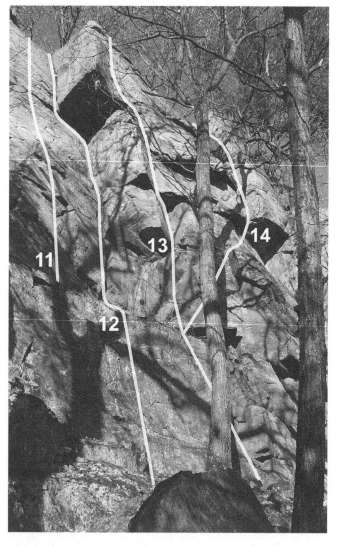

Red Nose Wall

RED NOSE WALL

DIAGRAM 16 E

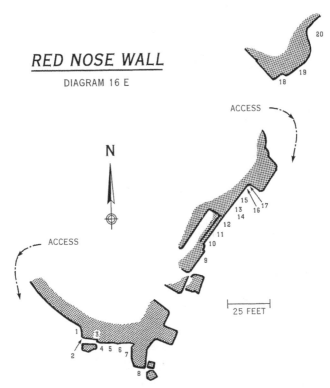

6 A GIRL NAMED SUE, 5.8. Climb face and shallow crack 8 feet left of inside corner. Avoid using cracks on either side.

7 JUDGMENT DAY, 5.11c. Climb face by a series of lay-backs and long reaches.

8 5.7. Start with a layback. Pass overhang on the right or climb face below upper corner. Finish on southeast corner.

9 VOYAGER, 5.11a. Start on ledge and climb upper over-hanging wall left of Cutting Edge (route 10).

10 CUTTING EDGE, 5.8. Start on ledge and climb easy lower part of wall to overhanging diagonal crack 15 feet below top. Follow crack to top.

11 SOLSTICE, 5.11c. Start on ledge and climb narrow face left of Bloodshed (route 12). Do not use Bloodshed crack.

12 BLOODSHED, 5.7. Climb lower face to ledge. Continue in inside corner, passing both lower and upper overhangs on the left.

13 WOUNDED KNEE, 5.10c. Climb to ledge and continue up past a couple of small overhangs until upper corner is reached. Finish on right side of upper corner.

14 LAUGHING SIOUX, 5.8. Same start as Wounded Knee (route 13). From ledge, climb up and right onto small platform at 20 feet. Finish in hanging inside corner.

15 OCTOBER COUNTRY, 5.9+. Climb crack and a couple of down-sloping projections. Very awkward.

16 LOOK MA, NO HANDS, 5.10b. Overhanging wall and groove between October Country (route 15) and Breaking Away (route 17).

17 BREAKING AWAY, 5.8. Inside corner. Watch for loose rocks.

18 5.5. Inside corner.

19 5.8. Climb crack system leading slightly left.

20 NO PROBLEM, 5.10d. Climb the flaring crack. It looks a lot easier than it is.

A number of short climbs and boulder problems can be found on the low walls above Red Nose Wall. These walls form a cirque above the Western Cwm boulderfield almost connecting with Vulture Lookout to the east.

Vulture Lookout (Diagram 17 E)

Vulture Lookout is at the top of the bluff above the Western Cwm boulderfield. This boulderfield has numerous rocks with white tops that resemble snow-covered peaks. These are the result of deposits by Turkey Vultures that like to sit on the rocks.

Approach: Vulture Lookout is best reached from the Ice Age Trail/Upland Trail, which follows the top of the bluff. Follow the CCC Trail from the CCC parking area to the top of the bluff. Above D'Arcy's Wall, walk 250 feet north through the woods to the East Bluff Woods Trail/Ice Age Trail. Follow the trail east for 350 feet to where the Upland Trail joins and the East Bluff Woods Trail turns north. Continue east on the Ice Age Trail/Upland Trail for 2,000 feet to a clearing at the top of the bluff and the Western Cwm boulderfield. Vulture Lookout is located 200 feet south of the trail at the northeast corner of the Western Cwm boulderfield. It is well hidden by trees.

A shorter route to the Ice Age Trail/Upland Trail is the unofficial Jack-in-the-Pulpit Trail. It joins the Ice Age Trail/Upland Trail near an obvious low point between the East Rampart and West of the Quarry Rocks. This faint trail starts across the road and 10 feet east of the group campground exit, (roughly 500 feet east of the CCC parking area) and goes north into the woods. Where the slope begins a large fallen tree lies directly on the trail. Traverse east around the tree and pick up the original track. Where the slope appears to ease the trail splits; follow the rocky gully (dry streambed) up and right. Near the top the trail becomes level and very indistinct. Continue northeast about 300 feet to the Ice Age Trail/Upland Trail. Turn right (east) and walk 1,200 feet to a clearing at the top of the bluff and the Western Cwm boulderfield. Continue as above.

Waypoint 25: Vulture Lookout
    UTM 16T 281061E 4810220N
Base Elevation: 1,356 feet
Top Elevation: 1,397 feet

ROUTES:
1   MISSING PIECE, 5.7. Climb slightly overhanging inside corner to big platform. Continue in crack to top.
2   DURACELL, 5.10a. Climb face right of Missing Piece (route 1). At 8 feet move left to crack close to Missing Piece.

VULTURE LOOKOUT

DIAGRAM 17 E

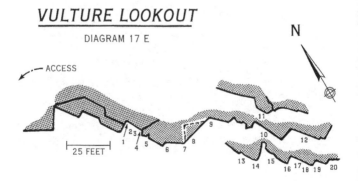

N

— ACCESS

25 FEET

3 MAGIC MUSHROOM, 5.12b/c. Climb face 3–4 feet left of route 4. Beware of the tree if you fall.

4 5.7. Crack system slightly overhanging at the start. Follow cracks straight to top.

5 5.6. Crack that joins route 4 at 20 feet.

6 DOUBLE JEOPARDY CRACKS, 5.9. Start in small inside corner. Climb to ledge 12 feet up and rest. Continue in left, right, or both cracks.

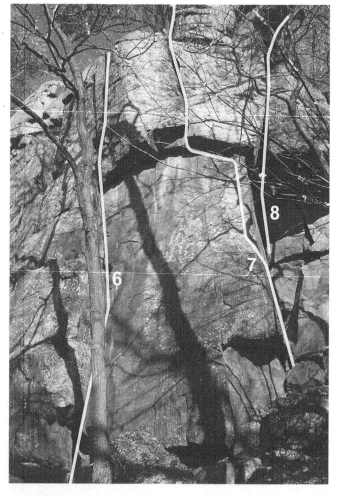

Vulture Lookout

7   THE ENERGIZER, 5.9. Start just right of corner. Climb up and move left around corner. At small overhang move 3 feet left and follow obvious crack (crux) to top.
Variation, 5.11a. Climb lower face just left of corner to small overhang and continue as above.

8   THE V, 5.10d. Climb to alcove, then up and out of the V.

9   5.8. Crack right of overhang.

10   5.7. Crack in center of wall.

11   5.8–5.10a. Two climbs on small tower with overhang.
5.8. Left corner.
5.10a. Thin cracks 6 feet right of corner.

12   5.8. Crack with small chockstone.

13   HARDER BY THE CLIMBER, 5.6. Inside corner that became harder after each climber.

14   SPLIT CORNER, 5.7. Corner with crack.

15   HIGH STEP, 5.11a. Short face and crack.

16   5.6. Inside corner.

17   TUBS, 5.10b. Crack.

18   MOSS MUFFIN, 5.9. Climb face and crack 3 feet right of Tubs (route 17).

19   5.6. Inside corner.

20   5.6. Inside corner.

West Terraces (Diagram 18 E)

West Terraces consists of Hidden Buttress, Juniper Wall, White Wall, Poison Ivy Wall, and Bird-Foot Buttress. The climbing walls in these five areas face south and are located one above the other.

Hidden Buttress is near the base of the bluff behind trees.

Juniper Wall is 75 feet above and slightly east of Hidden Buttress. It is a short wall with numerous juniper trees above and below.

White Wall has large white quart sections on the main wall. There is also a tower at the west end that resembles the stone faces on Easter Island.

Poison Ivy Wall has a very healthy population of poison ivy growing along the buttress, making topping out and setting up climbs a precarious operation.

Bird-Foot Buttress is the highest rock outcropping and named for the numerous bird-foot violets that grow along the top of the buttress.

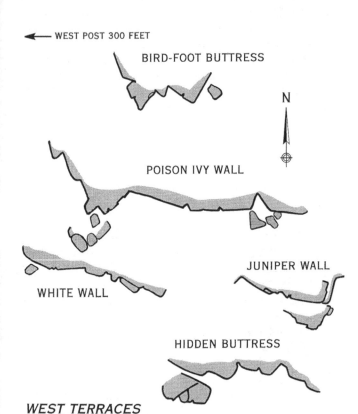

BIRD-FOOT BUTTRESS

N

POISON IVY WALL

JUNIPER WALL

WHITE WALL

HIDDEN BUTTRESS

WEST TERRACES
DIAGRAM 18 E

├────┤
50 FEET

Hidden Buttress (Diagram 19 E)

APPROACH: Refer to Diagram 18 E, West Terraces. From the CCC parking area, walk east on the South Shore Road approximately 1,000 feet to where the road begins to descend the moraine slope. Turn left and walk north through the trees to the base of the boulderfield, which splits down low. Hidden Buttress is just above the east margin of the west boulderfield, 350 feet from South Shore Road, hidden behind a few trees.

Waypoint 26: Hidden Buttress
    UTM 16T 280872E 4810121N

Base Elevation: 1,099 feet
Top Elevation: 1,151 feet

ROUTES:

1 5.7. Climb center of face.
2 CHARLIE BROWN, 5.6. Climb just right of southeast corner.
3 PEANUTS, 5.10a. Crack just left of southeast corner. *Variation*, 5.8. At 10 feet traverse left a few feet to another crack leading to large ledge. Continue near corner to top.
4 LINUS, 5.11b. Thin cracks in center of face.
5 THE FERN, 5.10b. Climb lower face 4 feet right of Nowhere Man (route 6). Continue in crack above.
6 NOWHERE MAN, 5.11c/d. Climb shallow groove/crack that ends 8 feet below top. Continue straight up on face.

Hidden Buttress

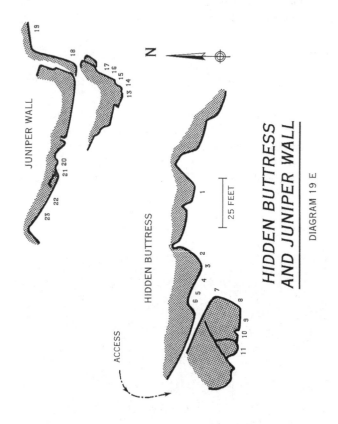

**HIDDEN BUTTRESS
AND JUNIPER WALL**

DIAGRAM 19 E

25 FEET

N

JUNIPER WALL

HIDDEN BUTTRESS

ACCESS

Variation, 5.8. Where groove/crack ends, traverse right 5 feet and follow crack to top.

Routes 7–11 end on a lower platform.

7 PINE SAP, 5.8. Climb right-slanting crack to small over-hang. Continue straight up to top.
8 5.9. Climb face. Avoid using left corner.
9 5.5. Broken face.
10 5.10a. Climb overhang directly.
11 5.6. Climb to ledge under large ceiling. Move right and up over overhang.

Juniper Wall (Diagram 19 E)

APPROACH: Refer to Approach for Hidden Buttress and Diagram 18 E, West Terraces.

Juniper Wall

Waypoint 27: Juniper Wall
    UTM 16T 280898E 4810144N
Base Elevation: 1,196 feet
Top Elevation: 1,240 feet

Routes:
13 5.7. Short face route.
14 HIVE, 5.7. Corner.
15 5.4. Crack 4 feet right of corner.
16 5.9. Face 3 feet right of route 15.
17 SQUIRM, 5.6. Inside corner. Very awkward.
18 5.7. Face.
19 5.9. Right-slanting diagonal crack. Start as low as possible.
20 5.8. Start on lower wall, finish on corner above.
21 5.8. Crack in shallow V-depression.
22 5.8. Climb lower wall to high point.
23 5.6. Start in crack on lower wall, finish on face above.

White Wall (Diagram 20 E)

Approach: Refer to Approach for Hidden Buttress and Diagram 18 E, West Terraces.

Waypoint 28: White Wall
    UTM 16T 280841E 4810159N
Base Elevation: 1,207 feet
Top Elevation: 1,243 feet

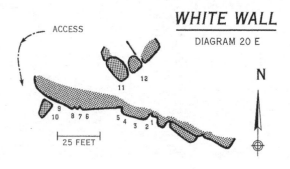

WHITE WALL

DIAGRAM 20 E

1 EXIT BLUES, 5.11c. Climb corner and face left of gully. Move right to overhang and continue up face to crux near top.

2 SHORT PEOPLE NEED NOT APPLY, 5.12a. Start near corner or in deep crack and climb to overhang two-thirds of the way up. Move left and climb face to top.

3 A MIDWESTERN CLIMB, 5.12a. Start 5 feet left of deep crack and climb center of white wall. Finish right of Purple Stripe (route 4) or on face as in Short People Need Not Apply (route 2).

White Wall

4 PURPLE STRIPE, 5.9. Start in crack below obvious recess. Climb crack and recess to 2-foot-wide ledge. Move right a few feet. Climb face and upper thin crack to top.

5 5.6. Start in crack and climb into recess. Finish in upper inside corner left of overhanging nose.

6 EASTER ISLAND, 5.7. Start on freestanding block. Climb face, finish in short crack near top.

7 5.8. Climb lower and upper inside corners, staying right of rib. Avoid holds on rib. Involves quite awkward stems at start.

8 UNSATISFACTORILY, 5.6. Crack left of rib.

9 BEHIND AKU, 5.4. Crack.

10 AKU AKU, 5.7. East face of tower. Avoid using corners.

11 5.9. Corner and face of tower.

12 5.7. Face of tower.

Poison Ivy Wall (Diagram 21 E)

Approach: Refer to Approach for Hidden Buttress and Diagram 18 E, West Terraces, or Approach for Vulture Lookout using the Jack-in-the-Pulpit Trail. When you reach the top of the small rocky gully/dry streambed on the Jack-in-the-Pulpit Trail, walk southeast (right). After 300 feet you reach West Post. Another 300 feet farther is Bird-Foot Buttress. Poison Ivy Wall is 75 feet directly below Bird-Foot Buttress.

Waypoint 29: Poison Ivy Wall
 UTM 16T 280887E 4810167N
Base Elevation: 1,258 feet
Top Elevation: 1,297 feet

Routes:
1 LOST ARROW, 5.6. Northeast side of tower.

2 RAMSES III, 5.8. Start on face just right of crack. Continue on south-facing ramp. Finish by climbing top overhang.

3 UNDER THE BOTTLE, 5.11b. Climb face right of center. There is an obvious undercling at 15 feet. Do not use upper left corner.

4 RAMSES II, 5.7. Wide crack with overhang at top.

5 RAMSES I, 5.7. Crack with overhang at top.

6 RIGHT OF BLANKNESS, 5.8. Face near inside corner.

7 BROKEN HOLD, 5.10a. Short face route.

8 5.6. Climb face, then finish on blocks at top.

9 PORTRAIT CORNER, 5.8. Start just left of corner. At 10 feet move right and follow corner to top.

10 SAY CHEESE, 5.10a. Climb center of face on small holds.

11 DECEPTION, 5.6. Wide, left-leaning crack.

12 5.5. Crack system.

FLYING SQUIRREL, 5.9. Narrow face between route 12 and route 13. Climb face without using vertical crack or holds on route 12 or route 13.

Poison Ivy Wall

13 5.8. Start in short, shallow V-crack left of wide chimney/crack (route 14). Climb to ledge with block. Finish on face above. Do not step on block.

14 5.5. Wide chimney/crack.

15 WEEPING QUARTZ LEFT, 5.8. Face 4–5 feet right of route 14.

16 WEEPING QUARTZ RIGHT, 5.6. Climb center of face.

17 5.7. Climb diagonally up just left of white quartz rock.

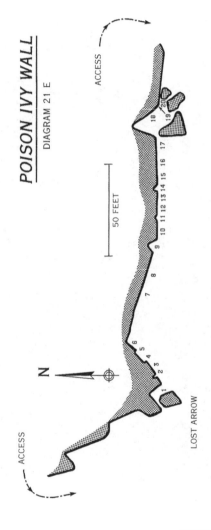

EAST BLUFF CLIMBS

Under the Bottle (Diagram 21 E, route 3). Climber: Peter Cleveland.
Photo: Alex Andrews.

Routes 18–20 start from a platform 10 feet up.

18 SLUGGO, 5.6. Crack in southwest face.
19 PETE'S 10, 5.8. Climb staying as close to corner as possible.
20 NANCY, 5.8. Face 4 feet right of Pete's 10 (route 19).

Bird-Foot Buttress, a.k.a. American Dream Area
(Diagram 22 E)

Approach: Refer to Approach for Hidden Buttress and Diagram 18 E, West Terraces, or Approach for Poison Ivy Wall using the Jack-in-the-Pulpit Trail.

Waypoint 30: Bird-Foot Buttress
 UTM 16T 280872E 4810193N

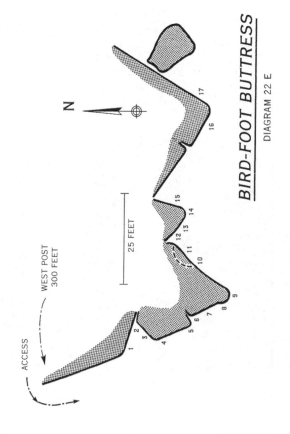

Base Elevation: 1,326 feet
Top Elevation: 1,364 feet

ROUTES:

  1 BIRD SEED, 5.9. Overhanging wall and crack.
  2 5.5. Chimney.
  3 PAY OFF, 5.7. Face.

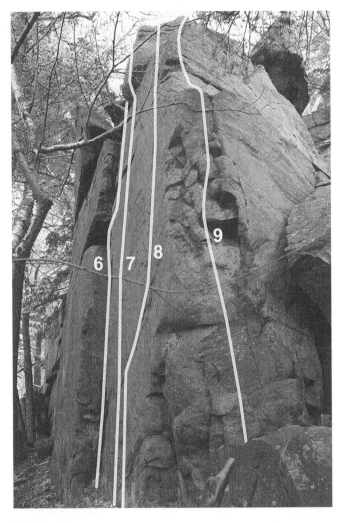

Bird-Foot Buttress

4 LITTLE BIRD, 5.8. Climb crack near southwest corner. Avoid using left corner.
Variation, 5.7. Climb on and left of corner.

5 SICK VULTURE, 5.8. Climb lower corner and upper face. Finish just right of center crack in overhang.
Variation, 5.10b. Start farther left. Avoid lower right corner.

6 SQUEEZE PLAY, 5.8. Start in chimney and climb to overhang. Climb out of chimney and step right, continue to top. Awkward.

7 PROCTO PETE AND THE ENDOS, 5.12b. Face just right of Squeeze Play (route 6).

8 MOTHER AND APPLE PIE, 5.9. Start in middle of face. Climb diagonally up and right to thin crack near corner. Follow crack to surprise near the top. Avoid using corner.

9 HARD NOSE, 5.8. Corner.

10 ELLIS ISLAND, 5.8. Start from block, climb up and right to top.

11 AMERICAN DREAM ROOF, 5.10d. Start above lower overhang. Climb 5-foot overhang directly, using finger-holds under roof and large bucket holds above.
Variation, AMERICAN DREAM DIRECT, 5.11a. Start on left side of lower overhang. Move right and up.

12 5.5. Chimney.

13 5.7. Face just right of chimney.

14 DOVE TAIL LEFT, 5.7. Corner.

15 DOVE TAIL RIGHT, 5.6. Crack just right of corner.

16 5.7. Climb corner, move left near top.

17 VULTURE NEST, 5.7. Face with thin start.

West Post (Diagram 23 E)

APPROACH: West Post is a small outcropping well hidden in the forest 300 feet west of Bird-Foot Buttress. All of the climbs are short. Refer to Approach for Hidden Buttress and Diagram 18 or Approach for Poison Ivy Wall using the Jack-In-The-Pulpit Trail.

Waypoint 31: West Post
UTM 16T 280757E 4810219N
Base Elevation: 1,255 feet
Top Elevation: 1,290 feet

ROUTES:

1 THE POST, 5.8. Face route near corner.
2 R.C., 5.10c. Overhanging inside corner and crack.
3 OUTSIDE R.C., 5.10d. Start 6 feet right of R.C. (route 2), climb into hanging inside corner.

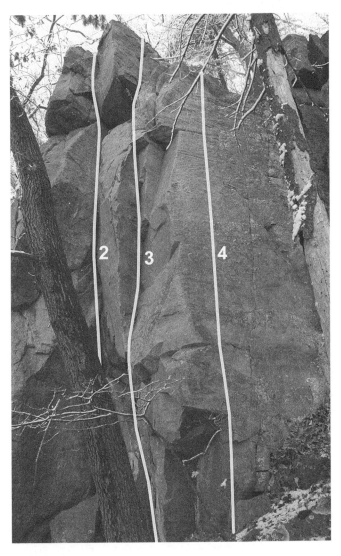

West Post

4 I SEE THE BUCKET, 5.10b. Face and left corner.
Variation, 5.11a. Avoid using left corner.

5 ROTTEN ATTITUDE, 5.8. Inside corner.

6 5.7. Crack.

7 5.9. Crack 3 feet right of route 6. Avoid using route 6 crack and right corner.

8 5.4. Crack.

9 5.4. Inside corner.

10 5.8. Crack 4 feet right of route 9.

11 5.9. Double crack.

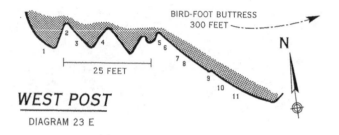

BIRD-FOOT BUTTRESS
300 FEET

N

25 FEET

WEST POST

DIAGRAM 23 E

THE GUILLOTINE

The Guillotine is a cluster of walls and towers situated below the east end of the East Rampart located approximately 0.5 mile east of the parking and picnic areas at the south shore of the lake.

The CCC Trail provides relatively easy access to The Guillotine, which is comprised of climbing areas on three levels above and east of the CCC Trail. The lower level is called No Sweat. Directly above No Sweat lies the middle level, Guillotine Wall. The upper level lies above Guillotine Wall and gives the area its name. It consists of towers with a suggestive wedge-shaped chockstone lodged between two of them. A considerable number and variety of short climbs (20–30 feet) are concentrated on the towers and on the walls below. This is a good area for beginners and large groups.

No Sweat (Diagram 24 E)

APPROACH: Follow the CCC Trail from the CCC parking area. No Sweat is the first rock outcropping along the trail located above three switchbacks in the wooded lower bluff.

Waypoint 32: CCC Parking Area
    UTM 16T 280525E 4810027N
Waypoint 33: No Sweat
    UTM 16T 280456E 4810229N
Base Elevation: 1,233 feet
Top Elevation: 1,286 feet

ROUTES:
  1 5.4 Rib/crack. Climb easy steps behind tree to west end of roof. Use crack above to take a high step and climb to ledge. This is a good point to start an ascent of the Guillotine ridge.
  2 NO SWEAT, 5.9. Climb strenuously through notch near center of roof.

No Sweat

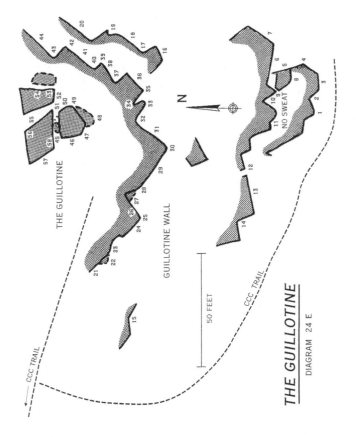

THE GUILLOTINE

DIAGRAM 24 E

3 NO SWEAT OVERHANG, 5.11a, a.k.a. THE BIRD. Start 5 feet right of No Sweat (route 2). Dyno past a very small (8-inch) notch between nose of overhang and No Sweat.

4 5.8. Balance from right onto rock projecting from east end. Step carefully high and left above roof.
Variation, 5.9. Start from below and avoid projecting rock.

5 5.8. A hand traverse. Start left of chimney. Traverse 6 feet left with handholds on a ledge, climb to ledge above.
Variation, 5.9. Climb straight up from bottom. Avoid the hand traverse.

6 5.7. Climb wall right of easy chimney onto mantelshelf. Balance onto upper ledge, then climb above or around right corner.

7   MONGO FURY, 5.10c. Climb cracks 3 feet right of corner.

8–14   A number of 15-foot climbs along the trail above the first ledge.

15   5.5. Traditional layback. A 15-foot, sharp-edged crack along the trail. A faint path branches east at this point.

16–20   Minor wall with short climbs.

Guillotine Wall (Diagram 24 E)

Approach: Guillotine Wall is located directly above No Sweat. Refer to Approach for No Sweat and Diagram 24 E.

Waypoint 34: Guillotine Wall
  UTM 16T 280446E 4810261N
Base Elevation: 1,324 feet
Top Elevation: 1,365 feet

Routes:

21   5.7. Overhanging nose. Climb on left side.

22   5.9. Climb wall into inside corner. Continue on nose above.

23   THE LITTLE THING, 5.1. Shallow chimney.

24   ANNIE'S OVERHANG, 5.7. Overhang/crack. Climb thin crack to overhang. Use hand jam in left crack above overhang and climb right crack to top.

25   POISON IVY, 5.5. Corner with small holds at first.

26   RHUS TOXICODENDRON RADICANS, 5.9+. Climb right of corner.

27   LEVITATION, 5.5. A little levitation may help you to get off the ground (the hardest part). Climb onto left side of slab. Stem past first overhang and finish on left wall.
Variation, 5.9. Same start. Continue on face left of Levitation.

28   LEVITATION, RIGHT SIDE, 5.6. Start at right side of slab. Continue fairly straight up about 5 feet right of inside corner.
Variation, 5.11d. Start same. At 8 feet stretch far right and move up. Avoid the holds on Labor Pains (route 29). Continue straight to top.

29   LABOR PAINS, 5.10b. Start at left limit of undercut section. The difficulty is concentrated in the first 6 feet.

30 5.7. Corner. Use layback and pinch hold on right side to gain first corner ledge. Continue up corner onto next small ledge. A mantelshelf problem.

31 BROKEN BOULDERS, 5.2. Crack starting from niche. *Variation*, 5.2. Begin farther right on slanting ledge.

32 THE LAYBACK, 5.4. Layback, jamming left leg in crack. *Variation*, 5.7. Climb as a pure layback. Very strenuous.

33 5.5. Corner.

34 BEGINNER'S CHIMNEY, 5.2. Chimney.

35 BEGINNER'S NOSE, 5.2. Nose.

36 BEGINNER'S FACE, 5.4. Climb 4 feet onto first ledge, then up left corner.

Guillotine Wall

Variation, 5.6. Climb directly up middle and right side of face.

37–44 East end of Guillotine Wall.

The Guillotine (Diagram 24 E)

APPROACH: The Guillotine is a cluster of towers sitting on a platform directly above Guillotine Wall. Refer to Approaches for No Sweat and Guillotine Wall.

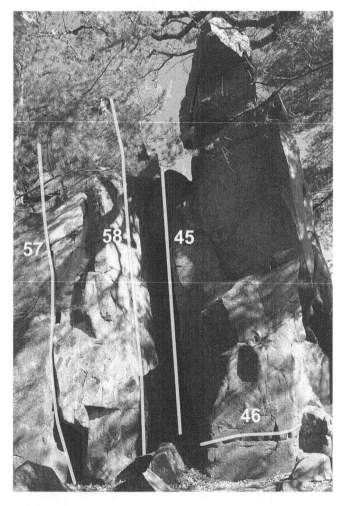

The Guillotine

Waypoint 35: The Guillotine
  UTM 16T 280456E 4810272N
Base Elevation: 1,366 feet

ROUTES:

45 GUILLOTINE WEST, 5.2. Chimney. Climb by bridging with back and feet or by stemming. The latter method is neater.
Variation, 5.2. From upper chockstone, traverse underneath top overhang on south tower.

46 5.4. Low-level traverse 2 feet off the ground.

47 5.7. Overhanging crack.

48 5.2. Ledges. Easy except for retable at top.

49 5.3. Corner with small balance holds.

50 BAREFOOT CRACK, 5.3. Face/cracks. A good climb to practice placing protection.

51 GUILLOTINE EAST, 5.2. Chimney featuring easy stemming practice.

52 5.8. Narrow face with small holds.

53 THE GOPHER, 5.7. Work up right side of corner onto small face holds, then grab for the top.

54 5.7. Crack starting behind block.

55 5.2. Chimney.

56 5.4. Corner. Climb straight up.

57 ANARCHIST CRACK, 5.4. Crack leading to upper ledge.

58 DECAPITATION, 5.7. Climb wall just right of corner to upper ledge. Continue on small holds to top.

East Bluff, East Rampart. Photo: Chuck Koch.

EAST RAMPART

The East Rampart (Diagram 25 E) is a rock outcropping 0.5 mile east of the South Shore parking and picnic area. The cliff band is almost continuous for 0.25 mile along the summit of the East Bluff. It averages 80 feet in height and is generally considered to have the finest climbing at Devil's Lake.

Climbers visit the East Rampart more frequently than any other area in the park. Because the area offers excellent climbing and a high concentration of longer climbs, it is often very crowded. Patience is often required, since there may be a wait for the most popular routes.

The Monster (Diagram 26 E)

APPROACH: Follow the CCC Trail from the CCC parking area. After passing the first rock outcropping, No Sweat, the trail skirts a scenic boulderfield and turns abruptly left (west) at the base of a short wall, The Monster.

Waypoint 32: CCC Parking Area
    UTM 16T 280525E 4810027N
Waypoint 36: The Monster
    UTM 16T 280427E 4810289N
Base Elevation: 1,364 feet
Top Elevation: 1,407 feet

ROUTES:
  1 THE FLATIRON, B1. This is a ghastly John Gill boulder problem (every area has at least one). Climb the center of the smooth, 15-foot-high rock slab where the trail reaches the base of a subsidiary wall just below the summit cliff. There are easier variations on the sides.
     Variation, B2. Climb using right crack only.
  2 5.9. Start at top of The Flatiron (route 1) and climb short wall above.

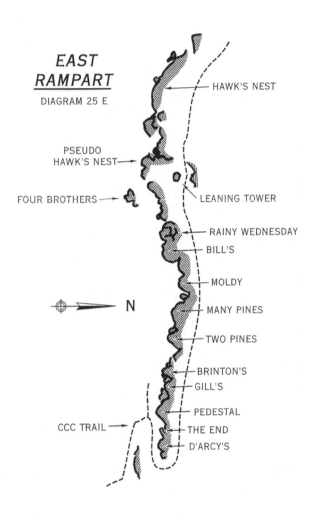

EAST RAMPART

DIAGRAM 25 E

HAWK'S NEST

PSEUDO HAWK'S NEST →

FOUR BROTHERS →

LEANING TOWER

RAINY WEDNESDAY

BILL'S

MOLDY

N

MANY PINES

TWO PINES

BRINTON'S

GILL'S

PEDESTAL

CCC TRAIL →

THE END

D'ARCY'S

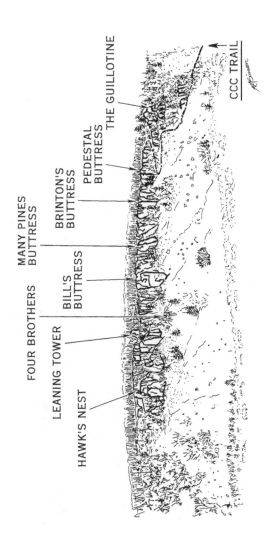

FOUR BROTHERS   MANY PINES BUTTRESS

LEANING TOWER   BILL'S BUTTRESS   BRINTON'S BUTTRESS   PEDESTAL BUTTRESS

HAWK'S NEST   THE GUILLOTINE

CCC TRAIL

EAST BLUFF

EAST RAMPART

3 FRANKENSTEIN, 5.12b. Climb corner with small over-hang.

4 THE MONSTER, 5.10c. Short, unfriendly crack. Start in shallow alcove in overhanging wall. Climb to top of alcove, continue in crack above.

5 THE THING, 5.7. A typical Devil's Lake paradox—how can it be so hard when it looks so easy? Start at base of chimney or groove (an approach from left or right is preferable to a direct attack) and climb groove to top.

6 THE ZIPPER, B2. Tight seam just left of The Thing (route 5).

7 CLOSE TO THE THING, 5.8. Climb left corner of wall.

8 ALSO CLOSE TO THE THING, 5.8. Climb cracks in middle of face.

9 THE BODY SNATCHER, 5.7. Start below shallow chimney capped by an overhang. Climb crack at left to ledge at base of chimney, then climb chimney. Step left and up to top. It would be well not to fall traversing out from the chimney.

The Monster

10 THE BODY SNATCHER DIRECT, 5.10c. Climb straight over the overhang. Avoid holds on The Body Snatcher (route 9).

11 THE BODY SNATCHER VARIATION, 5.7. Start on bench just left of The Body Snatcher (route 9). Climb flake and crack.

12 THE CRAB, 5.9-B1. The short wall just left of The Body Snatcher (route 9). It can be climbed several different ways.

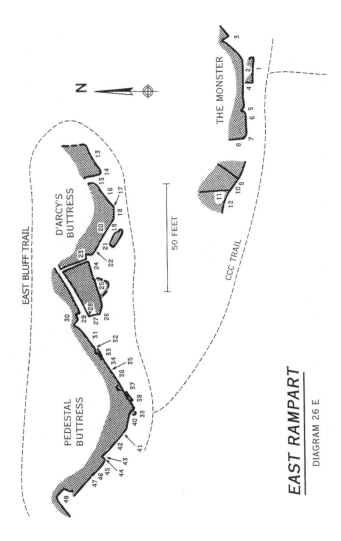

EAST RAMPART

DIAGRAM 26 E

D'Arcy's Buttress (Diagram 26 E)

Approach: Follow the CCC Trail past No Sweat and The Monster. The trail runs directly into the center of Pedestal Buttress. D'Arcy's Buttress is 100 feet east (right) of Pedestal Buttress.

Waypoint 37: D'Arcy's Buttress
   UTM 16T 280414E 4810314N
Base Elevation: 1,413 feet
Top Elevation: 1,458 feet

D'Arcy's Buttress, East Rampart

Routes:

13 CEMETERY WALL, 5.6. Short boulder problem. Start in center of face.

14 SHIP'S PROW, 5.6. Jutting nose. Likened to keelhauling.

15 30 SECOND CRACK, 5.3. For those who are bothered by exposure.

16 D'ARCY'S WALL, 5.8. Named for Ray D'Arcy, who never was able to make the last crux reach. Start on right side of wall near inside corner. Climb left to approximate center of wall, then up to top.

Variation, GRAND TRAVERSE, 5.8. From center of wall, traverse left around the corner to Last Gasp (route 18).

17 DEATH LEAP 2000, 5.10b, a.k.a. BLOW YOUR NOSE. Start 8 feet right of corner in thin crack. Traverse left to corner, then right onto large flakes of D'Arcy's Wall (route 16). Jump up and left for bucket hold on Last Gasp (route 18). Finish on face right of corner.

Variation, PICK YOUR NOSE, 5.10d. Avoid bucket hold on Last Gasp (route 18).

ZSCHIESCHE'S ROOF, B2. Same start, then climb overhang and thin seam near left edge of face without using left corner.

18 LAST GASP, 5.8. Many a climber has grasped the final ledge only to fall from utter exhaustion. Start in pit slightly left of corner (starting from adjacent rocks is strictly frowned upon). Struggle up to ledge, continue close to corner to top.

19 EASY OVERHANG, 5.4. This route offers an introductory course in the use of buckets. Climb to ledge behind large block. Traverse to right crack. Negotiate overhang, continue to top.

20 STRAWBERRY FIELDS, 5.9. Climb bulge left of Easy Overhang (route 19). Surmount overhang, then continue directly to top.

21 ZIG-ZAG, 5.5. This line follows the left crack behind the block. Climb to ledge behind large block. Zig left and zag right to clear overhang, continue in crack to top. Try to be one of Devil's Lake's select few who don't use the linden tree.

22 5.9. Climb corner left of Zig-Zag (route 21) to roof. Continue over roof to top.

23 DARKNESS AT NOON, 5.2. Stygian chimney.

24 SOMETIME CRACK RIGHT SIDE, 5.10b/c. Thin crack on right side of overhanging wall. Climb crack to alcove, then up left to Sometime Crack (route 25).

25 SOMETIME CRACK, 5.10a. When queried about whether they lead this climb, climbers typically give the evasive response "sometime." Start on slab 15 feet high at base of overhanging jam crack. Climb jam crack to intersection with horizontal crack. Traverse 5 feet right, then up to top. On top rope, watch for a severe pendulum.

BLOW-UP, 5.10b. At horizontal crack, hand traverse left to corner, then up crack to top.

SOMETIME DIRECT, 5.10d. At horizontal crack, continue up center of wall past big bucket hold to top. Not topping out avoids the last hard mantle move.

WELFARE LINE, 5.12b/c. Climb overhanging face between Sometime Crack and Sometime Left.

MODERN ART, 5.13a. Direct finish to Welfare Line. Climb Welfare Line to horizontal crack. Finish on face left of Sometime Direct.

SOMETIME LEFT, 5.11d. Start on platform 6 feet left of crack. Climb overhanging wall to horizontal crack. Traverse right and finish on Sometime Direct.

DYSLEXIA, 5.13d. Climb straight up steep face/corner between Sometime Left and Batman, a.k.a. The Dog (route 26).

26 BATMAN, 5.12a/b, a.k.a. THE DOG. Start under The End (route 27), traverse up and right around corner on good holds. Then traverse back left on thin holds to arête. Follow arête to top.

27 THE END, 5.10a. One's last lead at Devil's Lake? Start on block outside deep cleft. Traverse right to narrow overhanging wall, climb wall (if lucky) to top.

Variation, THE END DIRECT, 5.10b. Start on bottom, avoiding block.

28 END OF THE END, 5.10a. Start on same block as The End (route 27). Climb corner above, that is, left corner of The End.

29 CHIMNEY'S END, 5.4. Deep cleft behind The End (route 27). The cleft can be ascended as a chimney.

Pedestal Buttress (Diagram 26 E)

Approach: Follow the CCC Trail past No Sweat and The Monster. The trail runs directly into the center of Pedestal Buttress.

Waypoint 38: Pedestal Buttress
    UTM 16T 280375E 4810308N
Base Elevation: 1,387 feet
Top Elevation: 1,467 feet

Routes:
30 THE BEGINNING, 5.7. Groove or V-chimney.
31 THE STRETCHER, 5.9+/10a. Start on smooth face 10 feet right of Birch Tree Crack (route 32). Make a few long reaches, then continue up, up, up to top.

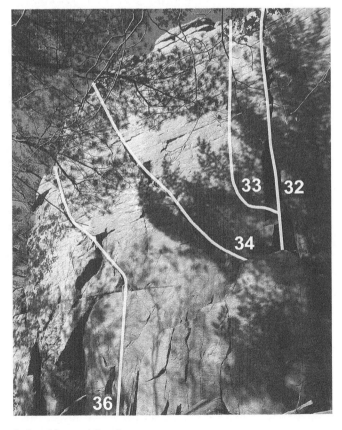

Pedestal Buttress, East Rampart

Variation, 5.10b. Same start, but climb up and slightly left near Birch Tree Crack (route 32).

PETE'S LAMENT, 5.12b. Climb blank-looking face right of The Stretcher.

32 BIRCH TREE CRACK, 5.8. This is a one-move climb. Without proper technique it becomes a no-move retreat. The birch tree that once grew here could not stand the continual abuse of falling climbers. Start on ledge 10 feet up. Climb into alcove, then up crack to top.

33 HOURGLASS, 5.11c. From higher blocks in Birch Tree Crack (route 32) alcove, traverse left onto face. Continue on face straight to top.

HOURGLASS DIRECT, 5.12a. Start from large ledge 10 feet up, just left of Birch Tree Crack (route 32). Move left and climb face straight to top.

34 UPPER DIAGONAL, 5.9. Start on same ledge as Birch Tree Crack (route 32). Climb left to diagonal crack and follow it to the top. Strenuous, but it can be well protected.

FLAKE ROUTE, 5.10d. Climb face left of Upper Diagonal to alcove with fixed pin. Here the route crosses Upper Diagonal. From alcove, move right to obvious flake, then up and slightly right to top.

ANGLE OF DANGLE, 5.12a. From flake, climb to thin crack. At the end of the crack, move left to face. This route is hard on the fingertips.

35 SWEATSHOP, 5.11b. Climb between Upper Diagonal (route 34) and Lower Diagonal (route 36).

36 LOWER DIAGONAL, 5.8. This route offers experience in placing protection on the run. Start 7 feet right of large alcove by tree stump. Climb to lower diagonal crack. Climb crack to ledge on left corner. Exit left.

Variation, THE TRICK, 5.8. From ledge, finish by climbing the wall directly, a bit left of the corner.

37 THE PEDESTAL, 5.4. A traditional two-pitch climb. *First pitch:* Start below detached flake. Climb right edge to top of flake (pedestal), traverse left around corner to hidden triangular belay ledge. *Second pitch:* Continue traversing left to pine tree. Climb crack to upper ledge, from which several finishes are possible.

38 CONDOLENCES, 5.7. A straighter version of The Pedestal (route 37). Start under left edge of flake. Climb crack

Upper Diagonal (Diagram 26 E, route 34). Climber: Lorene Marcinek. Photo: Alex Andrews.

and overhang, then up onto flake (crux). Traverse left to corner. Climb corner past bulges to ledge (same ledge as Lower Diagonal, route 36).

Variation, 5.11b. At 10 feet, climb short face with sharp fingerholds just left of The Pedestal (route 37) flake.

39 GOLDEN LEDGES, 5.11b. The gold is fool's gold, and so are the ledges. Start just left of corner. Climb into groove on corner, then up to traverse on The Pedestal (route 37). Continue straight up.

40 ALL THE WAY, 5.12b. There are no easy moves on this climb. Start in groove 5 feet right of Congratulations (route 41). Climb straight up face to The Pedestal (route 37) belay ledge. Continue straight up.

Variation, 5.11d. Start from left, avoiding groove.

41 CONGRATULATIONS, 5.10a. One of the classic *hard* routes, the scene of many falls. Climb steep crack leading to pine tree.

42 ASSUME THE POSITION, 5.12b. Thin face route left of Congratulations (route 41). The face is gained by a traverse from the left.

43 RICH & FAMOUS, 5.11d. Start up Ironmongers (route 44) and climb to small pedestal. Traverse 6 feet right under overhang, then up bulging overhang to top. Do not use the bucket hold on Pine Box (route 44 variation).

44 IRONMONGERS, 5.7. Start at base of tree. Climb into alcove, step left, and continue up crack to ledge.

Variation, PINE BOX, 5.10a. Climb straight up from alcove.

45 IRONMONGERS SUPER DIRECT, 5.11a. Start 5 feet left of Ironmongers (route 44). Everything but the corner is legal.

46 EVELYN BITES THE CRUST, 5.10b. Climb 12 inches left of Ironmongers Super Direct (route 45).

47 LETHE, 5.7. Climb slabby wall past overhang to ledge. An easy crack leads to top.

48 5.2. Easy climbs in upper recess.

Gill's Buttress and Brinton's Buttress (Diagram 27 E)

Approach: Where the CCC Trail meets Pedestal Buttress walk approximately 50 feet west along the base of the bluff on the climbers' trail to Gill's Buttress. Access the top by following the CCC Trail around the east end of D'Arcy's Buttress.

Waypoint 39: Gill's Buttress and Brinton's Buttress
UTM 16T 280357E 4810305N
Base Elevation: 1,384 feet
Top Elevation: 1,482 feet

ROUTES:

49 FANTASY, 5.9. Start at base of smooth wall. At 10 feet, move 8 feet right, then back left into notch at top of wall. *Variation,* WEASELS RIPPED MY FLESH, 5.12a. Climb straight up to upper notch.

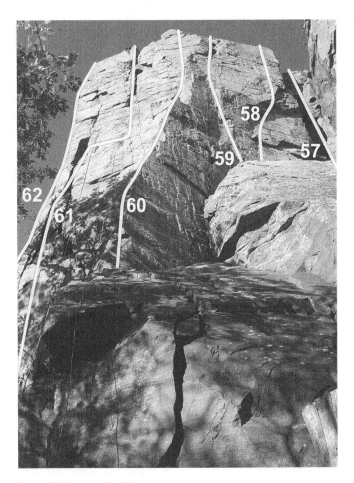

Brinton's Buttress, East Rampart

50 IN SEARCH OF THE LOST LIBIDO, 5.12b. Climb left of Fantasy (route 49).

51 THE SPINE, 5.4. Deep groove or chimney. Start at crack on left side. Climb into groove and up.

Variation, 5.6. Eliminate right wall of groove.

52 ACID ROCK, 5.12a. Smooth, high wall left of The Spine (route 51). Start on top of large block, climb 5 feet on right side of wall. Traverse up and left to flake, then up and farther left to good ledge near left corner. Continue up and right. Finish in center of wall.

Variation, SLUT FOR PUNISHMENT, 5.12b. Same start, but climb straight to top. Very thin.

53 PEYOTE BLUES, 5.12b. Start on block below Acid Rock (route 52). Step across to wall and traverse up and left to corner. Follow corner to top.

Variation, ICE, 5.13b. Start in chimney right of Gill's Nose (route 54). Climb face with a series of very thin moves to join Peyote Blues.

54 GILL'S NOSE, 5.11b. Start at base of corner, climb face just left of corner.

Variation, 5.11c. Near top, climb on corner.

55 GILL'S CHEEK, 5.11d/12a. Climb wall between Gill's Nose (route 54) and Gill's Crack (route 56). Avoid using holds on other climbs.

56 GILL'S CRACK, 5.10b/c. Start halfway up slab in Boy Scout (route 57). Climb crack in right-hand wall. A John Gill on-sight solo.

57 BOY SCOUT, 5.3. A standard *easy* route often crammed with beginners. Climb slab (many variations) to base of large chimney, then up chimney to top.

58 RUBBER MAN, 5.13a. Start on pedestal right of Cheap Thrills (route 59). The first move is a very hard mantle.

59 CHEAP THRILLS, 5.12b/c. Start at top left edge of Boy Scout (route 57) slab. Climb to top, staying right of corner.

60 CHIAROSCURO, 5.9+. Start at semicorner 10 feet right of Brinton's Crack (route 61) directly below Hilton Ledge (see Brinton's Crack description). Climb face left of corner to Hilton Ledge, then directly up wall to top.

Variation, 5.9. Start from left side of Boy Scout (route 57) slab. Climb thin crack to Hilton Ledge.

61 BRINTON'S CRACK, 5.6. A classic climb made worthwhile by a continuous series of exposed moves. It was first ascended in 1941; its crux still embarrasses many climbers. Scramble 20 feet up slabby rock to crack near left corner of buttress. Climb crack to just below rectangular niche. Traverse delicately right to (or almost to) platform (Hilton Ledge), then climb jam crack to top.
Variation, BRINTON'S DIRECT, 5.8. From rectangular niche, climb near corner to top.

62 BRINTON'S CORNER, 5.10a. Climb corner all the way to top.

63 ROCOCO VARIATIONS, 5.7. Start near right corner. Climb flake crack for 30 feet and join Berkeley (route 64).
Variation, STOOL PIGEON, 5.10b. At end of flake crack, continue straight up.

64 BERKELEY, 5.6. Another classic. Start at crack 20 feet left of corner. Climb crack 20 feet, then traverse right to ledge under first small overhang. Move up right, then somewhat left to exit crack leading into hanging chimney. This route can be varied considerably.

65 SOUTHSIDE, 5.12a. Climb through small overhang 5 feet right of niche. Avoid holds on Berkeley (route 64) and Chicago (route 66).

66 CHICAGO, 5.8. One of the earlier *hero* climbs. The quality of protection is poor. Start in same crack as Berkeley (route 64). Climb 25 feet to triangular niche (last protection until after crux). Continue up crack past the long, sustained crux. Surmount final overhang just below top.

67 EVANSTON TOWNSHIP, 5.10b. Start from platform at base of Puff 'n' Grunt Chimney (route 69). Climb thin crack parallel to Chicago (route 66).
Variation, 5.11b. Climb lower wall without using rock on left.

68 GOLF ROAD, 5.10d. Start on platform. Climb face right of chimney.

69 PUFF 'N' GRUNT CHIMNEY, 5.6. Climb one of two inside corners to base of chimney. Continue up chimney to top. Several wedged chockstones are useful.

70 THE RACK, 5.7. Start at right-curving crack capped by overhang. Follow crack to small platform on right corner. Step up left (crux), and climb corner blocks to ledge. Finish on wall right of corner.

Variation, 5.6. From small platform on right corner, traverse right 10 feet and climb wall to corner blocks.

71 THOROUGHFARE, 5.11a. Start 5 feet right of The Grotto (route 73). Climb inside corner with use of adjacent (right) crack. Continue up thin cracks in spectacular green wall above.

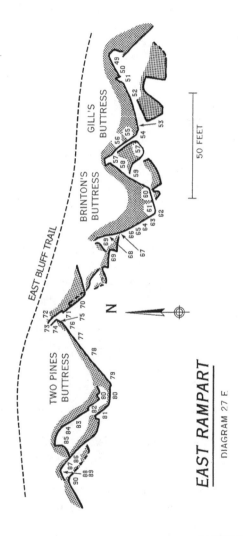

EAST RAMPART

DIAGRAM 27 E

CROSS TOWN TRAFFIC, 5.11d/12a. Start 4–5 feet right of Thoroughfare. Climb up and left to solution pocket. Continue using only right-hand crack. A difficult start leading to an arm-burning finish.

L.S.D., 5.11c. Climb using only left crack of Thoroughfare.

72 LUNAR ECLIPSE, 5.11a. Climb crack in right wall of The Grotto (route 73). Continue up through middle of higher, right overhang. When falling, watch your back.

Two Pines Buttress (Diagram 27 E)

Approach: Where the CCC Trail meets Pedestal Buttress walk approximately 150 feet west along the base of the bluff on the climbers' trail to Two Pines Buttress. Access the top by walking around the east end of D'Arcy's Buttress.

Waypoint 40: Two Pines Buttress
   UTM 16T 280329E 4810328N
Base Elevation: 1,388 feet
Top Elevation: 1,483 feet

Routes:

73 THE GROTTO, 5.4. Start in dark chimney. Climb past chockstones to platform on outside (top of chimney is filled with rock). Finish using crack or inside corner.

74 SOLAR ECLIPSE, 5.7. Climb left wall 4 feet inside the grotto.

75 MOUSE TRAP, 5.11d. Climb narrow face near corner right of Vacillation (route 76).

76 VACILLATION, 5.7. Climb crack with bulge 10 feet up. Two-thirds of the way up, move right to wide crack. Follow crack to top.

77 MOUSE'S MISERY, 5.10a. Face just left of Vacillation (route 76). Climb 25 feet up and left to overhang. Turn the overhang at left crack. Follow crack to top.

MOUSE TRACKS, 5.11a. Climb right side of overhang. Continue by using a heel hook into appalling-looking solution pockets above.

MOUSE'S TAIL, 5.11c. Climb Mouse's Misery to left side of low triangular roof on the right, about 15 feet up. Traverse right and up right side of arch. Continue between Mouse Tracks and Vacillation (route 76). Avoid using the good holds on Vacillation.

78 FULL STOP, 5.6. Another classic, originally called Two Pines. Climb thin crack leading to square niche. From niche, climb over elephant ear bulge. Move 5 feet left and up to hanging gully with several pine trees. (There may be loose rock on the ledge.) Traverse right onto broken section and continue to top.

BIG DEAL, 5.10a. Above elephant ear bulge, climb thin crack about 5 feet left of Mouse's Misery (route 77).

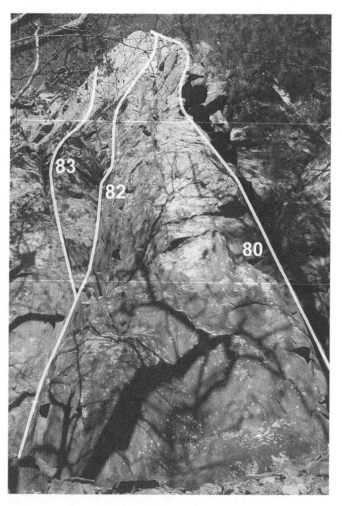

Two Pines Buttress, East Rampart

EAST BLUFF CLIMBS

79 REPRIEVE, 5.7. Start just right of corner, climb up (crux not high off ground) and left to a stance. Continue up face, staying right of corner.

80 SCHIZOPHRENIA, 5.6. Start below overhanging nose 25 feet up. Climb into dark pocket, then around left side of nose (or directly over it) and up ridge.

81 MODERATION, 5.4. Start up broken rock. Traverse right above nose on Schizophrenia (route 80), then up ridge.

Variation, 5.5. Same start, but continue straight up groove that intersects the ridge higher up.

82 BROTHER WITHOUT A BRAIN, 5.11a. Start partway up Moderation (route 81). Climb overhang and corner.

A rock-and-clay gully (5.2) angles steeply left from the start of Moderation (route 81). It provides access to routes 83–85 and the top.

83 TOUCH AND GO, 5.7. Start halfway up gully at the base of steep wall. Move up and right, then back left, following a set of small ledges to top of crackless green wall.

84 DYSPEPSIA, 5.6. About halfway up this wall you'll wish for your pills. Start in same gully as Touch and Go (route 83). Climb crack on left side of steep wall, ending just right of dark overhang near top.

PUSSY GALORE'S FLYING CIRCUS, 5.7. Start below flake (detached block) in line with dark overhang. Climb edge of flake, then continue until below right side of overhang. Traverse left on good footholds. Continue up (crux) to top.

85 JOLLY GENDARME, 5.4. Start in upper part of gully. Traverse left around gendarme on southwest side of gully to crack with tree stump. Climb crack.

86 GERITOL, 5.11c. Start at base of wall with dirty yellow lichen. Climb on very small awkward holds until below hanging corner. Continue up on right side of corner.

87 5.10a–5.10d. Two cracks on wall between Geritol (route 86) and Chlorosis (route 88). The right crack is 5.10a. The left crack is 5.10d.

Routes 88–90 start in the same inside corner.

88 CHLOROSIS, 5.7. Climb inside corner to overhang 30 feet up. Step right and climb overhang to crack above. Follow crack to top.

89 HYPOGLYCEMIA, 5.7. Same start as Chlorosis (route 88). Above overhang, climb overhanging crack and groove on right wall.

Many Pines Buttress (Diagram 28 E)

APPROACH: Where the CCC Trail reaches Pedestal Buttress walk approximately 250 feet west along the base of the bluff on the climbers' trail to Many Pines Buttress. Access the top by following the CCC Trail around the east end of D'Arcy's Buttress.

Waypoint 41: Many Pines Buttress
    UTM 16T 280301E 4810332N
Base Elevation: 1,364 feet
Top Elevation: 1,468 feet

ROUTES:
90 ANEMIA, 5.2. Originally called Many Pines. Same start as Chlorosis (route 88) and Hypoglycemia (route 89). Climb to ledge with first pine tree. Continue by one of several routes.

91 BROKEN LADDER, 5.7. Climb face to pine tree ledge. Continue by one of several variations.

92 PETER'S PROJECT RIGHT SIDE, 5.9. Climb face about 5 feet right of Peter's Project (route 93). The crack is off-limits.

93 PETER'S PROJECT, 5.7. Start in overhanging crack. Climb crack until the angle eases, then move fairly straight up face and cracks to top.

94 OSTENTATION, 5.10a. Start just right of corner with overhang 10 feet up. Climb to overhang and traverse left around corner. Continue up and right to good holds, then follow corner to top.

95 CALLIPIGEANOUS CRACK, 5.10a. An exercise in muscular laybacking. Climb (finger) jam crack, then exit right to corner.

Variation, CALLIPIGEANOUS DIRECT, 5.11b. From jam crack, continue straight up. Avoid good right-handholds.

96 ASLEEP IN A FUKNES DREAM, 5.12a, a.k.a. THE INDIAN. Climb between Callipigeanous Crack (route 95) and No Trump (route 97) all the way to top.

97 NO TRUMP, 5.11d. Start 3 feet right of Michael's Project (route 98). Stay within a few feet of crack all the way to top. Avoid holds in crack.

98 MICHAEL'S PROJECT, 5.7. Start in prominent groove and crack. At 10–15 feet up step right to easier holds, then back to crack until below overhang. Exit right to large ledge, from which there are a couple of ways to finish.

KAMA-KAZI, 5.8. Climb, worming your way up inside corner crack. Finish directly up overhang to top.

99 FLATUS, 5.11b. Easily identified by the lack of identifiable holds. Start below Black Rib (route 100). Climb up and right past three bolts approximately 20 feet up. Continue left under overhang and up.

Variation, FLATUS DIRECT, 5.11d. Do not traverse left under overhang. Climb straight up to top.

FLATUS TRIPLE DIRECT, 5.11d. Start directly below bolts and climb straight to top.

100 BLACK RIB, 5.11a. Getting off the ground is the first crux. Start in pit below dark section of wall, climb to hanging chimney.

101 DOUBLE CLUTCH, 5.12a, a.k.a. CHICKEN'S DON'T FLY. Face between Black Rib (route 100) and Man and Superman (route 102). Climb face, then over bulge to top.

102 MAN AND SUPERMAN, 5.10d. Corner. Finish left at top.

103 SUPERMAN, 5.12a. Face left of Man and Superman (route 102).

104 SEWING MACHINE, 5.6. An unusual climb for Devil's Lake. One's legs give out before one's arms, unless legs and arms give out together. Climb dirty flaring chimney to top. Loose rock near top.

105 5.9. Climb face starting from ledge partway up Sewing Machine (route 104).

106 JAMBOREE, 5.6. Start in chimney (which gives a 5.2 access route behind the small tower), then jam up deep cracks on right wall.

ALGAE, 5.4. Start left of chimney. Follow crack up and right to flake in chimney.

Variation, 5.9. From top of crack, climb left and up.

107 V8, 5.11a. Start in center of wall until a move right leads to a high step. Layback to top.

108 PLEASURES OF THE GROIN, 5.12b. Left side of tower. Same start as V8 (route 107), but follow a straighter line just to the left of V8.

109 5.4. Tower. Start near south corner.

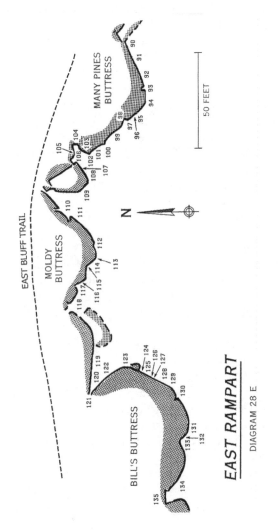

EAST RAMPART

DIAGRAM 28 E

Moldy Buttress (Diagram 28 E)

APPROACH: Moldy Buttress is located between Many Pines Buttress and Bill's Buttress.

ROUTES:

110 LICHEN, 5.2. Climb behind one of the large flakes and continue up wall to top.

111 FUNGUS, 5.7. Face left of flakes using crusty holds.

112 NINE-MINUS, 5.8. Start in shallow inside corner capped by an overhang. Climb up and exit right below overhang. Continue up and left.

TEN-MINUS, 5.10a. Climb face right of inside corner. Continue left as in Nine-Minus.

ELEVEN-MINUS, 5.10d. Same start as Ten-Minus, but continue directly up face.

113 HALES CORNER, 5.10d. Start right of corner. Climb up and left to corner.

114 MOTHER OF PEARL, 5.10c. Only climb face on right side of inside corner.

115 CUL-DE-SAC, 5.8. A deceptive line that is much harder than it looks. Start in inside corner capped by square overhang. Climb up and right past overhang. Scramble up short chimney to ledge, then to top.

Variation, CUL-DE-SAC EXIT, 5.11d. Mantle at roof, then follow corner to top.

116 FIBULA CRACKS, 5.12a/b. Start in shallow inside corner 5 feet left of Cul-de-Sac (route 115). Climb straight up 35 feet and pass overhang on right.

117 TIBIA CRACK, 5.8. Start in crack leading to hanging chimney between two overhangs. Climb crack, enter chimney, and exit right.

118 HORTICULTURE, 5.4. There are large rotten overhangs high up on this line. Several starts. The most interesting is on the outside of semiattached pillar. Climb pillar, then inside corner beneath the overhangs. Exit right to top.

Variation, ROOFUS, 5.8. Same start. Exit left to top.

Bill's Buttress (Diagram 28 E)

APPROACH: Where the CCC Trail reaches Pedestal Buttress walk approximately 375 feet west along the base of the bluff on the climbers' trail to Bill's Buttress. Access the top by following the CCC Trail around the east end of D'Arcy's Buttress.

Waypoint 42: Bill's Buttress
  UTM 16T 280260E 4810308N
Base Elevation: 1,340 feet
Top Elevation: 1,471 feet

ROUTES:

119 DOG LEG, 5.4. Start in dirt gully near base of The Dark Corner (route 121). Climb groove that angles right and then turns straight up. Continue on ledges to top.

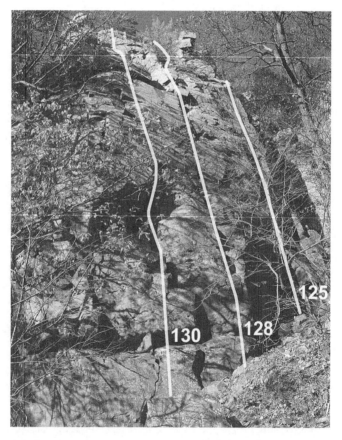

Bill's Buttress, East Rampart

EAST BLUFF CLIMBS

Cheatah (Diagram 28 E, route 125). Climber: Jim Boeder. Photo: Alex Andrews.

120 PROPHET'S HONOR, 5.9. Same start as Dog Leg (route 119). Climb overhanging wall to right of The Dark Corner (route 121).

121 THE DARK CORNER, 5.4. Dark, stygian chimney.

122 BREAKFAST OF CHAMPIONS, 5.8. Climb long jam crack to huge flake. Continue up and left to top.

123 IGNOMINY, 5.4. Start near corner. Climb broken crack up and right to northeast wall of buttress (white rock), then up wall for 10 feet. Continue up ledges into upper inside corner with pine tree, then to top.

124 TIGER, 5.12a. Face just right of Cheatah (route 125). The bucket hold on the right is out of bounds.

125 CHEATAH, 5.10b. An exceptionally continuous route. Climb long crack that ends with a difficult layback (crux) near right corner.

The following two climbs cross partway up.

126 PUSSY CAT, 5.11a. Climb face left of Cheatah (route 125) using flake at the start. Pull past small overhang, then move left. Continue up right of Push-Mi, Pull-Yu (route 128) to top.

127 TOM CAT, 5.12a. A difficult start just left of Pussy Cat (route 126). Start 8 feet left of Cheatah (route 125) crack. Climb over arch, move slightly right, and continue up a few feet left of Cheatah crack.

128 PUSH-MI, PULL-YU, 5.6, a.k.a. THREE PINES. An old classic and popular lead with excellent protection. Climb (several ways) to crack beginning 20 feet up with a pine tree above. Climb crack to pine tree, then scramble up ledges to top.

129 TALK TO THE ANIMALS, 5.10a. Face left of Push-Mi, Pull-Yu (route 128).

130 AGNOSTIC, 5.7. Climb into prominent alcove. Step left onto ledge, then climb face and thin crack directly above alcove.

131 GRAND INQUISITOR, 5.7. An indistinct line that prohibits traversing to the easier climbs on either side. Start at lowest point of Bill's Buttress. Climb 10 feet to ledge, then up (slightly left) 15 feet into shallow groove or trough (obscure from the ground). Continue on easier rock to overhanging layback crack. Climb up crack and end on small tower.

132 MR. BUNNEY MEETS THE POULTRY MAN, 5.11a. Face right of Coatimundi Crack (route 133). Climb overhang at top.

133 COATIMUNDI CRACK, 5.6. Climb prominent groove and crack past overhanging section, then step right onto ledge. Climb to base of corner with small tower above. Continue up near corner or step left to ledge and stem up inside corner (V-chimney). Ends behind tower.

Variation, 5.10a. Same start. At top, climb finger crack on small tower.

OVEREXTENSION, 5.6. Exit left from groove, angling up to first ledge on Escalation (route 134).

134 ESCALATION, 5.6. Climb crack 20 feet to ledge and pine tree. Continue to another ledge and pine tree, then to top.

Variation, 5.6. From first ledge, traverse right on narrow exposed ledge. Join either of the two preceding routes.

Variation, 5.9. From left side of first ledge, climb narrow southwest face. Finish on lichen-covered narrow buttress.

135 THE OUTHOUSE, 5.7. Ugly climb. Start under overhang between the two buttresses. Climb either side of both overhangs. The second overhang is a huge wedged block.

Rainy Wednesday Tower to Leaning Tower Gully
(Diagram 29 E)

APPROACH: Where the CCC Trail meets Pedestal Buttress walk approximately 450 feet west on the climbers' trail to Rainy Wednesday Tower. Access the top by Leaning Tower Gully. The bottom of the gully is a series of rock steps somewhat hidden by a small juniper. An alternate access to the top is to follow the CCC Trail around the east end of D'Arcy's Buttress.

Waypoint 43: Bottom of Leaning Tower Gully
    UTM 16T 280187E 4810317N
Waypoint 44: Rainy Wednesday Tower
    UTM 16T 280236E 4810318N
Base Elevation (Rainy Wednesday Tower): 1,354 feet
Top Elevation (Rainy Wednesday Tower): 1,457 feet

136 5.10b. Climb corner in gully behind upper section of Rainy Wednesday Tower.

137 FALSE ALARM JAM, 5.6. Southeast side of Rainy Wednesday Tower. Start on broken rock, climb to obvious crack in red rock. Climb crack to ledge, then up either side of slab boulder. Continue on southeast face to top of tower.

Rainy Wednesday Tower, East Rampart

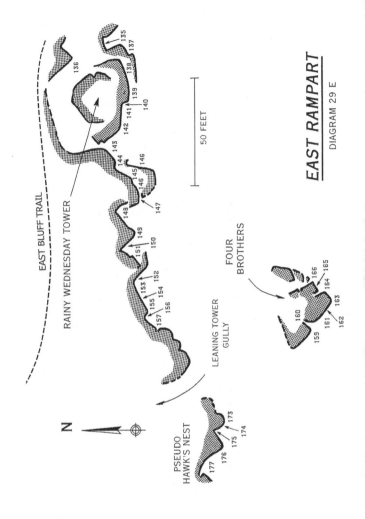

Descent route. Climb down short chimney on northeast side and jump down behind tower. Continue down chimney west of tower to base of cliff.

138 RESURRECTION, 5.10a. Start on large block at base of smooth face (pointed ceiling above). Climb face near right edge until able to move left and up into bowl-shaped area. Continue up to ceiling and exit right.

Variation, 5.11d/12a. Climb center of smooth face, then step left and climb into bowl as above.

RESURRECTION RIGHT, 5.11c/d. Face right of Resurrection.

139 LAUNDRY CHUTE, 5.11d. Climb left side of face past two small overhangs. Continue up and under right side of large overhang. Climb hanging chute in overhang.

NO STARCH, 5.11b/c. Avoid chute. Pass overhang on the right.

140 EAVE OF DESTRUCTION, 5.9+. Same start as Double Overhang (route 141). When under ceiling 30 feet up, step right and continue straight up. Finish left of upper corner. *Variation*, 5.7. Step right about 15 feet below ceiling, then up corner.

141 DOUBLE OVERHANG, 5.4. A well-protected route sufficiently exposed to maintain interest. Start in inside corner below ceiling and climb crack in corner. Exit left and up to platform. Climb right onto *lemon squeezer* block, then up into recess beneath right side of upper overhang. (**NOTE:** If you climb directly up from the platform toward the overhang, it is necessary to step right around a rib to attain this recess.) Step left and up into notch in overhang, then to top of tower.

Variation, 5.7. At the *lemon squeezer*, traverse right 10 feet. Step around corner into groove and climb to top.

142 5.4. Climb face directly to platform.

143 OUT OF THE WOODS, 5.8. Southeast face.

144 BIRNAM WOOD, 5.7. Climb crack hidden and jealously guarded by tree.

145 NEW LIGHT WAVES, 5.12b. Cracks and overhang right of Green Bulge (route 146). Climb slabs to the first crack (25 feet up). Move left to pass overhang, then back right. Follow thin cracks to top.

Variation, 5.12b. At overhang continue straight up on very thin holds and a long reach. Finish as above.

146 GREEN BULGE, 5.7. Start at prominent red slab. Climb slab (various routes) to base of green bulge, then up bulge (from left or right) to ledge. Continue up and finish on small tower.

147 MISS PIGGY'S PLEASURE, 5.8. Wall and short tower left of Green Bulge (route 146).

148 THE BALCONY, 5.4. Climb inside corner past a band of fairly unconsolidated rock.

149 THE MEZZANINE, 5.4. Start on outside of minor buttress that reaches halfway up the wall. Climb buttress to base of groove. Continue in groove to top.

150 SECOND BALCONY, 5.4. Inside corner/chimney. Climb inside corner past band of fairly unconsolidated rock.

151 HIRSUTE, 5.7. Face and two overhangs.

152 CEREBRATION, 5.4. Inside corner with overhang near top. Pass overhang on right.

Variation, 5.4. Start at short jam crack right of inside corner, then up broken rock.

153 RESOLUTION, 5.9. Start 4 feet left of Cerebration (route 152). Climb straight up and join Second Coming (route 154) at 20-foot ledge.

154 SECOND COMING, 5.7. Start at base of steep face. Climb layback crack 20 feet to ledge on right. Continue until it's possible to traverse left and up to top.

Variation, 5.8. Instead of traversing, continue straight up to top.

155 ORGASM DIRECT, 5.11b. Climb 4 feet right of corner.

156 ORGASM, 5.8. Try not to become overly excited by this intimidating line. Climb inside corner below large ceiling. Continue up to smooth wall, mantle, then step right around corner. Continue to top.

CLIFF'S COITUS, 5.7. Face between Orgasm and Foreplay (route 157).

157 FOREPLAY, 5.6. Climb crack to pine tree. Step right to inside corner left of ceiling on Orgasm (route 156), then up past overhang to top. Watch for loose rock on top.

158 THE FRICTION SLAB (not on diagram). One of several boulder problems below Orgasm (route 156).

Four Brothers (Diagram 29 E)

APPROACH: Four Brothers is a cluster of rock located along the top of the large boulderfield that covers the bluff below the East Rampart. Four Brothers is easily reached by descending Leaning Tower Gully from the East Bluff Trail. From the bottom of the gully continue down (south) 50 feet. A slower approach is to traverse along the base of East Rampart on the climbers' trail.

Waypoint 45: Four Brothers
UTM 16T 280204E 4810282N
Base Elevation: 1,295 feet
Top Elevation: 1,345 feet

ROUTES:

159 FAMILY JEWELS, 5.7. Start from pedestal left of corner. Step right around corner to hidden dihedral. Climb
dihedral and finish in jam crack.

THE MIC, 5.11a. Same start. At 10 feet move right and
climb overhang, then climb face and arête to top.

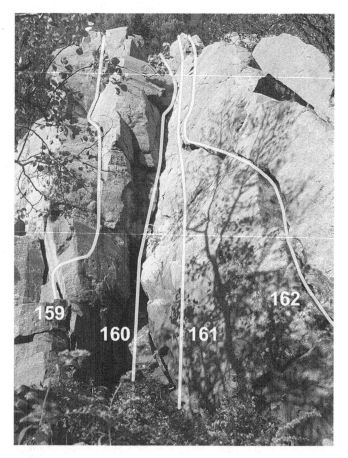

Four Brothers

EAST BLUFF CLIMBS

160 GRAVEL PIT, 5.4. Climb inside corner. Layback past overhang into gravel.

161 MARY'S FACE, 5.9. Face left of Foliage (route 162).

162 FOLIAGE, 5.4. Crack that angles left across face.
Variation, 5.7. Same start, but step onto right corner and climb corner to top.

163 ZOT, 5.9. Start below corner overhang. Climb corner to top.

164 CATALEPSY, 5.6. Start in crack. Climb into prominent groove above.

165 5.9. Climb face up over small roof.

166 DECADENCE, 5.4. Follow grungy crack up to overhanging block. Exit left when your belayer isn't looking.

Leaning Tower (Diagram 30 E)

Approach: Leaning Tower is a massive block located along the East Bluff Trail above the top of Leaning Tower Gully.

Waypoint 46: Leaning Tower
UTM 16T 280180E 4810338N
Base Elevation: 1,441 feet

Routes:

167 SOUTH FACE, 5.2. Climb center or either corner of face.

168 WEST FACE, 5.8. Start at right edge and climb smooth face without using prominent holds on left (specifically, the triangular niche).
Variation, 5.2. Start at left corner (above low platform). Climb up and right to top.

169 NORTHWEST FACE, 5.7. Start in center of narrow face. Climb up and right to top.

170 NORTH FACE, 5.11a. Start in center of smooth, overhanging face. Dyno to ledge, continue up to small pocket, then up and left to another pocket and top.
Variation, COSMIC CRINGE, 5.11b. Direct start.

171 EAST FACE, 5.7. Start at right edge. Climb up and left to top of overhanging wall.
Variation, 5.7. Start at left edge of face.

172 THE TOMBSTONE. Many variations are possible on this low wall across the trail from Leaning Tower. Some are very difficult.

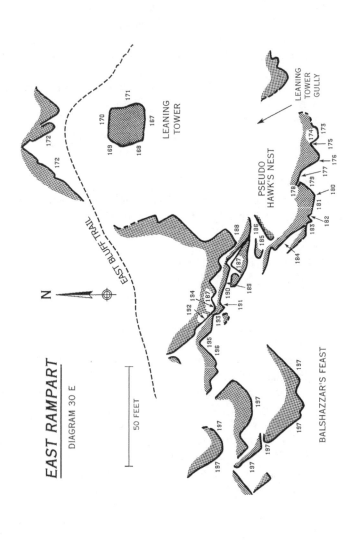

EAST RAMPART

DIAGRAM 30 E

50 FEET

N

EAST BLUFF TRAIL

LEANING TOWER

PSEUDO HAWK'S NEST

LEANING TOWER GULLY

BALSHAZZAR'S FEAST

Leaning Tower

Pseudo Hawk's Nest (Diagram 30 E)

APPROACH: Pseudo Hawk's Nest begins immediately west of Leaning Tower Gully. *From above*—Walk the East Bluff Trail to Leaning Tower. Descend Leaning Tower Gully and turn west to reach the base of the climbs. *From below*—Follow the CCC Trail to Pedestal Buttress, then take the climbers' trail at the base of the bluff west past Leaning Tower Gully to the base of the climbs.

Waypoint 47: Pseudo Hawk's Nest
    UTM 16T 280183E 4810303N

Base Elevation: 1,351 feet
Top Elevation: 1,441 feet

ROUTES:

173 WILD HORSES, 5.8. Start at corner below right side of overhanging nose. When above overhang continue up slab or left corner. Erosion and rock breakage keep making this climb harder.

174 IMMACULATE CONCEPTION, 5.10a. Steep narrow wall just right of The Pretzel (route 175). Climb using only the face.

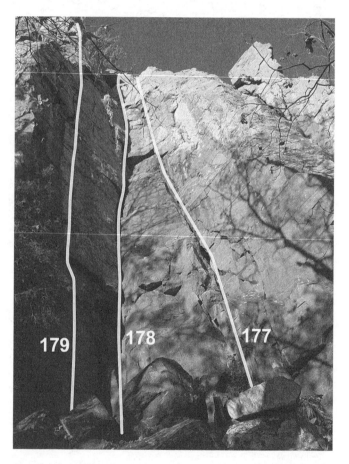

Pseudo Hawk's Nest, East Rampart

175 THE PRETZEL, 5.6. Is the name of this climb also a description of the climber on it? Start in inside corner, which is very steep for 15 feet, then follow crack to top.

176 DRUNKEN SAILOR, 5.5. Many climbers lose their bearings on this route. Start left of nose. Move up and right 15 feet to a stance, then wander up broad, rounded ridge to top.

177 EPIPHANY, 5.9. Climb left-leaning crack starting 12 feet right of inside corner. Avoid using left wall.

178 CRACKING UP, 5.6. Prominent inside corner and crack.

179 BAGATELLE, 5.12c/d. Climb mini-overhang to crack, then up left of crack to a temporary rest stance at 20 feet. Move right and zigzag up and past an 8-inch overhang at 35 feet. Climb center of face to top.
PHLOGISTON, 5.12d. Climb left crack in the same wall. Avoid use of left corner.

180 BEGINNER'S DEMISE, 5.11a. Start at base of steep wall just left of corner. Climb wall near or on corner to easier rock above. The difficult bulge can be passed by a few unusual moves.

181 ABM, 5.11a/b. This route is often mistaken for Beginner's Demise (route 180). It runs 4–6 feet left of Beginner's Demise. Start on short, difficult wall and continue up over easier rock.

182 CHICKEN DELIGHT, 5.7. Start just right of sharp, narrow rib. Climb layback crack for 15 feet. Continue straight up past overhanging block at 35 feet, then to top.
CHICKEN TONIGHT, 5.8. Steep and hard crack left of Chicken Delight.

183 BEGINNER'S DELIGHT, 5.4. An aptly named climb. Several variations are possible at the start. Climb 30 feet to detached block. Traverse right to corner or climb crack to below overhanging block, then traverse and climb corner to top.
FULL MOON OVER BARABOO, 5.9. Climb wall and roof above start of Beginner's Delight.

184 HERO'S FRIGHT, 5.7. Climb lower wall to base of crack visible near upper left corner. Follow crack to top.

185 COUCH OF PAIN, 5.12a. Climb center of wall on small holds to top.

186 SOFA-ISTICATED-LADY, 5.10d. Climb left side of wall through small niche.

187 DEATH AND TRANSFIGURATION, 5.4. Climb (any way) onto large, narrow blocks detached from wall. Step into prominent dihedral and climb past black bulge of loose rock to broad ledge. Walk off right or climb to top in crack 20 feet left.

Variation, 5.8. Start on right block (near auxiliary access gully) and climb bulging wall.

188 FALLEN BIRCH, 5.5. Cracks and overhang.

189 DEATH AND DISFIGURATION, 5.8. Start on left detached block. Climb thin crack to broad ledge.

190 DEGRADE MY SISTER, 5.11a. Face right of Prime Rib (route 191). Start from block. Climb up and right, then left to obvious undercling. Finish 5–6 feet left of pine tree.

Variation, 5.12a. Direct start. Climb face just right of inside corner.

191 PRIME RIB, 5.9+. Climb rib until it fades at level of Bloody Mary (route 193) overhang. Continue slightly left past small niche to broad ledge.

Variation, 5.11d. Direct start.

Variation, 5.9. Climb right of rib using a series of laybacks.

192 5.11b. Face on upper level above Bloody Mary (route 193).

193 BLOODY MARY, 5.8. Look for a large bulge of loose rock with a meaty crack through the center. Climb groove directly below the bulge. Surmount overhang by hand jams and face holds to an awkward stance, then up left to ledge left of prominent upper corner. Finish on wall above.

Variation, THE FAKIR, 5.7. Same start. Climb left crack 20 feet to platform. Traverse up and right to awkward stance. Continue as above.

194 THARSIS, 5.11c. Start on upper ledge. Climb crack right of corner. Move left to corner, and continue to top.

195 OCTOBER FIRST, 5.7. Strenuous layback up inside corner that degenerates after the first few moves.

196 ANCHOR'S AWAY, 5.6–5.8. Steep, short wall with two cracks. The left crack is 5.6.

Balshazzar's Feast (Diagram 30 E)

Approach: Balshazzar's Feast is west of Pseudo Hawk's Nest.

Routes:

197 BALSHAZZAR'S FEAST, 5.4–5.7. A veritable feast of climbing presented in three courses. There are many variations, especially on the lowest wall.

Hawk's Nest (Diagram 31 E)

Approach: Hawk's Nest is the west end of the East Rampart. Refer to Approach for Pseudo Hawk's Nest. Use Leaning Tower Gully to access the top, or walk around the west end of the East Rampart.

Waypoint 48: Hawk's Nest
   UTM 16T 280133E 4810312N
Base Elevation: 1,329 feet
Top Elevation: 1,438 feet

Routes:

198 R. EXAM, 5.9. Follow the black watermarks. Pass the 8-inch overhang on the right.

199 HAPPY HUNTING GROUNDS, 5.11a. Climb thin, steep crack. Continue to ceiling high on wall, then over right side to top. Leaders who fall on this climb may go to the Happy Hunting Grounds.

200 FLAKES AWAY, 5.11d/12a. Wall 4–5 feet left of Happy Hunting Grounds (route 199).

201 DOUBLE HERNIA, 5.12a. Climb thin crack to ledge at 20 feet. Continue right of corner without using corner.
NICE CORNER, 5.10a. Start 6 feet right of Bucket Brigade (route 202). Follow corner to top.

202 BUCKET BRIGADE, 5.6. Start in the funnel, a cleft or groove 25 feet high. Climb to broken rock, where two main variations branch. Bucket Brigade is the right (east) alternative. Continue almost straight up for 30 feet to ledge at base of prominent inside corner. Climb inside corner past overhang to top.
Variation, HALLUCINATION, 5.4. At the 30-foot ledge, step right to outside ledge, then up and left to exit crack in wall.

Variation, THE RAMP, 5.6. From top of the funnel, climb left wall for 15 feet to base of low-angle slab. Climb either side of slab to broad ledge. (The ledge system to the west is commonly used to traverse off the wall.) Climb obvious chimney at east end of ledge or wall west of chimney (several variations possible).

Variation, WALPURGISNACHT, 5.6. From broad ledge, traverse right into hanging groove and climb to top.

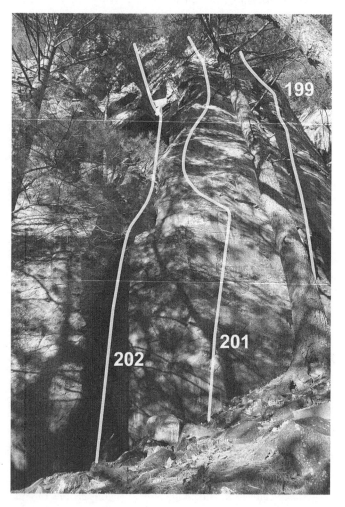

Hawk's Nest, East Rampart

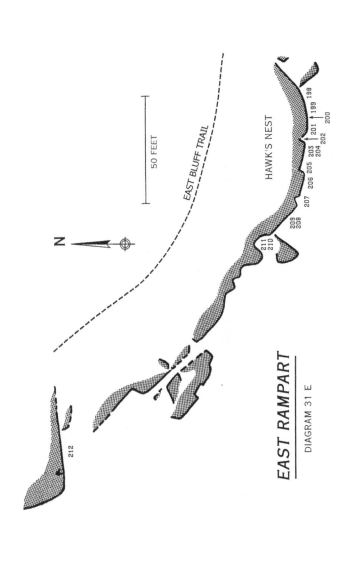

EAST RAMPART

DIAGRAM 31 E

50 FEET

EAST BLUFF TRAIL

N

HAWK'S NEST

198
199
200
201
202
203
204
205
206
207
208
209
210
211
212

203 NO FRUIT PLEASE, 5.11b. Start left of the funnel in Bucket Brigade (route 202). Climb face straight to top.

204 PIEPLATE, 5.11a/b. Same start as No Fruit Please (route 203). Climb up and left a few feet on pieplate holds, then straight to top.

Variation, 5.11a/b. Direct start that begins with a lunge.

205 VIVISECTION, 5.11a. This climb has an unforgettable start, particularly if you lose your fingers on it. Start beneath overhang 5 feet off the ground. Conquer overhang onto small slab. Pass smaller overhang, then straight up cracks to top.

206 ALPHA CENTAURI, 5.10d. Start a few feet left of Vivisection (route 205) on slightly overhanging, disjointed crack and layback system. Climb 10 feet (crux). Continue up steep ledges, as in Vivisection.

YELLOW PAGES, 5.11a. Start from top of block. Let your fingers do the walking, and join Alpha Centauri at 12 feet. Use care at the start when top roping.

207 ANOMIE, 5.8. Climb into alcove 15 feet off the ground. Climb out to the right and follow shallow trough or concavity that angles slightly right.

Variation, MOTHER FLETCHER'S, 5.8. From alcove, climb up and left to join Charybdis (route 208). There is no easy way out from this alcove.

208 CHARYBDIS, 5.7. A magnificent line with continuous climbing that can be well protected. Start 15 feet right of inside corner formed by large block. Climb straight up for 15 feet, then up thin crack, angling slightly right. Continue up to exit ledge and top.

209 SCYLLA, 5.7. Same start as Charybdis (route 208). At 15 feet climb slightly left to comfortable ledge 30 feet up. Climb into dark overhang or dihedral that rises steeply to the right and follow it to highest overhanging point. Or step right from comfortable ledge and climb face to same point. Continue to top.

210 CORONARY, 5.7. You can walk or climb to the start on large block at west end of wall. Move up and right, then mantle onto Scylla (route 209) ledge. Step left and up to a possibly loose block between two prominent overhangs, then up shallow right groove. There is a left groove accessible by stepping left from the loose block.

Variation, ANGINA, 5.9. Same start. Climb up toward overhang and exit right to left groove of Coronary.

211 ANGINA II, 5.9. Pass Angina (route 210 variation) overhang on left. Continue in hanging inside corner.

There is a buttress 150 feet northwest of Angina II (route 211) with a steep south face and overhang. The rocks between are rather shattered.

212 LAND'S END, 5.6–5.7. Several interesting variations are possible on this weathered wall.

The low outcroppings farther west have a couple of interesting climbs.

East Bluff, Balanced Rock and Doorway Rocks Areas. Photo: Chuck Koch.

DOORWAY ROCKS

The Doorway Massif is perhaps the most expansive cliff area at Devil's Lake. When one sees it from the parking and picnic area at the south end of the lake, its 200-foot height captures the eye and staggers the imagination. Despite its first appearance, the area is quite broken up. The tallest vertical walls are about 60 feet. The unique feature of the area is the possibility of multiple-pitch climbing, with mountain-type scrambling and route finding. A large gully divides the two main sections of this massif into Major Mass and Minor Mass.

Major Mass includes the distinctive Devil's Doorway formation and is further divided into the Upper Band and the Lower Band. The two bands are separated by a terrace and ledge system that in places contains a 20-foot middle band of rocks. The Devil's Doorway formation has several interesting climbs on its twin pillars. It is the scene of many dramatic demonstrations of rock-climbing technique to passing hikers.

Minor Mass consists mainly of a single large buttress with two distinct levels. The lower (south) level reaches a high point known as the South Tower. The saddle behind the South Tower is accessible by a short climb from either side.

Red Rocks is east of Doorway Rocks on the Potholes Trail. This accessible area is often used by beginner groups, though its location right on a hiking trail is an unfavorable feature.

Ramsay's Pinnacle is located 150 feet west of Devil's Doorway. This area consists of many low walls and towers with a great number of short climbs. You may find it interesting to explore, following the various terraces and gullies that give the area a rock-garden character.

Major Mass, Upper Band (Diagrams 32 E and 33 E)

APPROACH: *From below*—Ascend the talus slope to the base of Major Mass or hike partway up the Potholes Trail to just below Red Rocks, then traverse 300 feet west to the base of Minor Mass. Continue past the lowest part (south end) of

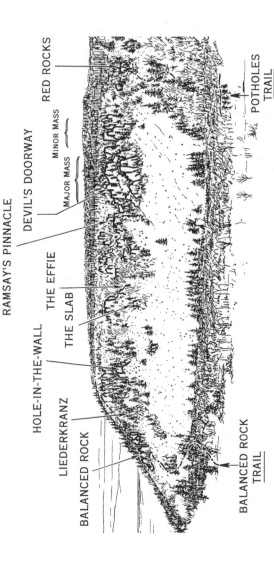

RAMSAY'S PINNACLE

DEVIL'S DOORWAY

MINOR MASS

MAJOR MASS

RED ROCKS

POTHOLES TRAIL

THE EFFIE

HOLE-IN-THE-WALL

THE SLAB

LIEDERKRANZ

BALANCED ROCK

BALANCED ROCK TRAIL

EAST BLUFF

BALANCED ROCK AND DOORWAY ROCKS AREAS

Minor Mass to ascend the gully between Major Mass and Minor Mass. The Keyhole is visible from portions of this gully. *From above*—Hike the short, scenic Devil's Doorway Trail, which loops down from the East Bluff Trail. Devil's Doorway is located near the west end of this trail. Reach the lower level by descending the gully between Major Mass and Minor Mass, located 90 feet east of the Devil's Doorway formation, or descend the broken rocks west of Major Mass.

Waypoint 49: Top of gully east of Major Mass (between Major Mass and Minor Mass)
   UTM 16T 279811E 4810408N

Devil's Doorway, Major Mass

Waypoint 50: Major Mass, Upper Band (at Devil's Doorway)
   UTM 16T 279785E 4810401N
Base Elevation (at Devil's Doorway): 1,397 feet

ROUTES:

The northwest corner, Romper (route 1), or Doorway Chimney (route 3) is usually used to ascend Devil's Doorway to set upper belays.

1 ROMPER, 5.2. Climb ledges at northwest corner of formation.

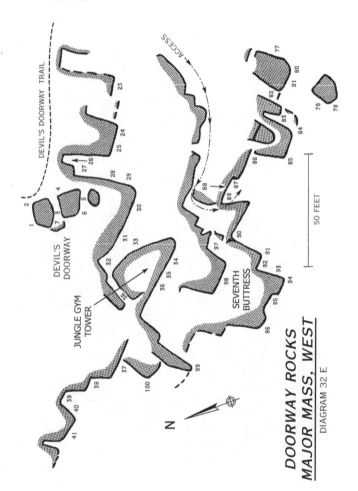

DOORWAY ROCKS
MAJOR MASS, WEST
DIAGRAM 32 E

2 LAZY DAY, 5.7. Climb north face near left edge.

3 DOORWAY CHIMNEY, 5.2. The chimney walls have been worn smooth by the boots and butts of many climbers. Those with long legs may feel unpleasantly cramped.

4 IMPOSSIBLE CRACK, 5.8. Start on wall below crack. Climb overhang to crack, then jam or layback to top. *Variation*, 5.7. Start inside Devil's Doorway. Climb left to crack (half the battle), then follow crack to top.

5 UP YOURS TOO, 5.8. Climb south end of south pillar.

6 BLOODY FINGER, 5.6. Climb southwest side of south pillar. A fall from this knife-edge crack can be messy.

7 5.6. Climb southwest side of north pillar.

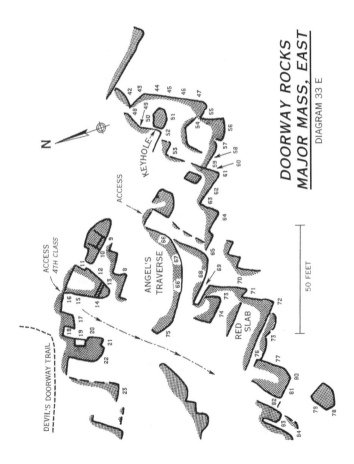

DOORWAY ROCKS
MAJOR MASS, EAST
DIAGRAM 33 E

Several gullies can be used to descend from the trail to the base of the Upper Band. The most convenient descent is by route 16.

8 5.5. Crack.

9 5.2. Crack.

10 THE THREE KINGS, 5.7. Three large blocks form a ridge at the east end of the Upper Band. Climb the short, strenuous layback between the west and middle king.

11–15 This small buttress has several short routes. The MAGICAL MYSTERY TOUR is for beginners. Start at low point near south corner (route 13), climb southeast side to base of huge detached block. Traverse around south end of buttress onto slanted ledge (route 14), then up behind the detached block. Scramble to top.

16 *Access route*, 4th class.

17 HIDDEN WALL, 5.8. The headwall between two prominent buttresses. Climb face and overhang.

18 THE CRYPT, 5.2. Is it actually possible to escape from this rock tomb? Start in gully below and climb narrow chimney past chockstone into The Crypt.

19 5.4. From base of The Crypt, traverse left to an open alcove and stem to top.

20 FAITH, HOPE, AND CHARITY, 5.4. Start from bottom of east face. Follow crack past small overhang.

21 ANGEL'S CRACK, 5.6. Dihedral marked by a steep, arrowhead slab. Climb past slab and exit right to top.

22 THE JOLLY ROGER, 5.8. Climb southwest face, following crack system past two small niches.

23 5.4. Crack and corner.

24 MARY JANE, 5.8. Climb right side of south face to last ledge. Step onto toehold on right corner (crux) and reach for a finger jam.
Variation, 5.6. Same start. Traverse left to good ledge at west corner. Mantle to top.

25 ROSEMARY'S BABY, 5.12b. Climb face 8 feet left of Mary Jane (route 24).

26 5.2. Chockstone chimney. A possible access route.

27 VAMOS ALA KAMA, 5.5. Crack.

28 INDECISION, 5.4. Climb cracked face. Two distinct lines are possible, but most climbers zigzag, finding the easiest way.

29 SPLIT DECISION, 5.7. Climb crack and face 3–4 feet left of Indecision (route 28) to large ledge. Finish in notch above ledge.

30 CEDAR TREE WALL, 5.6–5.7. There are two crack climbs on this wall. Climb right crack to top. Climb left crack, then short wall to top.

31 CANNABIS SATIVA, 5.8. Climb face on small holds. Finish in crack above.

JUNGLE GYM TOWER (routes 33–36) stands out slightly from the wall behind it. To reach the climbs from above, descend the gully (route 32) on the east side of the tower.

32 *Descent route,* 4th class.

33 5.4. Climb east face of Jungle Gym Tower from gully.

34 JUNGLE GYM, 5.4. Start on top of Seventh Buttress (western buttress) of Lower Band. Climb jam crack to ledge, then up to sloping platform. Mantle on west side of platform and climb to top of tower.

35 DANCES WITH FIBS, 5.7. Climb face left of bulge to overhang. Mantle the overhang (crux) and continue to top.

36 JUNGLE GYM CHIMNEY, 5.4. Start climb below pine tree. At 15 feet traverse left across slab using flake handholds. Continue up chimney behind west side of Jungle Gym Tower.

37 THE PLAYGROUND, 5.5. Don't forget to look over there! A not-too-steep face to practice small-hold technique.

38–41 Short climbs.

Major Mass, Lower Band (Diagrams 32 E and 33 E)

APPROACH: Refer to Approach for Major Mass, Upper Band.

Waypoint 51: Major Mass, Lower Band (between the Keyhole and Red Slab)
  UTM 16T 279806E 4810358N
Base Elevation: 1,241 feet

ROUTES:
Routes 42–59 ascend the Keyhole, the easternmost buttress of the Lower Band. Most of these climbs cross one of two platforms on the north and south sides of the opening giving this buttress its name.

42 SUNKEN SLAB, 5.6. Start at recessed section, well up along the base of the buttress. Climb approximate center of lower slab to overhang. Step up onto lip of overhang and climb slab to a stance. Traverse left to short jam crack beneath highest overhang. Exit left.

43 PROSPERITY, 5.4. Begin in crack just left of Sunken Slab (route 42), then angle left, following good holds on corner.

44 HAMMER CRACK, 5.8. There was a tradition (best forgotten) of using a wedged piton hammer to aid this climb. Climb crack straight up to north platform.
Variation, 5.6. Start a few feet right and traverse left to crack 5 feet up.

45 MEAT HAMMER, 5.12b. Start with one good handhold. Continue straight to top on face with very thin holds a few feet left of Hammer Crack (route 44).

46 HAMMER CASE, 5.12a. Same start as Meat Hammer (route 45). From good hold, climb up and left, following crack to top.

47 HAMMER MASTER, 5.11d. Climb small overhang, then move left and follow crack on left part of wall.

48 INSECT PARTS, 5.5. At north edge of platform, climb up and right above Sunken Slab (route 42).

49 DARKEST HOUR, 5.7. Start in slabby groove. Climb to overhanging crack that leads to an inside corner. Continue in corner.

50 TOP SHELF, 5.7. Start on face just left of the Keyhole and climb to an undercling. Move left and up to ledge under roof. Traverse left, escape the roof to a sloping shoulder, and continue on southeast ridge above the Keyhole.

51 NONCONFORMIST, 5.7. Start on ledge level with base of the Keyhole. Climb southeast face of the Keyhole pillar.

52 KEYHOLE CHIMNEY, 5.4. Scramble up ledges to base of the Keyhole. Move up crack to reach a hold and swing into the chimney. Alternatively, traverse around the outside of the Keyhole pillar and enter chimney from the north. Exit chimney onto south face and climb to top of buttress, or climb awkwardly high inside the Keyhole and exit northeast.

53 5.4. Inside corner leading to slab at top of Keyhole buttress.

54 5.4. Climb mostly broken rock above east end of south platform to ledge where Nonconformist (route 51) starts.

It is interesting to traverse right onto the steep east face and climb past the small pine tree to reach the same ledge.

55 STETTNER'S OVERHANG, 5.6. Start below right side of ceiling. Use holds right of deep crack (staying in crack is harder). Climb past ceiling, then follow crack over an easy overhang to south platform.

56 5.2. Face route to south platform.

57 EASY STREET, 5.0. Easiest route to south platform. Climb obvious block-filled chimney.

58 5.6. Thin crack.

59 HARD TIMES, 5.4. Inside corner with small overhang 20 feet up.

The following two climbs, King's Corner (route 60) and Wicker Man (route 61), cross partway up.

60 KING'S CORNER, 5.6. Same start as Hard Times (route 59). At 12 feet traverse right to corner. Climb corner past overhang and step right to hanging crack in east face (can be avoided by staying left of corner). Climb crack, then regain corner and follow it to top of crowning pinnacle. *Variation*, 5.8. From left side of first ledge of Dippy Diagonal (route 62), traverse right onto corner 12 feet up. Continue as above.

61 WICKER MAN, 5.12b. Climb overhanging corner directly. At 20 feet, move right to narrow east face. Continue up face with thin cracks, avoiding wide hanging crack in King's Corner (route 60). Finish on face of top pinnacle.

62 DIPPY DIAGONAL, 5.7. Climb crack that angles slightly left.
Variation, 5.8. Start on first ledge to the right of Dippy Diagonal (15 feet up). Climb face and thin crack, then through niche. Continue in crack above to large ledge.

63 KENOSIS, 5.4. Climb crack and inside corner to second large ledge with pine tree, then up between awkward blocks above the inside corner.

64 SURE SHOT, 5.3. Climb broken buttress left of Kenosis (route 63).

65 5.1. Access couloir.

66 ANGEL'S TRAVERSE, 5.4. The traverse is on an exposed ledge, usually used for walking, that spans the upper mass of the high, rounded buttress. Start traverse from head of access couloir (route 65). At far (west) end of traverse, climb chimney 20 feet to top of buttress.

67 5.7. Climb buttress starting in middle of Angel's Traverse (route 66).

68 MINDLESS DRIBBLE, 5.8. Start on ledge 30 feet below Angel's Traverse (route 66). The ledge is reached easily from Congestion Chimney (route 69). Climb crack to west end of Angel's Traverse.

The Lower Band of Major Mass

Variation, 5.7. Same start. Climb diagonally right until a section with no holds forces you farther right toward access couloir (route 65).

69 CONGESTION CHIMNEY, 5.2. Chimney.

70 INNOCENCE, 5.7. Steep east face of Red Slab Buttress. Start near dihedral in Puffs Plus (route 71), climb 15 feet, then move right and climb center of face to slabbier rock above.

71 PUFFS PLUS, 5.4. Climb dihedral or adjacent crack to top of Red Slab.

72 EARNINGS SUMMARY, 5.4. Start at lowest point below southeast corner of buttress. Climb left onto pedestal, then step right to corner and up Red Slab.

73 RED SLAB, 5.4. Climb slightly overhanging system on good holds, then up slab. Move right around corner and climb southeast corner.

74 5.4. Same start as Red Slab (route 73). Finish on short southwest-facing wall by doing a mantle and using a balance step to reach the top.

75 5.9. Short face (boulder problem).

76 CHOCKSTONE CHIMNEY, 5.6. Climb inside corner, then stem past large chockstone into chimney above. Continue to top.
Variation, 5.4. Start by walking up ledges on right to reach inside corner/chimney.

77 TM OVERHANG, 5.9+. Climb tough layback crack on east face to resting place just below overhang. Reach for good holds above overhang, then merely pull yourself up until footholds are found.
Variation, 5.8. Exit left of overhang.
Variation, 5.10b. At overhang, move right and continue straight up to top.

78 LAYBACK BOULDER, 5.6. This is a large boulder that impedes travel along the base of the Lower Band. Start on southwest side, swing right to south slab, then layback to top. Descend on northeast side of boulder.

79 5.4. Short jam crack.

80 COOKIE CUTTER, 5.6. Start on slabby rock at southeast corner of buttress. Climb onto shelf above first overhang, then traverse left onto southwest face. Continue as in Archway Cookie (route 81).

81 ARCHWAY COOKIE, 5.8. Start on southwest face above large boulder. Climb past bulge using friction handholds, then up under arching overhang. Traverse right around arch, then climb to top of buttress.

82 5.2. *Descent route* from Archway Buttress.

83 5.4. Chimney.

84 BLUE SLAB, 5.4. Start at southeast corner (pine tree on first ledge). Ascend giant staircase to blue slab at top.

85 WEST MICHIGAN, 5.4. Start at west corner, climb up and right more or less as in Blue Slab (route 84).
Variation, 5.5. Same start. Climb left to wide, angling crack on west face.

86 LOCO HEAD, 5.4. Chimney.

87 MICROWAVE DINNER, 5.4. Inside corner crack.

88 MENTAL BLOCK, 5.12a/b. Start on left side of overhanging red wall, climb up and right to center of wall, then directly to top.

89 Access gully to top of Lower Band. Start from little inside corner. Climb into dirt gully, then up and right to top of band.

90 CAT WALK, 5.7. Start in inside corner. Climb up and traverse left on irregular ledge, then continue up near left corner.

91–96 SEVENTH BUTTRESS, 5.3–5.7. This is the last or westernmost buttress of the Lower Band. It is the start of an easy four-pitch route that includes Jungle Gym Tower. The lower section of the buttress is broken with many short, closely spaced routes.

97 5.7. Climb inside corner (an unpleasant layback) or adjacent crack that leads to the inside corner.

98 NO REST FOR THE WICKED, 5.8. Start just left of pine tree. Climb southwest face past three triangular pockets.

99 RIGHT ON, 5.4. Narrow, tall buttress or ridge. Start at inconspicuous point behind oak tree, climb past overhang. Finish on either corner of the more prominent upper section.

100 5.7. Corner 10 feet left of upper section of Right On (route 99).

Minor Mass (Diagram 34 E)

APPROACH: *From below*—Ascend the talus slope to the base of Minor Mass or hike partway up the Potholes Trail to just below Red Rocks, then traverse 300 feet west to the base of Minor Mass. *From above*—Hike the short, scenic Devil's Doorway Trail, which loops down from the East Bluff Trail. Devil's Doorway is located near the west end of this trail. Descend the gully between Major Mass and Minor Mass located 90 feet east of Devil's Doorway to the base of Minor Mass.

Waypoint 52: Minor Mass
   UTM 16T 279854E 4810365N
Base Elevation: 1,286 feet
Top Elevation: 1,394 feet

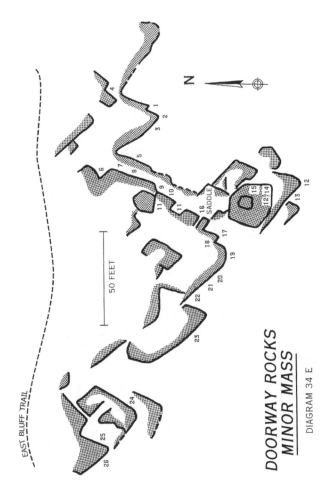

DOORWAY ROCKS
MINOR MASS

DIAGRAM 34 E

Routes:

1–4 East Buttress of Minor Mass. This small formation is separated from the main buttress by a grungy gully and has a few easy climbs.

5 OBDURACY, 5.6. Start right of oak tree. Climb short wall to ledge.

Minor Mass

Routes 6–8 start from the same ledge.

6 DISINCLINATION, 5.4. Start on ledge left of grungy gully. Climb to large dead pine tree, then up inclined chute behind tree.

Variation, 5.6. Climb overhanging blocks right of dead tree.

7 POWER OF A GOOD HAIRCUT, 5.12b. Start 10 feet right of Ladyfingers (route 8). Climb straight to top.

8 LADYFINGERS, 5.10a. Climb wall into shallow groove. Follow groove to top.

9 PIGEON ROOF, 5.6. Climb crack leading to prominent roof. Pass roof easily to wide crack above. The crack is that perplexing in-between width, too small to chimney and too large to jam.

Variation, 5.8. Traverse left under roof and continue to top.

10 NO STRANGER TO THE FIST, 5.12d. Climb face and overhang left of Pigeon Roof (route 9).

11 FLOTSAM AND JETSAM, 5.4. This is actually two climbs, both starting in the recess. The left chimney is obstructed by a partially toppled tree. The right inside corner is longer, with an interesting finish on the small tower.

12 B-MINOR MASS, 5.4. Delightful two-pitch climb to top of south tower. Begin on south corner (lowest point of Minor Mass). Climb to first good ledge, traverse left to small overhang. Continue up overhang or 5 feet farther left to next ledge. Traverse right and climb inside corner.

13 5.6. Climb face on southwest side to first ledge.

14 5.7. Start on ledge, climb southeast corner.

15 IN THE HEAT OF THE SUN, 5.10a. Start on first ledge and climb center of east face.

16 5.4. This chockstone chimney is the obvious route from the saddle, giving access to (or from) the scree ledges above.

17 Á CHEVAL, 5.6. Start in gully below saddle. Climb sharp corner (avoid using left inside corner). Near the top you may find it helpful to mount up and ride.

18 5.3. From saddle, traverse left along narrow ledge to second inside corner, then up a set of ledges.

19 5.7. Start on rounded corner and climb slabby wall past right end of upper overhang.

20 GREEN LEDGES, 5.7. Wall with three ledges 8–10 feet apart. From upper ledge, go right around corner, climb to overhang, then in groove above.

21 MR. WIZARD AND TUTOR TURTLE, 5.10d. Start up face right of Manhandler (route 22). At overhang, climb up and left to top.

22 MANHANDLER, 5.9. Start 5 feet right of inside corner below formidable overhang. Climb up and right to overhang, climb overhang, and continue in crack above.

23–26 Short climbs.

Red Rocks (Diagram 35 E)

APPROACH: This small area is located on the Potholes Trail where it passes between a tower and the main wall, about halfway up the bluff. *Please give hikers the right-of-way.*

Waypoint 53: Red Rocks
   UTM 16T 279931E 4810367N
Base Elevation: 1,326 feet
Top Elevation: 1,353 feet

ROUTES:
   1 5.3. Climb lower crack, then continue on short ridge.
   2 THE CLEFT, 5.4. Ascend the cleft by stemming. Either of the opposing walls can be climbed separately (5.8–5.9).

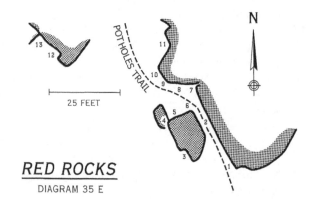

RED ROCKS
DIAGRAM 35 E

3 5.4. Climb southwest dihedral. Once on top, step across cleft to opposite wall.

4 5.2. *Access or descent route.*

5 5.8. Overhanging face/crack.

6 5.8. Corner of tower.

7 5.3. Chimney.

8 FIRST NINE, 5.9. Overhanging wall just left of route 7.
5.8. Climb corner just right of route 9.

9 5.4. Ledge and jam crack.

10 5.8. Climb corner to top. Avoid holds on route 9.

Red Rocks

11 5.3. Inside corner.
12 JEFF, 5.4. Left-slanting crack.
13 BILL, 5.4. Left-slanting crack.

Ramsay's Pinnacle (Diagram 36 E)

APPROACH: Walk approximately 375 feet west of Devil's Doorway, first on the Devil's Doorway Trail, then on the East Bluff Trail, to the top of an access gully that descends to the Ramsay's Pinnacle climbing area. The pinnacle is 235 feet southeast of the top of the access gully.

Ramsay's Pinnacle

West of the Ramsay's Pinnacle gully, a low intermittent summit band continues to Balanced Rock Trail. A number of short routes can be found on these rock outcroppings.

Waypoint 54: Access gully above Ramsay's Pinnacle
    UTM 16T 279694E 4810471N
Waypoint 55: Ramsay's Pinnacle
    UTM 16T 279741E 4810415N
Base Elevation: 1,335 feet
Top Elevation: 1,439 feet

Routes:
1 5.7. Overhang and crack.
2 5.4. Inside corner.
Variation, 5.8. At 8 feet, move left and climb left side of face and upper corner.
3–5 5.3–5.4. Crack and corners.
6 5.5. Inside corner and narrow upper face.
Variation, 5.9. Start near left corner (avoid using right inside corner crack).
7 BLOODY SHIN, 5.7. Hanging inside corner. Climb to roof 15 feet up, then move right and up to ledge. Continue in upper inside corner to platform below Ramsay's Pinnacle.

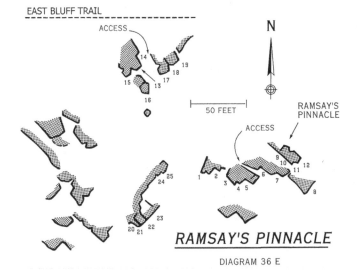

RAMSAY'S PINNACLE

DIAGRAM 36 E

8 SUPER VGA, 5.9. Overhanging face. Start at low point near left corner. Climb diagonally up and right to vertical crack. Follow crack to top.

AROUND THE CORNER, 5.4. Start around corner (west) from start of Super VGA. Climb close to corner to top.

9 5.4. Crack.

10 MONOCHROME, 5.8. Climb face over both lower and upper overhangs. Finish left of chockstone.

11 RAMSAY'S RAMP, 5.7. Climb series of overhanging, sloping steps. Finish at chockstone.

12 5.7. Narrow face.

13–16 5.3–5.7. Don't overlook the climbs in or around the access gully.

17 5.7. Nice smooth face. Avoid using the crack or corner.

18–19 5.3–5.7. Don't overlook these climbs.

20–25 5.3–5.9. The routes west of the gully provide a great variety of short climbs. Routes 21–23 offer the biggest challenges.

BALANCED ROCK AREAS

The Balanced Rock Areas are located at the south end of Devil's Lake directly above the parking and picnic area, where the East Bluff makes a right-angle turn to the north.

The main climbing interest is on Balanced Rock Wall. There are many routes; a few are 60 feet in length. A drawback to climbing here is the heavy trail traffic along the base of the wall. Box Canyon, an alcove behind the east end of Balanced Rock Wall, contains some entertaining short climbs. There are scattered rock outcroppings on the upper half of the bluff, mostly east of Balanced Rock Wall.

Balanced Rock Wall (Diagram 37 E)

APPROACH: The Balanced Rock Trail starts across the railroad tracks at the north end of the South Shore parking and picnic

Balanced Rock Wall

area. The trail leads directly to Balanced Rock Wall and continues to the top of the East Bluff.

Waypoint 56: Balanced Rock Wall
   UTM 16T 279365E 4810413N
Base Elevation: 1,190 feet
Top Elevation: 1,267 feet

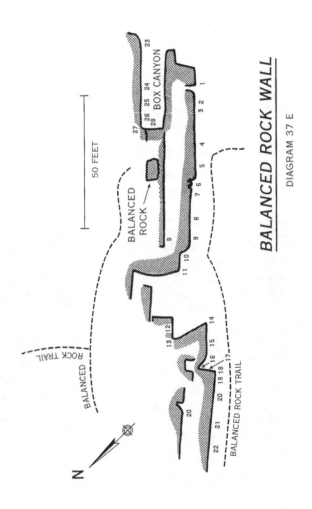

BALANCED ROCK WALL

DIAGRAM 37 E

Routes:

1 BASSWOOD CHIMNEY, 5.2. The chimney is a bit awkward until a ledge at 20 feet. After that it is quite easy.
Variation, 5.5. Climb to ledge as above, then climb crack 5 feet right of chimney.

2 MORNING AFTER, 5.10d. Start at left edge of basswood thicket. Climb face to reach a bucket hold at 20 feet.

3 NIGHT BEFORE, 5.11d. Climb face between Morning After (route 2) and Watermarks (route 4) on thin holds.

4 WATERMARKS, 5.8. The classic climb of the area. It appears on the "must-do" list of every aspiring climber. Start where the trail from below joins Balanced Rock Wall. Climb 10 feet to ledge, then right to crack with two triangular pocket holds. Follow crack past bulge (crux), continue to top.
WATERMARKS DIRECT, 5.10a/b. Start directly below triangular pockets and climb straight up.
WATERMARKS LEFT SIDE, 5.8. Same start as Watermarks. At ledge climb up and slightly left into small inside corner below overhang. Step right, and the rest is easy.

5 DER GLOTZ, 5.9. Start on the face 10 feet left of Watermarks (route 4) below a faint, slanting dihedral a few inches wide. Follow this line past left end of overhang in Watermarks Left Side (route 4 variation).
DER GLOTZ DIRECT, 5.9. Same start. Climb straight up, staying close to left corner of wall (avoid left corner).

6 SUNKEN PILLAR, 5.5. Start at double cracks. Stem up until cracks diverge, then follow either crack. Climb ends near base of Balanced Rock.

7 AAHRG, 5.9+. Start 3 feet left of Sunken Pillar's (route 6) left crack. Climb face straight up to pulpit.

8 RED PULPIT, 5.6. Start at thin crack 7 feet left of Aahrg (route 7) start. Climb crack (harder for shorter people), then step right onto pulpit 20 feet up. Continue left and up past a juniper to top.

9 FEAR AND TREMBLING, 5.9. Start on face just right of corner. The first 10 feet are quite difficult. Continue up crack and wall (close to the corner) to large ledge 15 feet below top. Finish on or near corner of upper 15-foot wall.
Variation, 5.10d. Climb center of upper 15-foot wall through flaring crack.

10 NEW BOX, 5.4. Climb inside corner until it becomes a crack. Continue up crack or step right to easier rock.

11 MR. NEUTRON, 5.6. Wall and corner. Stay left of inside corner.

12 5.9. Start from dirt and rock slope on left side of gully. Climb wall a few feet right of inside corner into shallow dihedral (crux), then to top.

13 5.4. Inside corner with projecting chockstone.

14 GRANDMA'S STAIRCASE, 5.6. Climb corner on easy ledges to overhang (leave Grandma here). Step right and climb face left of route 13 inside corner to top.

15 SPRING FEVER, 5.8. This is not a clearly defined line. Start up center of steep lower slab to overhang. Do not go into the notch of Bifurcation (route 16); instead, step up right past overhang. Continue by laybacking steep, narrow section above (note loose flake hold).

16 BIFURCATION, 5.2. Climb left side of slab through notch (chockstone in notch) into alcove. Step left to boulder bench, continue to top.
Variation, 5.6. Climb right crack inside alcove.

17 MOONDUST, 5.11b. Overhanging wall with crack. Avoid using right wall.

18 JOY RIDE, 5.9. Overhanging corner.

19 RIDERS ON THE STORM, 5.10c. Face between Joy Ride (route 18) and Invitation (route 20).

20 INVITATION, 5.6. Start below obvious crack. Climb crack to bench above. Walk off or climb onto sharp block and retable to top.
INVITATION DIRECT, 5.8. Same start. Follow thin crack left into notch at top of wall.

21 R.S.V.P., 5.9. Climb straight up wall into notch in Invitation Direct (route 20).

22 5.8. Climb short wall 5 feet from west end.

Box Canyon (Diagram 37 E)

ROUTES:

23 5.4. A relatively long route that starts at the low point of the north wall. Climb corner and somewhat slabby wall 35 feet to ledge. Continue up easy inside corner to another ledge. Take any of several continuations to top.

Variation, 5.6. At ledge 35 feet up, step left and climb obvious jam crack.

24 WHAMUS, 5.4. Right crack in north wall.

25 HITCH HIKE, 5.4. Left crack in north wall.

26 BALANCE CLIMB, 5.7. Climb smooth wall about 5 feet right of The Gargoyle (route 27) until level with Balanced Rock platform. Continue on the same line over bulge to platform above.

27 THE GARGOYLE, 5.4. Inside corner. Climb past projecting chockstone or traverse left to Balanced Rock.
Variation, 5.4. Start from Balanced Rock, perform a "blind" traverse to inside corner, then climb past projecting chockstone.

28 5.6. Short jam crack that leads to Balanced Rock.

Balanced Rock Ridge (No Diagram)

This ridge is a series of walking and scrambling pitches leading from Balanced Rock to the top of the bluff 200 feet above. Balanced Rock itself can be ascended on the east side or the northeast corner. It is a one-move climb, especially if you are tall enough to reach the top.

Rocks East of Balanced Rock Wall (No Diagram)

Approach: Refer to Approach for Balanced Rock Wall. Walk around the east end of Balanced Rock Wall and up the gully for 100 feet. On the right is a 45-foot-high outcropping with an overhanging summit block and a south-facing lower wall.

Waypoint 57: Liederkranz
UTM 16T 279411E 4810426N
Base Elevation: 1,278 feet
Top Elevation: 1,325 feet

Routes:

1 LIEDERKRANZ, 5.9. Climb right crack and ledges on south wall. At horizontal crack, just above lower overhanging block, traverse left to west corner and follow to top.

2 BEAR HUG, 5.11c. Same start as Liederkranz (route 1). Climb south face of lower overhanging block to horizontal crack. Finish on west corner.

3 KRANZ, 5.6. Climb left layback crack leading up west side of outcropping.
Variation, 5.9. Halfway up, climb overhang on west side of lower block. Finish on west corner.

Hole-In-The-Wall (Diagram 38 E)

APPROACH: This small area is located 300 feet east of Balanced Rock. The wall faces southeast and has a few interesting climbs.

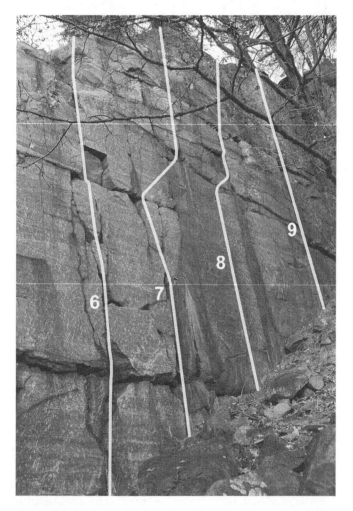

Hole-In-The-Wall

Waypoint 58: Hole-In-The-Wall
  UTM 16T 279492E 4810420N
Base Elevation: 1,345 feet
Top Elevation: 1,384 feet

ROUTES:

1 5.2. Chimney.

2 5.3. Climb left edge of flake. Continue in wide crack on upper wall.

3 DON'T LEAN ON THE TREE, 5.8. Overhanging wall with thin crack on the outside of the flake.

4 5.7. Crack.

5 5.3. Climb leaning block using chockstone behind right edge.

6 HOLE-IN-THE-WALL, 5.6. Climb crack to niche. To pass niche, reach high for jam hold in left crack. This is an attractive climb on smooth, clean rock. The wall is slightly overhanging.

7 SURPRISE, 5.8. Start 4 feet right of Hole-In-The-Wall (route 6) and climb a series of cracks running diagonally upward. When level with niche, move right a couple of feet and continue to top. Do not use edge of Hole-In-The-Wall niche.

8 LEFT ARM, 5.10a. Thin crack and flake system. Take great care when using the flakes; they might peel off.

9 RODIN'S INSPIRATION, 5.7. Crack. The upper shallow inside corner is surprisingly harder than it looks.

10 THE WHITE CLOUD, 5.8. Face route starting 5 feet left of route 11.

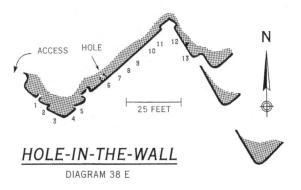

HOLE-IN-THE-WALL

DIAGRAM 38 E

I I 5.4. Crack leading to shallow chimney.

I 2 5.4. Short face with several cracks.

I 3 5.5. Corner and face. Climb on or just left of corner.

Rocks East of Hole-In-The-Wall (No Diagram)

APPROACH: Hike up the talus slope midway between Balanced Rock and Devil's Doorway. The Slab is located above the boulderfield. The Effie is 25 feet above The Slab.

Waypoint 59: Top of The Slab
   UTM 16T 279606E 4810398N

The Effie

Waypoint 60: The Effie
  UTM 16T 279609E 4810405N
Base Elevation: 1,313 feet
Top Elevation: 1,351 feet

ROUTES:
There are two 5.4 climbs on The Slab.

I THE EFFIE, 5.7. The name is a memorial to Effinger Beer, once brewed in Baraboo. Climb the inside corner/jam crack that starts with an overhang. Negotiate the overhang without using the large detached block on the right.
2 WHERE IS THE BEER, 5.10d. Climb overhang and face just right of The Effie (route 1). Avoid using good holds on right.
3 NO FOAM, 5.7. Face directly above the block on The Effie (route 1).

The face left of The Effie has two routes.

4 5.11a. Right side of face.
5 5.10a. Left side of face.

East Bluff, Railroad Tracks. Photo: Sven Olof Swartling.

RAILROAD TRACKS AREAS

Above the east shore of Devil's Lake, roughly midway between the south and north shores, are several rock outcroppings that afford excellent climbing. Many of the climbs are down low, a feature that is appreciated on hot summer days. The major outcroppings are Railroad Amphitheater, Birthday Rocks, and Horse Rampart. These are all near the "electric fence," a net running parallel to the railroad tracks for several hundred feet that used to give trains a warning in the event of a rock fall onto the tracks. Above the major outcroppings are numerous low rock outcroppings with many nice climbs. They are scattered in a line from above Waterfall Wall to near Balanced Rock.

Railroad Amphitheater is at the bottom of the bluff, 150 feet north of the electric fence. It is notable for its overhanging north wall and two fairly long climbs on its south wall.

Waterfall Wall above Railroad Amphitheater is a formation with rounded ledges and contours.

Birthday Rocks is above the electric fence. The main southwest wall starts 50 feet above the fence and angles up (southeast) to a prominent tower.

Horse Rampart is above the large boulderfield just south of the electric fence. It is a higher southward continuation of the band that forms the upper part of the Railroad Amphitheater and Birthday Rocks. The culminating point at the south end of the rampart is Teetering Tower.

Other rocks in the area include Lothar's Ledges, a series of rock steps on the boulderfield above and south of the electric fence, and Squirrel's Nest Tower, a 50-foot formation 300 feet south of Horse Rampart.

Railroad Amphitheater (Diagram 39 E)

APPROACH: Railroad Amphitheater is located a few feet from the railroad tracks that run along the east shore of the lake, 150 feet north of the electric fence.

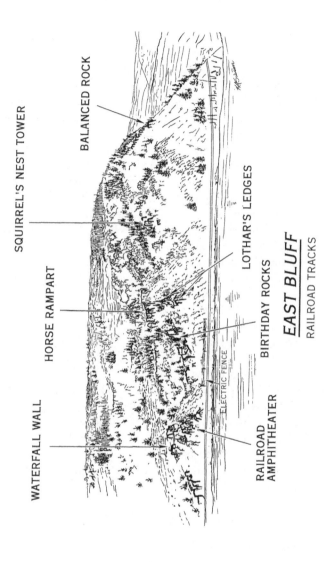

WATERFALL WALL

HORSE RAMPART

SQUIRREL'S NEST TOWER

BALANCED ROCK

LOTHAR'S LEDGES

BIRDHAY ROCKS

ELECTRIC FENCE

RAILROAD
AMPHITHEATER

EAST BLUFF
RAILROAD TRACKS

Waypoint 61: Railroad Amphitheater
 UTM 16T 279216E 4810861N
Base Elevation: 999 feet
Top Elevation: 1,079 feet

ROUTES:

1 SNEDEGAR'S NOSE, 5.7. Ridge route. Start on right side of corner, step up left to block at base of ridge. Stem 10 feet on right side and continue with steep slab climbing on or just left of corner.

2 JACK THE RIPPER, 5.10c. For those who enjoy self-abuse. Start below diagonal gash, jam up gash, and reach ridge about halfway up wall.

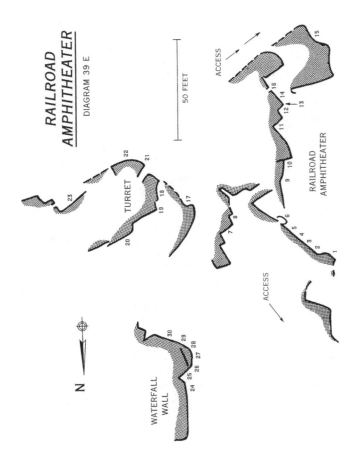

3 COP RIPPER, 5.12b. Difficult climb between Jack the Ripper (route 2) and Cop-Out (route 4).

4 COP-OUT, 5.11a. A study in combinatorial climbing. Start 10 feet left of The Pillar (route 6). Climb thin cracks for 35 feet into inside corner beneath overhang. Step to right corner and climb to top.

5 CATENARY CRACK, 5.9. A swooping curve that yields to deep analysis. Start 5 feet left of The Pillar (route 6) and climb crack to top.

6 THE PILLAR, 5.6. Climb or chimney up to top of standing block. Step across to upper half of Catenary Crack (route 5).
Variation, 5.8. From The Pillar, climb upper wall right of Catenary Crack.

Railroad Amphitheater

7–8   Climbs on 20-foot wall above northeast side of Railroad Amphitheater.

9   PINE TREE STEP-ACROSS, 5.6. Start 5 feet left of inside corner (Pine Tree Dihedral, route 10). Climb to first sloping ledge, then shuffle left to corner. Continue up and right to overhanging block with pine tree. Step far left and feel for a handhold to pull yourself across. Continue up slabby rock to top.

Variation, 5.6. Start in inside corner, traverse left on black rock, then up to overhanging block with pine tree.

10   PINE TREE DIHEDRAL, 5.5. Climb inside corner below block with pine tree. Move right under overhang and up to next ledge. Continue in inside corner past two more ledges to top.

11   RIGHT OF THE EYE, 5.4. Inside corner.

12   5.7. Inside corners obscured by trees.

13   OLD SHOES, 5.10c. Climb corner to overhang, pass overhang on the right. Continue on corner to top.

14   FACE-OFF, 5.9. Start on upper right end of detached block. Step left onto face. Move up and left toward corner where climbing becomes easier.

Lumby Ridge (routes 15–18) forms the southern arm of Railroad Amphitheater. It is named after Harry Lumby, a former CMC president who suffered a heart attack on these rocks on a hot Saturday morning while exerting himself on a layback. The ridge consists of short pitches. The start is only a few feet from the railroad tracks.

15   5.4. Climb onto loose upright plate, then in crack to first platform.

16   5.5. Climb chimney from the bottom or traverse into it from adjacent inside corner to next platform. Step across gap to the north, going around and into short chimney and up. Walk to next low wall for start of route 17.

17   5.4. Climb to sloping platform.

18   5.4. Start from large slab. Step up on left end of large displaced block. Go right and up to a little slab, then up to summit platform. A hole in the platform gives access to a scramble route down the south side.

ONE MOVE, 5.6/7. Climb southeast face of displaced block.

19 5.4. Short corner.

20 5.5. Climb short face or right inside corner.

21 BLOCKY, 5.5. Corner next to wide chimney.

22 THE TURRET, 5.7. Start on south corner in crack below overhang. Climb overhang, continue on corner to top.
TURRET RIGHT, 5.7. Start 5 feet right of The Turret. Climb past right end of overhang, continue on face, and finish in upper hanging inside corner.

23 5.3–5.7. Short wall with two crack routes and one inside corner.

Waterfall Wall (Diagram 39 E)

APPROACH: Ascend the talus slope on the north side of Railroad Amphitheater.

Base Elevation: 1,059 feet
Top Elevation: 1,116 feet

ROUTES:

24 5.7. Start up the right diagonal ledge, then up crack to ledge beneath notched overhang. Retable through notch and continue up short steep wall to top.

25 5.6. Inside corner and chimney.

26 DISAPPEARING LEDGE, 5.7. Climb corner to large ledge. Move right and step up on wall above. Traverse left on disappearing ledge, then up and left around corner.

27 5.9+/10a. Start 8 feet right of corner. Climb straight to top over upper overhang.

28 CHARLOTTE'S WEB, 5.10a. Start between blocks, then climb V-niche to top. Avoid use of large ledge on route 29.

29 5.8. Start on block and climb left to large ledge. Continue up and right, staying close to southwest corner.

30 SLIMER, 5.12a. Climb middle of overhanging wall.

Birthday Rocks (Diagram 40 E)

APPROACH: Ascend the slope near the north end of the electric fence.

Waypoint 62: Birthday Rocks
UTM 16T 279239E 4810739N

Base Elevation: 1,079 feet
Top Elevation: 1,146 feet

ROUTES:

I HORNER'S CORNER, 5.4. Climb crack 20 feet to a bench. Continue up west wall and southwest corner, climbing from ledge to ledge. Beware: sitting on a ledge is indecorous and subject to a penalty.

Birthday Rocks

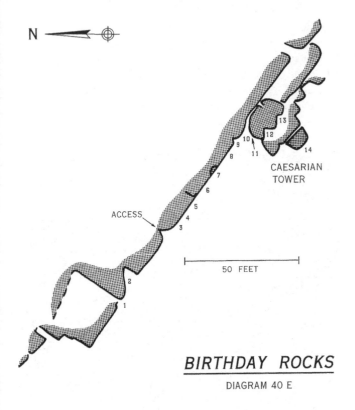

N

BIRTHDAY ROCKS

DIAGRAM 40 E

CHESTER'S CHIMNEY, 5.5. Wide chimney 35 feet north-west and below Horner's Corner.

2 5.7. Thin crack in recessed section.

3 PEAL OFF, 5.7. Climb crack system with shallow niche.

4 BOWING TO THE UNDERCLING, 5.12a. Short face with horizontal crack.

5 5.4. Ledges and crack that end left of 15-foot upper corner.

6–7 THE TWINS, 5.7. Both climbs are in shallow inside corners leading to an overhang.

8 GREAT WHITE HOPE, 5.11a. Difficult face left of Birthday Crack (route 9).

9 BIRTHDAY CRACK, 5.7. Prominent crack with overhang at ledge one-third of the way up.

10 BIRTHDAY CHIMNEY, 5.3. Long chimney leading to top.

Birthday Crack (Diagram 40 E, route 9). Climber: Jan Marion.
Photo: Alex Andrews.

11 CAESARIAN WEST FACE, 5.12b/c. Climb center of face, moving left to pass small overhang. After a hard fingertip mantle to ledge, follow crack, then traverse left and up to flake. Continue up and left to corner.

12 CAESARIAN TOWER, 5.8. Start on first ledge. Climb sharp west corner or adjacent groove to higher ledge on northwest side. Climb right to overhanging upper corner (the key is keeping a hand in the left crack). Shinny to top of tower.

13 SPECIAL DELIVERY, 5.6. Chockstone crack in hanging inside corner.

14 BIRTHDAY BOULDER, 5.9–5.10a. Face route with several variations.

Horse Rampart (Diagram 41 E)

Approach: Horse Rampart is located above the boulderfield south of the electric fence. Portions of the rampart are visible from the railroad tracks. Ascend the boulderfield, passing Lothar's Ledges on either side.

Waypoint 63: Horse Rampart
  UTM 16T 279301E 4810697N
Base Elevation: 1,182 feet
Top Elevation: 1,249 feet

Routes:

1 MOBY DICK, 5.8. Corner above low slab.

2 BETWEEN THE SHEETS, 5.12c. Climb overhang, then up and left past pin. Continue on face to top.
AAA, 5.12a. Climb overhang on corner to top.

3 5.7. Climb inside corner below first overhang. Exit right onto south shoulder, then step left to exposed west face. Climb face, ending on northwest shoulder left of capstone.

4 MONARCH, 5.9. Climb steep slab (5.7) to vertical upper wall. Continue up small overhang into small dihedral. Traverse left to crack in sunken face.

5 THE HORSE, 5.4. Start 8 feet left of corner. Climb to left (east) end of large flake (the horse). Step right and mount the horse (or vice versa). Continue on corner to top.

6 PULLMAN CAR, 5.7. Start near corner, then climb past west end of the horse.

7 ARCHERY, 5.8. Climb face and crack 8 feet left of Roger's Roof (route 8) to the horse.

8 ROGER'S ROOF, 5.8. Climb rib to small ledge below crack in roof. Jam over roof, using your knee if it helps. Finish on face above.

9 WOGERS WOOF WIGHTSIDE, 5.11c. Wander up to roof. Climb overhang right of Roger's Roof (route 8). Finish on face.

10 TREACHERY, 5.7. Waltz up 10 feet to ledge just right of alcove. Step up left, painfully jamming your left foot. Continue up narrow rib into easy chimney.
Variation, 5.7. Climb lower wall, staying 6 feet right of alcove.

Horse Rampart

11 LECHERY, 5.8. Climb crack to ledge at 25 feet. Finish in thin crack on upper wall.

12 DEBAUCHERY, 5.8. Pure climbing deficient in protection. Climb on or near corner for 25 feet, then move a few feet left and pull onto comfortable ledge. Above this point the corner is ill defined. Continue slightly right into shallow concavity for final 20 feet.

Variation, 5.8. Climb lower face right of corner to comfortable ledge and join Debauchery.

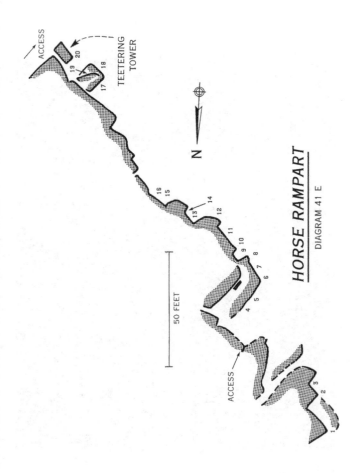

HORSE RAMPART
DIAGRAM 41 E

Variation, 5.11d. Same start as first variation, but avoid comfortable ledge and climb over bulge. Join Debauchery at the shallow concavity.

13 PRIMAK'S SURPRISE, 5.?. To rate this climb would spoil the surprise. Every 10 feet you think you've passed the crux. Climb inside corner, switchbacking holds on either side when helpful.

14 PLETHORA, 5.11a. Stem inside corner past slight bulge on left wall to ledge 20 feet below top. Climb ugly overhanging crack to cedar tree.

PTOLEMY, 5.10d. Start just right of corner. Climb face until under roof. Step up left around corner without using Plethora crack. Move up right and over roof. Continue on Plethora, Primak's Surprise (route 13), or route 15.

15 5.5. Climb inside corner onto left block. Continue up fractured rock to top.

16 VIA APIA, 5.7. Jam crack.

17 MUNG, 5.9. Crack system in northwest face.

18 PEANUT BUTTER, 5.8. Climb lower face to ledge. Continue on left corner.

19 MOTHER SMUCKER'S JAM, 5.8. Overhanging jam crack.

20 TEETERING TOWER, 5.7–5.9. A 40-foot tower separated from the main wall by a jumpable gap. The climb on the northwest corner is 5.7, except for the start, which is 5.9. There was an easier start at the south corner until a hold broke off.

Lothar's Ledges (No Diagram)

This area is named for Lothar Kolbig, a former CMC president who was active in the 1940s and 1950s. It is a series of three rock steps on the boulderfield above and south of the electric fence and below Horse Rampart. There are a number of short climbs, including a fall-across from the first tower to the next wall. It is a good place for beginners, since each step has at least one easy climb.

Squirrel's Nest Tower (No Diagram)

Approach: Squirrel's Nest Tower is a 50-foot outcropping midlevel on the bluff 300 feet south of Teetering Tower (route 20) on Horse Rampart. It can also be approached from the opposite direction by contouring 600 feet north from Balanced Rock Wall. The closely spaced routes are on the southwest side. They are listed from right to left.

Waypoint 64: Squirrel's Nest Tower
    UTM 16T 279331E 4810566N

Squirrel's Nest Tower

Base Elevation: 1,201 feet
Top Elevation: 1,253 feet

ROUTES:

1 5.7. Inside corner and hanging chimney near south corner.
2 5.7. Wide crack with remains of tree stump.
3 5.7. Inside corner and overhanging crack 3 feet left of route 2.
4 5.8. Overhang with two cracks 6 feet left of route 3.
5 5.9. Start from ledge on northwest side. Step right to west corner, then up corner.

NORTH END OF THE EAST BLUFF

There are several small rock outcroppings at the north end of the lake on the East Bluff that offer a number of interesting short climbs (20–30 feet). They are located close to the East Bluff Trail and are best approached from the north. North to south they are Cabin Rocks, Elephant Rocks, Tomahawk Rocks, and Monolith Blocks.

The north end of the East Bluff Trail begins at the northeast corner of Devil's Lake. From the north shore park entrance, drive east across the railroad tracks and turn right (south) to the second or third parking area. The trailhead is located across the road between these parking areas. The trail forks a short distance from the trailhead. Stay right and follow the East Bluff Trail (not the East Bluff Woods Trail) to the climbing areas.

Two park-named rock formations along the East Bluff Trail are used to locate the climbing areas, though both formations are somewhat separated from the actual climbs. Elephant Rock is a boulder located 1,850 feet from the start of the East Bluff Trail. Tomahawk Rock is 550 feet south of Elephant Rock.

Cabin Rocks (No Diagram)

The Cabin Rocks area is named after the one hundred cabins that used to occupy the current North Shore picnic and parking areas between the railroad tracks and the bluff. The cabins were removed in the 1960s after their one hundred–year leases expired.

Cabin Rocks consists of four small, low outcroppings located above and just east of the last parking area at the northeast corner of Devil's Lake. The outcroppings start at parking-area level, 150 feet south of a restroom building, and rise gradually to the south. The southernmost outcropping is located 250 feet north of Elephant Rock, 75 feet west of the East Bluff Trail. It has a couple of interesting climbs.

Routes:

1 5.8. An obvious, slightly overhanging, south-facing inside corner.
2 5.11a. Narrow face just left of the inside corner.

Elephant Rocks (Diagram 42 E)

Approach: From the north end of the East Bluff Trail, walk 1,850 feet to Elephant Rock. The small climbing area is located west and across the trail from Elephant Rock.

Waypoint 65: Elephant Rocks
    UTM 16T 279404E 4811681N
Base Elevation: 1,128 feet
Top Elevation: 1,190 feet

Routes:

1 5.5. Inside corner.

Elephant Rocks

2 TRANSCENDENTAL DISFIGURATION, 5.10d. Sharp corner with crack.

3 CLEARASIL SPATTERED FANTASIES, 5.9. Start in alcove, then climb thin crack straight to top.
Variation, 5.8. Same start, but follow diagonal crack up and right.

4 5.8. Face route with down-sloping ledges 5–6 feet left of route 5.

5 5.7. Crack.

6 DUMBO, 5.9. Start in lower inside corner. Continue on hanging pillar to top. Avoid stepping on right platform.

7 THE TRUNK, 5.7. Climb rib 20 feet to inside corner. Continue in corner to top.

8 TOMB OF THE UNKNOWN HOMO, 5.7. Crack and chimney.

9 TWO FINGER CRACKS, 5.10a. Climb, staying close to two thin cracks. Don't wander right.

10 5.7. Broken-up face and crack.

11 ROMANCING THE BONE, 5.12b. Overhanging wall.

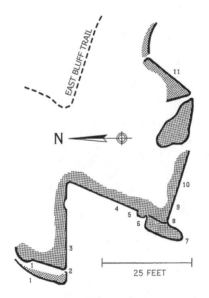

ELEPHANT ROCKS

DIAGRAM 42 E

Tomahawk Rocks (Diagram 43 E)

APPROACH: Follow the East Bluff Trail 250 feet south of Elephant Rock to the north end of Tomahawk Rocks. This long, low outcropping stretches south for 300 feet. It is named for the tomahawk-looking rock (Tomahawk Rock) located 150 feet south of the climbs. Most of the climbs are located on the northern half of the outcropping.

Waypoint 66: Tomahawk Rocks
    UTM 16T 279431E 4811613N
Base Elevation: 1,217 feet
Top Elevation: 1,246 feet

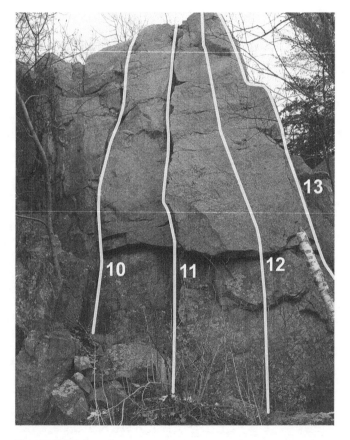

Tomahawk Rocks

Routes:

1 5.5. Crack.
2 5.4. Crack in inside corner.
3 5.8. Overhang with crack.
4 5.9. Short face route on lower part of wall.
5 WINNEBAGO, 5.8. Nice face and crack route leading to top of wall.
6 5.10a. Climb short slab and face.
  Variation, 5.7. Same start, then move right and follow corner to top.

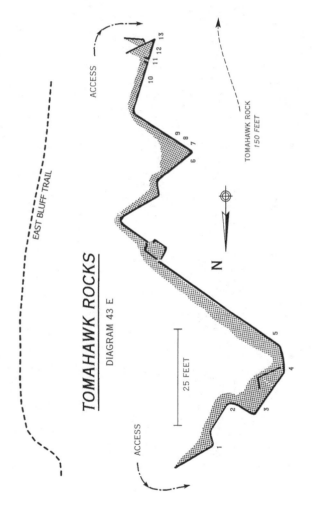

TOMAHAWK ROCKS

DIAGRAM 43 E

7 BRAVE, 5.9. Start in crack. When the crack ends, move left and up.

8 TEPEE, 5.9. Thin, awkward crack.

9 5.8. Jam crack.

10 5.7. Thin crack starting with a layback.

11 PUZZLEMENT, 5.7. Crack too wide to jam and too narrow to chimney.

12 5.9. Narrow face just right of Puzzlement (route 11).

13 MOHAWK, 5.8. Sharp corner.

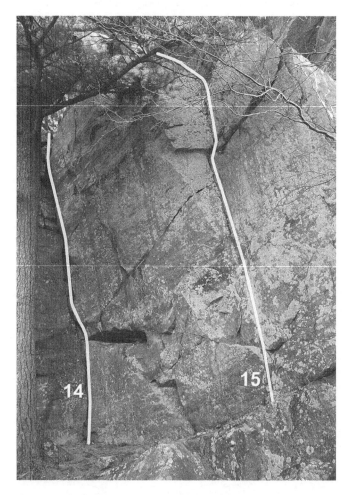

Tomahawk Rocks (two climbs not shown on diagram)

Two additional climbs are located 75 feet south of Mohawk (route 13). These climbs are not shown on the diagram. Tomahawk Rock is located 80 feet farther south–southeast.

14 5.5. Inside corner facing south and west.
15 HO-CHUNK, 5.8. Face with right-facing hanging dihedral.

Monolith Blocks (Diagram 44 E)

APPROACH: Follow the East Bluff Trail 750 feet south of Tomahawk Rock. The trail passes above the climbs.

Waypoint 67: Monolith Blocks
  UTM 16T 279461E 4811371N
Base Elevation: 1,321 feet
Top Elevation: 1,340 feet

ROUTES:
1 5.7. Crack with a few nice layback moves.
2 THE QUILL, 5.9. Climb, staying on corner to top.

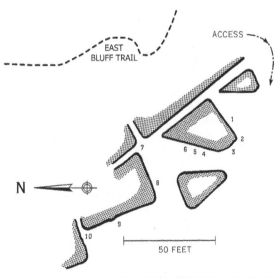

MONOLITH BLOCKS

DIAGRAM 44 E

3 PORCUPINE, 5.9. Narrow face. Avoid using either corner. *Variation*, 5.8. Same start, but make use of left corner.

4 5.9. Face just right of Foil (route 5). Do not use crack.

5 FOIL, 5.8. Climb lower face to crack. Continue in crack to top.

6 RAPIER, 5.11c. Climb face without using right crack or left corner.

Monolith Blocks

EAST BLUFF CLIMBS

7 5.4. Wide crack/chimney.

8 5.6. Wide, interesting crack.

9 SURFING WITH THE ALIEN, 5.11b. Start near left chimney. Climb up and right on weakness in face.

10 5.4. Chimney.

The climbs described below are not shown on the diagram.

11 RUSTY CRACK, 5.8. Climb rust-colored crack 25 feet north of route 10.

12 5.8. Corner 6 feet left (north) of Rusty Crack (route 11).

There is a small pink-and-purple buttress of weathered rock 150 feet south–southeast of Monolith Blocks with the following climb.

13 RAINBOW CRACK, 5.9. Climb slightly overhanging jam crack hidden by trees.

Ten feet left (north) of Rainbow Crack (route 13) are a couple of climbs.

14 5.5. Tight chimney.

15 5.8. Crack.

A few feet farther left (north) is a short wall with an overhang.

16 PINK PANTHER, 5.11b/c. Climb left of corner.

From Rainbow Crack (route 13) a broken band of rock outcroppings continues south about 500 feet. Several short climbs can be found on these rocks. There are a few longer climbs at the southern end of this band.

STEINKE BASIN ROCKS

The Steinke Basin rock outcroppings are located east of the north shore of Devil's Lake above and north of the creek draining Steinke Basin. There is significant distance between the climbing areas, which form an almost straight southeast-to-northwest line approximately 3,000 feet in length. One advantage, besides the solitude, is the relatively small elevation gain between the Steinke Basin parking area and these out-croppings.

There are four major outcroppings, with most climbs 20–25 feet. From southeast to northwest the climbing areas are Cibola Wall, Triple Tower Wall, Steinke Wall, and Storm Wrack Wall.

There are several lower outcroppings, including one to the north that is slightly larger. Unfortunately, they offer no worthwhile climbs.

Cibola Wall (Diagram 45 E)

APPROACH: From the Steinke Basin parking area, follow the East Bluff Woods Trail (service road) south to where the Steinke Basin Loop Trail crosses, then continue 350 feet south. If you reach the north branch of the creek, you have gone too far. Turn right and walk west 1,250 feet through an open white oak forest to Cibola Wall. Cibola Wall is 200 feet long but only 25 feet high. Since this approach brings you to the top of the wall, it is easy to miss.

Waypoint 68: Cibola Wall
   UTM 16T 280200E 4811403N
Base Elevation: 1,271 feet
Top Elevation: 1,294 feet

ROUTES:
   1   5.7. Inside corner. Harder than it looks.
   2   CONVERGENCE, 5.8. Cracks and ledges 2–3 feet left of inside corner (route 1).

3 FURTHER CONSIDERATION, 5.10a. Thin cracks 3 feet left of Convergence (route 2).

4 ELEPHANT EAR, 5.11a. Start in shallow crack below elephant ear block. From top of ear, climb crack and ledges.

THE TRINITY (routes 5–7). Three cracks diverge from their start at ground level. The easiest route uses a combination of the cracks.

5 RIGHT CRACK, 5.9+. Climb using only the right crack.

6 CENTERFOLD, 5.12a. Climb using crack and narrow faces between Right Crack (route 5) and Left Crack (route 7). The crux is halfway up.

7 LEFT CRACK, 5.8. Jam/layback crack.

8 ON YOUR KNEES, 5.9+. Corner just left of Left Crack (route 7).

9 5.10a. Climb into niche, then up inside corner and crack.

10 5.8. Cracks right of steep gully. Avoid holds in gully.

Cibola Wall. Photo: Pete Mayer.

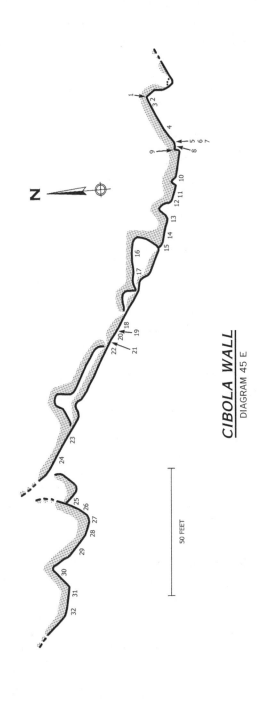

CIBOLA WALL
DIAGRAM 45 E

50 FEET

11 5.7. Center of face on narrow buttress.

12 5.6. Jam/layback crack. Use only the crack just left of route 11.

13 UNDER THE TREE, 5.4. Southeast corner.

14 HI-JINKS, 5.6. Climb center of buttress.

15 HEAD SCRATCHER, 5.7. Southwest corner and cracks.

16 5.4. Climb to large ledge. From ledge, climb crack to top.

17 LOST IN THE WOODS, 5.10a. Climb to large ledge. Continue in center of face.

18 BARBED WIRE, 5.6. Climb right crack.

19 SECOND CRACK, 5.5. Crack 4 feet left of Barbed Wire (route 18).

20 THIRD CRACK, 5.7. Right-slanting crack. Same start as Face Holds Only (route 21).

21 FACE HOLDS ONLY, 5.8. Narrow face between cracks. Avoid using cracks.

22 ATTITUDE PROBLEM, 5.4. Climb left crack.

23 SIDE DISH, 5.4. Crack and ledges.

24 MAIN ENTRÉE, 5.5. Start below high point of buttress. Climb straight to top.

25 5.6. Start in inside corner. Continue climb in crack above.

26 5.9. Face 8 feet left of inside corner (route 25). Climb to highest large ledge. Finish left of overhanging bulge.

27 5.9. Overhanging corner and cracks. Of the two overhanging sections, the second one is the hardest.

28 5.5. Crack and niche on right side of smooth face.

29 LOWER THE THERMOSTAT, 5.7–5.8. Climb smooth face with several cracks. Many variations are possible.

30 CUP OF TEA, 5.6. Face and cracks 6 feet left of inside corner.

31 5.10a. Climb cracks to rock projection. Pass it on the right.

32 TWIN BEAKS, 5.10a. Two large projections cap this route. Climb lower wall/cracks and finish between projections.

Triple Tower Wall (Diagram 46 E)

APPROACH: From the Steinke Basin parking area, walk west on the East Bluff Woods Trail. The trail parallels Highway DL to the top of a hill and then turns south. At the junction with the Steinke Basin Loop Trail, continue on the East Bluff Woods Trail for another 1,400 feet. Shortly after the trail curves right (northwest), the top of Steinke Wall will be visible

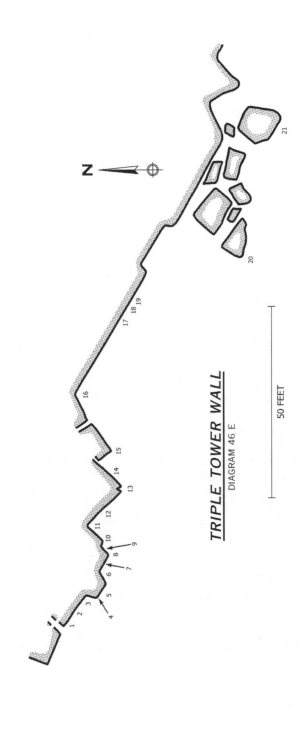

TRIPLE TOWER WALL

DIAGRAM 46 E

50 FEET

75 feet south (left) of the trail. Triple Tower Wall is 250 feet southeast of the east end of Steinke Wall.

Waypoint 69: Triple Tower Wall
 UTM 16T 279989E 4811736N
Base Elevation: 1,238 feet
Top Elevation: 1,258 feet

ROUTES:

1 5.7. Crack on left side of wall.
2 5.10a. Face left of inside corner. Avoid use of cracks (routes 1 and 3).

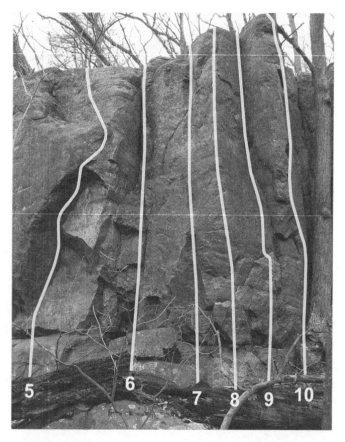

Triple Tower Wall

3 5.8. Inside corner. Harder than it looks.

4 5.9+. Climb left corner of smooth face.

5 GOOD GRIEF, 5.10a. Climb right-slanting dihedral past small white quartz-covered slab to upper right corner ledge. The ledge is smooth and rounded. Continue to top.

6 5.4. Crack and inside corner.

7 5.7. Face just right of route 6.

8 5.9. Corner between route 7 and Long Enough (route 9).

9 LONG ENOUGH, 5.9. Climb to top of large creaking flake near the ground. Continue in smooth dihedral.

10 TOO LONG, 5.10a. Corner and face right of Long Enough (route 9).

11 5.5. Inside corner (behind tree).

12 ARRESTED LAYBACK, 5.7. Climb sharp layback crack.

13 NO HOLDS BARRED, 5.7. Narrow V-shaped inside corner. Interesting if only the crack is used.

14 NO BOBBLING, 5.7. Climb face 3 feet right of No Holds Barred (route 13).

15 5.4. Corner and cracks.

16 5.5. Inside corner.

17 TIEBACK, 5.10a. Overhanging thin crack 4 feet left of route 18.

18 5.6. Crack with small niche in center of face.

19 COMMITTEE CLIMBING, 5.10b. Start 5 feet right of route 18. Climb overhanging wall with nice layback at top.

20 SLAP HAPPY, 5.11b. Overhanging southwest corner of tower. One good pull hold is near the top.

21 5.8. Crack on south side of tower.
Variation, 5.7. Same start. Climb southwest corner and overhang.

Steinke Wall (Diagram 47 E)

APPROACH: From the Steinke Basin parking area, walk west on the East Bluff Woods Trail. The trail parallels Highway DL to the top of a hill and then turns south. Continue on the East Bluff Woods Trail for 1,400 feet past the junction with the Steinke Basin Loop Trail. Shortly after the trail curves right (northwest), the top of Steinke Wall will be visible 75 feet south (left) of the trail.

Waypoint 70: Steinke Wall
UTM 16T 279937E 4811836N
Base Elevation: 1,212 feet
Top Elevation: 1,245 feet

ROUTES:
1. 5.5. Inside corner.
2. 5.6. Inside corner.
3. DOUBLE PINCH, 5.10a. Face right of route 2.
4. 5.9. Corner and crack.

Steinke Wall

5 5.8. Face and crack just left of route 6.

6 5.4. Wide crack.

7 5.7. Face and crack right of route 6.

8 5.7. Climb corner.

9 5.4. Crack in center of face.

10 5.7. Corner.

11 5.6. Crack.

12 MUD LEDGE, 5.8. Climb to ledge and retable. Then climb to top and retable again.

13 TUNING FORK, 5.5. Deep crack.

14 5.8. Nice crack. Don't step left or use right corner.

15 5.9. Corner.

16 GREASE SPOT, 5.9. Climb just right of corner.

17 5.8. Start below left end of large triangular ledge. Continue in inside corner.

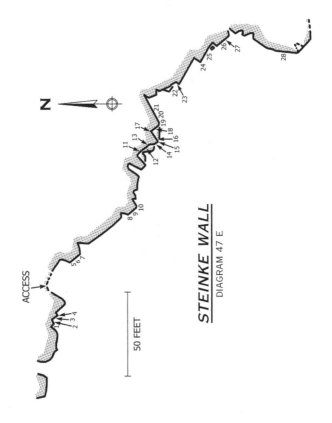

STEINKE WALL

DIAGRAM 47 E

50 FEET

18 5.9. Face just right of route 17.

19 5.9. Corner.

20 5.8. Overhanging cracks and chimney.

21 JACK BACKWARDS, 5.?. Unfinished project. Overhanging crack leading to hanging inside corner.

22 5.8. Start in crack, climb to ledge, then continue on obtuse corner.

23 5.9. Climb short inside corner to ledge. From ledge climb straight up to top crack.

24 VERY GREEN, 5.8. Obtuse corner with very green lichen at the start.

25 5.5. Face with several cracks.

26 5.9. Face with small, sharp holds. Avoid using right crack and upper niche.

27 5.8. Climb diagonal crack. Finish in upper niche.

28 5.8. Start from block, climb slightly left, then up.

Storm Wrack Wall (Diagram 48 E)

APPROACH: Refer to Approach for Steinke Wall. Storm Wrack Wall is 1,150 feet northwest of the west end of Steinke Wall, 200 feet south (left) of the East Bluff Woods Trail. Steinke Wall

Storm Wrack Wall. Photo: Pete Mayer.

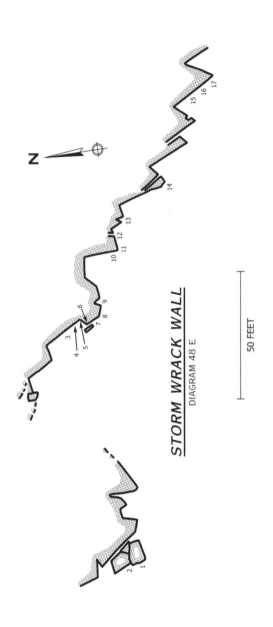

STORM WRACK WALL
DIAGRAM 48 E

50 FEET

N

may also be approached from the west. Start at the amphitheater in the Northern Lights Campground and follow the East Bluff Woods Trail 1,000 feet to where the trail is almost level. Storm Wrack Wall will be on your right.

Waypoint 71: Storm Wrack Wall
   UTM 16T 279619E 4812098N
Base Elevation: 1,114 feet
Top Elevation: 1,134 feet

ROUTES:
1 MISSING FOOTHOLD, 5.9. Climb lower face and upper inside corner.
2 5.4. Chimney.
3 5.8. Climb layback crack to funnel at top.
4 5.11a. Narrow face between routes 3 and 5.
5 5.7. Inside corner and crack.
6 NOT SHORT ENOUGH, 5.11a. Climb corner. At start do not use inside corner crack (route 5).
7 5.11a. Climb blank-looking face. Avoid the pedestal.
8 ZIGZAG CRACK, 5.6. South corner and crack.
9 STUMBLING BLOCKS, 5.5–5.7. Climb cracks on either side of blocks.
10 5.7. Face just left of corner.
11 5.6. Start near left corner and climb slab leading to inside corner.
12 5.1. Deep crack.
13 5.3. Shallow V-crack.
14 5.3. Shallow inside corner.
15 5.5. Crack on left side of face.
16 5.6. Climb middle of face between routes 15 and 17.
17 5.5. Crack near corner.

WEST BLUFF CLIMBS

West Bluff. Photo: Chuck Koch.

WEST BLUFF

The West Bluff parallels the west shore of Devil's Lake for 1 mile and has over thirty significant climbing areas. Climbing here has the same general character as climbing elsewhere at Devil's Lake. The outcroppings are widely scattered and often obscured by trees, giving the area a feel closer to the Quarry Rocks than to the nearly continuous East Rampart.

The West Bluff outcroppings show a banded structure that dips to the north in the same manner as the outcroppings on the opposite shore. For the most part, the bands are continuous; they consist of rock patches interrupted by wooded slopes. In a few places the outcroppings form vertical extensions, providing continuous, multipitch ascent routes for 200–300 feet (e.g., Turk's Head Ridge and Prospect Point Towers).

Two maintained hiking trails and one unofficial trail provide access to the climbing areas. The Tumbled Rocks Trail follows the base of the bluff along the shore of the lake. The West Bluff Trail mostly follows the top of the bluff. The unofficial trail (Old West Bluff Trail) is convenient for reaching some of the southern rock outcroppings since it more closely follows the edge of the bluff. This trail ends at Cleo Amphitheater.

There is a parking area at the southwest corner of the lake across the road from the boat launch. The West Bluff Trail's southern trailhead is a short distance northwest of the parking area at the junction of Cottage Grove Road and South Shore Road. The northern end of the West Bluff Trail is on Park Road near the Nature Center, where parking is also available. The Tumbled Rocks Trail's southern trailhead is at the end of the 0.25-mile Cottage Grove Road; the northern end is near the beach at the northwest corner of the lake.

Major Climbing Areas of the West Bluff

Following is a summary of the climbing areas described from south to north.

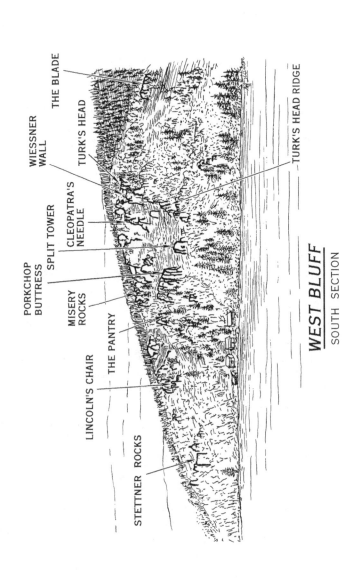

PORKCHOP
BUTTRESS

WIESSNER
WALL

THE BLADE

SPLIT TOWER

CLEOPATRA'S
NEEDLE

TURK'S HEAD

MISERY
ROCKS

LINCOLN'S CHAIR

THE PANTRY

STETTNER ROCKS

TURK'S HEAD RIDGE

WEST BLUFF

SOUTH SECTION

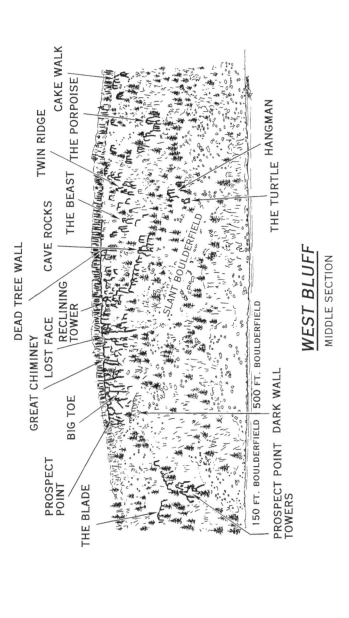

PROSPECT
POINT

DEAD TREE WALL

GREAT CHIMINEY

LOST FACE

CAVE ROCKS

TWIN RIDGE

CAKE WALK

THE BEAST

THE PORPOISE

RECLINING
TOWER

BIG TOE

THE TURTLE

HANGMAN

THE BLADE

SLANT BOULDERFIELD

150 FT. BOULDERFIELD   500 FT. BOULDERFIELD

PROSPECT POINT   DARK WALL
TOWERS

WEST BLUFF
MIDDLE SECTION

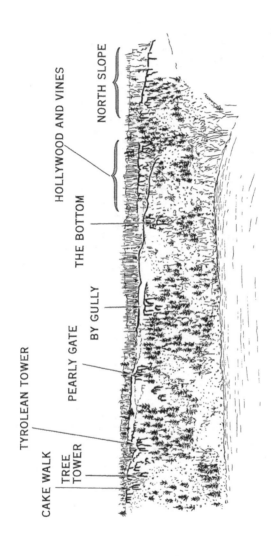

CAKE WALK

TYROLEAN TOWER

TREE TOWER

PEARLY GATE

BY GULLY

THE BOTTOM

HOLLYWOOD AND VINES

NORTH SLOPE

WEST BLUFF
NORTH SECTION

Stettner Rocks is located at the far south end of the West Bluff. It has southeast exposure, low elevation, and the advantage of a short approach. The rocks form a reddish band 200 feet long. Most of the climbs are short (20–30 feet high), but there is considerable variety. The area is often used for instruction.

Lincoln's Chair is a minor rock cluster 600 feet north of Stettner Rocks on a relatively low section of the bluff. The climbs are on several levels and range in height from 20 to 30 feet, making it another area suitable for instruction.

Misery Rocks is above the cottages at the southwest corner of Devil's Lake. The traditional Fat Man's Misery climb is on the 40-foot summit band. The area is distinguished by a large reclining block, The Pillow, that creates a cavelike enclosure. Directly below the summit wall is The Pantry, an outcropping with an alcove, ancillary walls, and towers on two levels.

Dutchman Rampart is 100 feet north of Misery Rocks across Misery Gully. It features a prominent high roof at the west end, a south-facing wall, and The Frigate, a three-sectioned tower. At a lower level are Dungeon Wall, Porkchop Buttress, and Split Tower. Porkchop Buttress is an impressive formation with relatively long climbs, approximately 60–70 feet high. Split Tower is an isolated 40-foot outcropping 150 feet north of Porkchop Buttress.

Cleo Amphitheater is part of the summit band on the south section of the West Bluff. The amphitheater is 200 feet across and partly surrounds a 50-foot spire, Cleopatra's Needle. These rocks are densely covered with routes.

Wiessner Wall and Turk's Head form a northerly extension of Cleo Amphitheater and are the most prominent of the southern rocks. Wiessner Wall is over 60 feet high and is naturally broken into two pitches by the Wiessner Ledge. Turk's Head can be seen in jutting profile from points along the south shore.

The Blade is a separate outcropping 300 feet to the north of Turk's Head.

Turk's Head Ridge ascends most of the bluff below Turk's Head, ending at Turk's Tooth. It provides a nearly continuous sequence of easy to moderate pitches.

Prospect Point Towers forms a ridge that extends up the middle third of the bluff below Prospect Point. It is a magnificent formation with many fine climbs.

Prospect Point Rampart is the summit band in the middle section of the West Bluff. The band continues for 400 feet from Prospect Point north to Lost Face with an average height of 80 feet. The lower section is broken by many benches and ledges. In a few places it provides long, continuous climbs, notably at Great Chimney and Lost Face. Dark Wall is at its base near the south end.

Reclining Tower and Dead Tree Wall are short, separate sections of the summit band north of Prospect Point Rampart. The latter is the more impressive formation, consisting of a steep wall with climbs up to 60 feet.

Cave Rocks Rampart descends northeast from the lower, northern end of Reclining Tower. Halfway down the bluff it ends at Cave Rocks.

Hangman Towers, north of Dead Tree Wall, consists of a group of towers, including Twin Ridge, Go-Go Tower, and The Porpoise. The towers are scattered over several hundred feet on the upper half of the bluff. The climbs are all in the short category, up to 30 feet high.

Tree Tower and Tyrolean Tower are 175 feet apart; both are a little below the crest of the bluff. Behind Tree Tower there are summit walls of interest. The top of Tyrolean Tower was first reached by Tyrolean traverse.

North of Tyrolean Tower there are only a couple of isolated climbs until above the north end of the lake. The most southerly, By Gully, has a few routes. Hollywood and Vines and North Slope are more extensive, each extending several hundred feet immediately beneath the West Bluff Trail with climbs 30–40 feet high.

West Bluff Approaches

Following is an overview of approaches to the climbing areas from south to north. See each climbing area for a more detailed description.

Old West Bluff Trail

This unofficial, faint trail starts near the third utility pole along Cottage Grove Road, approximately 325 feet east of South Shore Road.

Stettner Rocks is 300 feet from the trailhead on a bench 100 feet northeast of the trail.

Lincoln's Chair is below a small vantage point 600 feet farther north.

Misery Rocks is 300 feet farther north below an obvious vantage point.

The Old West Bluff Trail merges with the West Bluff Trail 300 feet past Misery Rocks above Cleo Amphitheater.

West Bluff Trail

Cleo Amphitheater is located below the junction of the Old West Bluff Trail and the West Bluff Trail. A couple of short gullies leading down to Cleopatra's Needle are found by walking north along the rim. Wiessner Wall and Turk's Head are located 200 feet north.

There is an unmarked path that leaves the West Bluff Trail above Turk's Head. The path gradually descends north for 400 feet. It passes above The Blade, then turns down and disappears in the gully adjacent to Prospect Point Towers.

Prospect Point is located 1,000 feet beyond Cleo Amphitheater at a vantage point with a panorama that includes the entire lake. Prospect Point Rampart is the summit band below and north of this point. To the south there is a broad summit boulderfield that creates a break in the contour of the upper bluff. Great Chimney is 250 feet farther north, 50 feet south of the geodetic survey marker and the park service road that joins South Shore Road to the west. Lost Face is 100 feet northeast of the survey marker.

Reclining Tower is 175 feet north of the survey marker.

Dead Tree Wall is 250 feet north of Reclining Tower.

Go-Go Tower is 425 feet north of Dead Tree Wall, 100 feet below the trail. Twin Ridge is 150 feet south of Go-Go Tower. These and other rocks of Hangman Towers are not visible from the top of the bluff. On the upper bluff about 200 feet north of Go-Go Tower is a small boulderfield that reaches almost to the summit.

Tree Tower is 425 feet north of Go-Go Tower. Though only 50 feet off the summit, the tower is easy to miss because of intervening trees. It has a small pine tree near its top.

Tyrolean Tower is 175 feet north of Tree Tower. It is about 75 feet below the trail and not visible from above. When approaching from the south, there is a short rise in the trail.

The rocks immediately below an obvious vantage point 325 feet farther north have no interesting climbs.

Pearly Gate is 150 feet north of the obvious vantage point and not visible from the trail. From the trail a narrow, descending cleft leads 25 feet to the top of the wall.

By Gully is located 350 feet north of the obvious vantage point (200 feet north of Pearly Gate). Where the trail dips and crosses a large, steep gully, descend 100 feet to reach the wall.

Hollywood and Vines is 525 feet north of By Gully.

North Slope is 650 feet farther north on the descending section of trail with exposed rock slabs. It is approximately 225 feet long, and the final rock band before the West Bluff Trail ends 375 feet farther north at Park Road.

Tumbled Rocks Trail

The Tumbled Rocks Trail starts at the south end of the West Bluff at the north end of Cottage Grove Road. Park by the South Shore Boat Launch. This trail provides the most convenient approach for climbing areas below the summit band. The best way to reach areas on the summit band is by descending from the West Bluff Trail.

Misery Rocks, The Pantry, and Dutchman Rampart: Walk up on the least overgrown talus 200 feet before the north end of Cottage Grove Road. Walking straight up (west) leads to the gully south of The Pantry and Misery Rocks. Walking west–northwest leads to the gully between Misery Rocks and Dutchman Rampart.

Double Chimney and Porkchop Buttress: Both are located 200–300 feet above the start of the Tumbled Rocks Trail. Follow the trail 100 feet north, turn left (west), and follow a faint path.

Turk's Head Ridge: The First Pitch, a small tower 200 feet up the bluff, is 350 feet north of the start of the Tumbled Rocks Trail.

Prospect Point Towers: The 150-Foot (wide) Boulderfield is the first open boulderfield that the trail crosses. Ascend the south edge of the boulderfield to reach Prospect Point Towers or follow a faint trail in the woods just south of the boulderfield that leads almost to the base of the towers.

Prospect Point and Great Chimney: The 500-Foot (wide) Boulderfield is the second open boulderfield that the trail crosses. Ascend the south edge of the boulderfield. At the top continue up, over, and between large blocks to the Slant Boulderfield on the upper portion of the bluff. Follow the Slant Boulderfield southwest toward Prospect Point or go up through the trees to the summit band in the vicinity of Great Chimney.

Cave Rocks Rampart, Reclining Tower, and Dead Tree Wall: Ascend the north edge of the 500-Foot Boulderfield. Near the top bear somewhat north to avoid most of the trees past a 25-foot rock with a steep slab climb. This brings you to Cave Rocks Rampart. Follow the rampart southwest to Reclining Tower or cross it northwest to Dead Tree Wall.

The Turtle, Cave Rocks Rampart, and Hangman Towers: North of the 500-Foot Boulderfield the trail passes through a gradually narrowing strip of trees. Near the north end of the trees, above on the Slant Boulderfield, is the Turtle, a large, sloping rock with a small boulder on top. Cave Rocks Rampart is about 250 feet southwest of the Turtle. Hangman Towers covers an extensive area above the Turtle.

The Porpoise and Tree Tower: The third boulderfield that the trail crosses is the Slant Boulderfield. It extends diagonally up and south, practically uninterrupted, to Prospect Point. Where the Tumbled Rocks Trail emerges from the trees, go up across this boulderfield and continue up on fairly open talus to The Porpoise, a rock band two-thirds of the way up the bluff. Veer north across a higher boulderfield to reach the top of the bluff in the vicinity of Tree Tower.

Stettner Rocks (Diagram 1 W)

APPROACH: There are three options to reach Stettner Rocks:
1. From the parking area at the southwest corner of the lake (across the road from the boat launch), walk north along South Shore Road to Cottage Grove Road. Follow Cottage Grove Road 325 feet to near or before the third utility pole. Turn left and hike up the faint Old West Bluff Trail. The trail crosses a low, sometimes-wet area before heading up the bluff. Approximately 300 feet from the road the trail reaches a bench above the first minor rock band. Follow the path 100 feet northeast to the base of Stettner Rocks.
2. Continue on the Cottage Grove Road 325 feet past the third utility pole. After the road turns north, just before a hill, a faint trail goes up (west) to the east end of Stettner Rocks.

3. Hike the West Bluff Trail about 600 feet and then turn right (east) on a faint trail to Stettner Rocks.

Waypoint 72: Old West Bluff Trailhead
    UTM 16T 278217E 4810406N
Waypoint 73: Stettner Rocks
    UTM 16T 278202E 4810497N
Base Elevation: 1,072 feet
Top Elevation: 1,118 feet

Stettner Rocks

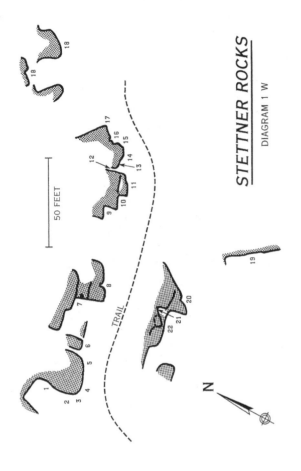

Routes:

1.   5.8. Short face climb.
2.   PAUL, 5.6. Overhang at southwest corner of west buttress. Climb left of small, sharp rib underneath overhang. *Variation*, 5.8. Climb right side of rib.
3.   5.2. Climb southwest corner on good ledges to top.
4.   JOSEPH, 5.4. Climb 15 feet into easy upper chimney.
5.   THE BROTHERS, 5.7. Southeast side of west buttress. Climb the relatively unbroken face on small ledges.
6.   WALK-UP, 5.1. Easy walk-up on this separate low buttress. 5.7–5.8. Face left of route 7. More difficult if left corner is not used.

The upper wall between routes 6 and 7 has a few easy climbs.

7 5.5. Inside corner.
8 5.3. Wide crack.
9 5.5. Inside corner.
   UNTIED SHOES, 5.7. Crack/face right of route 9. Climb crack in lower face and center of upper face.
10 THE NICHE, 5.5. Climb inside corner to niche. Retable to the left or hand traverse farther left for an even easier ascent.

There is a traverse just off the ground between routes 10 and 12.

11 THE MANTLE SHELF, 5.8. Climb middle of wall to first ledge. The crux is climbing onto the smaller ledge 5 feet higher. This can be done directly or indirectly by traversing onto the ledge from either end.
12 5.3. Chimney.
13 5.5. Follow bucket holds 2 feet right of chimney. The route is a bit overhanging.
14 5.9. Overhang south of Beastly Bulge (route 15).
15 BEASTLY BULGE, 5.7. Overhanging nose on lower wall.
16 5.4. Wide crack.
17 5.5. Corner.
18 5.2. Climb buttress with easy ledges. Continue on wall above.

The following climbs are on some rather overgrown, dirty rocks below Stettner Rocks called the Lower Band.

19 5.4. Crack in the southwest-facing wall.
20 OLD PEW, 5.7. Start in diagonal crack. Climb to first ledge, balance up carefully beneath overhang, reach into notch above and grope for a hold, then surmount overhang.
21 5.4. Slabby chimney.
22 5.7. Detached block on upper wall. Follow midline of block as closely as possible.

Lincoln's Chair (Diagram 2 W)

Approach: Refer to Approach for Stettner Rocks. From the top of Stettner Rocks follow the Old West Bluff Trail for 600 feet to a small vantage point, then descend 100 feet to Lincoln's Chair. Lincoln's Chair can also be reached by hiking 200 feet due south from The Pantry. It is at the same level as The Pantry.

Waypoint 74: Lincoln's Chair
    UTM 16T 278254E 4810614N
Base Elevation: 1,150 feet
Top Elevation: 1,192 feet

ROUTES:

I   LINCOLN'S CHAIR SOUTH ARM, 5.4. The two arms are 30 feet high and 10 feet apart. Start on left corner. End somewhat left, around the corner.

LINCOLN'S CHAIR

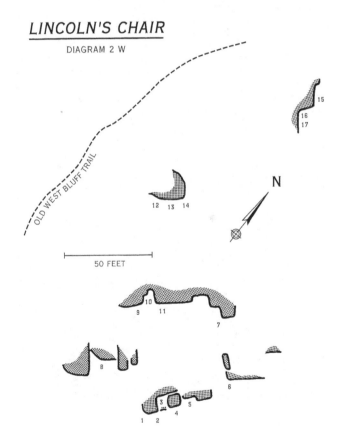

DIAGRAM 2 W

50 FEET

2 5.5. Southeast face of south arm. Start this slightly over-hanging face from the right side, where there is a hold that looks ready to break off.

3 5.2. Short inside corner crack above the seat of the chair.

4 LINCOLN'S CHAIR NORTH ARM, 5.4. Start on left corner of arm or, a bit harder, start on little ramp on right corner. Climb about halfway up, then move right to pass overhang.

5–7 5.2–5.4. Short climbs.

Lincoln's Chair

8 5.2. Recessed slab. Climb face of slab or slant chimney on left side.

9 5.4. Chockstone crack.

10 5.3. Climb south wall of alcove. The north chimney of the alcove is a scramble.

11 5.2. Of several variations, the best route on this 35-foot wall is 10 feet north of the alcove. Farther north the wall is broken into short steps.

12 5.7. Climb face 4 feet left of route 13.

13 5.4. Wide crack.

14 TWO TOAD CORNER, 5.8. Climb just left of corner to top.
Variation, 5.8. Start on right side of corner. At 6 feet, move left to corner.

Climbs 15–17 are on a minor wall 60 feet north.

15 5.7. Climb 20-foot jam crack in smooth face.

16 5.4. Inside corner.

17 5.7. Two cracks crossing a wide ledge.
Variation, 5.9. Climb lower left crack.

Misery Rocks (Diagram 3 W)

This wall forms the summit band in the region above the cottages. It is distinguished by a large reclining block, called The Pillow, that forms a cavelike enclosure.

Approach: There are several ways to approach Misery Rocks. From Stettner Rocks, follow the Old West Bluff Trail approximately 900 feet to the overlook above Misery Rocks. An alternate route is to follow the paved West Bluff Trail for 1,750 feet from its southern trailhead, then turn right (east) on a climbers' trail leading to Misery Rocks. A third approach is to follow Cottage Grove Road to the southernmost cottage, about 200 feet before the road ends. Ascend the talus slope straight up (west) to a gully that passes south of The Pantry or ascend west–northwest to a gully that passes north of The Pantry. Either gully leads to the bottom of Misery Rocks.

Waypoint 75: Climbers' Trail to Misery Rocks (from the West Bluff Trail)
UTM 16T 278109E 4810751N

Waypoint 76: On Cottage Grove Road below Misery Gully
    UTM 16T 278352E 4810650N
Waypoint 77: Misery Rocks
    UTM 16T 278256E 4810705N
Base Elevation: 1,250 feet
Top Elevation: 1,308 feet

Routes:

I 5.7. Start with a layback in the small inside corner, then
   climb easy rock above.

Misery Rocks

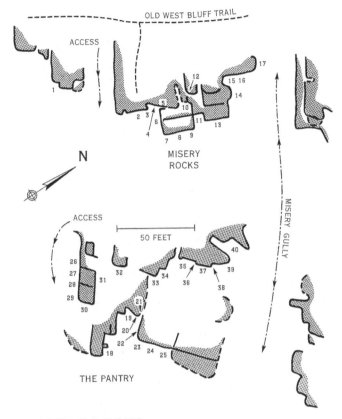

MISERY ROCKS

DIAGRAM 3 W

2 WEEPING WALL, 5.9. Start at a slight, ground-level niche. Climb up and somewhat left on small holds, then move back right, staying a few feet left of False Perspective (route 3) crack.

3 FALSE PERSPECTIVE, 5.8. Shallow V-chimney and crack. Climb chimney or on left corner. When chimney and corner join, follow crack to top without reaching or stepping left.

Variation, 5.6. When chimney and corner join, move left and continue on face.

4 WAILING WALL, 5.10c. Narrow wall between False Perspective (route 3) and Fat Man's Misery (route 5). Do not use crack of False Perspective or holds on Fat Man's Misery. The lower part of the wall is slightly overhanging.

5 FAT MAN'S MISERY, 5.4. Start 10 feet inside "the cave" behind The Pillow. Climb the west wall for 10–12 feet, then climb the chimney, facing east until forced out of the cave. Climb into the tight chimney above. The upper chimney becomes any man's misery if he becomes trapped by leaning in too far.

6 PILLOWS EDGE, 5.8. Start on pointed rock at south end of The Pillow. Climb narrow south end of lower and upper blocks. Do not use holds on either corner.
Variation, 5.9. Start on ground right of pointed rock. Avoid use of pointed rock.

7 THE PILLOW, 5.6. Southeast corner and overhang. Climb corner to overhang formed by upper block. Climb overhang by moving a bit right and taking a high step.

8 5.3. Follow good holds left of center on The Pillow. Escape right at overhang.

9 5.5. Climb at or near north edge of The Pillow.

10 SMOKE HOLE, 5.2. Climb deep chimney behind The Pillow. Exit through hole at top.

11 5.2. Wide recess with large blocks.

12 5.2. Narrow prominence above north end of The Pillow. Climb on south side or on southeast ledges.

13 5.4. Climb crack past three 10-foot steps. The crack widens at each step.

14 5.7. Climb 10 feet to ledge with large tree. Continue up right-hand corner. Go head first into the tight, awkward chimney or climb just right of chimney.

15 5.6. Long crack in left side of a dirty chute.

16 5.7. Overhanging wall. Start near north end. Climb left on ledges, then up to highest ledge.

17 5.8. Climb north end of overhanging, lichen-covered wall.

The Pantry (Diagram 3 W)

APPROACH: The Pantry is located directly below Misery Rocks. Refer to Approach for Misery Rocks and Diagram 3 W.

Waypoint 78: The Pantry
   UTM 16T 278285E 4810674N
Base Elevation: 1,164 feet
Top Elevation: 1,209 feet

Routes:

18 5.6. Corner/crack. Climb just left of corner to gain corner
   ledge, then angle right and up wide diagonal crack.
   Variation, 5.8. Start 5 feet right of corner and climb to
   wide diagonal crack.

The Pantry

19   PANTRY SHELF, 5.8. Step up to sloping shelf on lower part of wall. Continue straight up and over top overhang near right corner.

Variation, 5.7. Same start, but follow sloping shelf up and left to inside corner. Continue up inside corner. Pass overhang on left.

20   PANTRY RIGHT, 5.9. Start 2 feet right of the lower end of the sloping shelf in Pantry Shelf (route 19). Climb near right edge of wall to top.

21   5.1. Chimney with easy stemming.

22   5.3. North wall of The Pantry. Climb either of two cracks.

23   PANTRY CORNER, 5.4. A pleasant climb on well-spaced holds.

CALLOUS INDIFFERENCE, 5.10a. Face just right of Pantry Corner (route 23). Avoid use of holds on Pantry Corner and Bread Board (route 24).

24   BREAD BOARD, 5.10b. Climb center of wall. Start in niche and finish in flaky crack in highest part of wall. Avoid use of right corner.

25   5.4. Cracks.

26   5.2. Crack and inside corner.

27   K2, 5.9. Narrow face just left of Special K (route 28). Start with a very long reach or, more likely, a jump to reach the first hold. Continue on face above to base of small tower. Avoid using left upper corner.

28   SPECIAL K, 5.6. Climb shallow chimney, overhang, and crack, ending at ledge near base of small tower.

29   5.8. Corner. Start behind pine tree and climb corner to top.

30   5.4. Climb the southeast side of the tower in three short pitches.

31–34   5.3–5.4. Short climbs.

35   5.7. Inside corner with small overhang.

36   5.2. Cracks.

37   5.5. Crack that is narrowest at the bottom.

38   5.6. Overhang. Climb around north end of overhang to inside corner.

39   5.7. Start on face or in angling crack just left of northeast corner. Climb 15 feet to ledge, then up northeast corner on sloping holds.

40   5.4. Right wall of wide chimney.

Fifty feet below and southeast of The Pantry (not shown on the diagram) are several small buttresses with some interesting short climbs.

Dutchman Rampart *(Diagram 4 W)*

The rocks of Dutchman Rampart include the routes listed below as well as The Frigate, Dungeon Wall, Porkchop Buttress, and Double Chimney. Though detailed separately, these climbing areas are clustered close to one another along the north edge of Misery Gully.

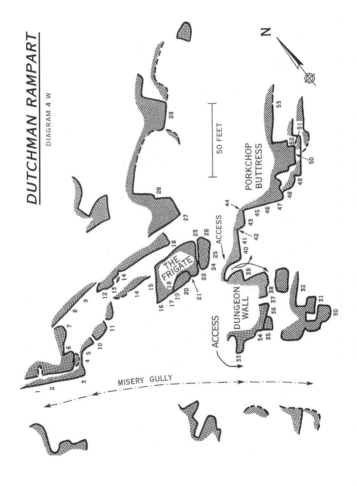

APPROACH: Refer to Approach for Misery Rocks. From Misery Rocks, walk 100 feet north across Misery Gully to Dutchman Rampart.

ROUTES:

1 5.6. Overhanging crack.

2 5.4. Deep, covered chimney. Getting out at the top is a messy procedure.

3 5.6. Ledges/crack. Start left of corner and climb to second large ledge. Finish using a finger crack in groove left of Oh Rats (route 4).

4 OH RATS, 5.8. Traverse north from the second large ledge on route 3 and climb a layback crack underneath the large upper overhang/roof. Escape by traversing to the right (north) corner. End with delicate climbing just around the corner.
   Variation, 5.11d. Climb the large upper overhang/roof directly.

5 5.3. Chimney with jutting overhangs. Imposing in appearance but easy to climb.

6 5.5. Narrow chimney that provides a continuation for route 5.

7–11 5.2–5.4. Short climbs up to and above the bench that crosses Dutchman Rampart.

12 5.6. Prominent upper section with overhang. Climb groove that leads behind a projecting block. Surmount overhang on substantial holds.

13 SUN SPOT, 5.7. Climb prominent section near the right corner. The hardest move is just below the top.

14 5.2–5.4. Short climb below and above the bench that crosses Dutchman Rampart.

The Frigate (Diagram 4 W)

APPROACH: Refer to Approach for Misery Rocks. From the base of Misery Rocks, walk 100 feet north across Misery Gully to the dramatic southwest corner of The Frigate. There is no easy access to the top of The Frigate. Descend by routes 18 or 21.

Waypoint 79: The Frigate
   UTM 16T 278281E 4810726N

Base Elevation: 1,220 feet
Top Elevation: 1,285 feet

ROUTES:

15 POOPER, 5.9. Overhanging west wall. Climb to small triangular niche, traverse right, then continue up very strenuous hanging crack that widens into a chimney.

The Frigate

Variation, 5.12c/d. Same start. At triangular niche, continue straight up near center of face.

CODE OF THE SEA, 5.12a. Start from block 10–12 feet up left of crack on Pooper. Climb overhanging face to top, staying left of Pooper.

16 THE STERN, 5.8. This climb ends on the high west end of The Frigate. Start on left corner, then at 10 feet move right and continue on right corner. Finish in crack on south face.

17 CAN-CAN, 5.5. Climb into the niche at 20 feet. Exit using a high left foothold. End in the chimney that splits the high west end of The Frigate.

18 5.3. *Descent route.* Climb short crack or step across to saddle north of The Frigate.

19 5.8. Climb lower overhanging block to platform. Continue in thin layback crack above west end of platform.

20–21 5.2. Easy cracks up to platform and above.

22–23 5.2. Chimney routes on north and south sides of The Frigate.

24 THE JIB, 5.10b. Climb the overhanging section near the left corner. Join Flying Dutchman (route 25) above the overhang.

25 FLYING DUTCHMAN, 5.10a. Climb up under right part of southeast overhang. Move left and up into a tight notch, then up a nice face to the summit block. Surmount the block by a dynamic move at the southeast corner.

26 THE BOWSPRIT, 5.8. Northeast corner of The Frigate. Start at the east corner. Climb 15 feet, angling to the northeast corner adjacent to the north chimney (route 23). Climb corner to base of summit block. Traverse left across the northeast side, balance onto a toehold, and retable to the top.

27 5.2. Buttress with mostly easy ledges on south side.

28 5.4. Inside corner with a crack variation.

29 5.4. Two routes on the 40-foot wall split by a crack.

Dungeon Wall (Diagram 4 W)

Approach: Dungeon Wall is located immediately below The Frigate. Refer to Approach for Misery Rocks and Diagram 4 W.

Waypoint 80: Dungeon Wall
 UTM 16T 278304E 4810724N

Base Elevation: 1,168 feet
Top Elevation: 1,219 feet

ROUTES:

30–32 Broken rocks at the base of Dungeon Wall. The dungeon has an entrance via a chimney (route 31) and an escape window to the south.

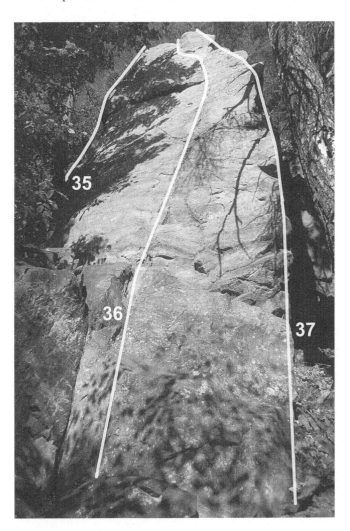

Dungeon Wall. Photo: Pete Mayer.

33 5.5. Protruding section. Stay on the outside.

34 BLARNEY STONE, 5.2. Broken chimney.

35 5.4. South corner. It makes for a pleasant line.

36 DUNGEON WALL CRACK, 5.7. Climb thin crack 5 feet left of corner. Near top, move left and finish in center crack. The face route avoids the right corner, Nutz Lice (route 37).

Variation, 5.7. Climb the lower face 5 feet left of the thin crack.

37 NUTZ LICE, 5.7. Corner. Start on sloping steps, then follow corner to top.

38 5.5. Face opposite small tower. Start on left side of face, then angle up and right to small inside corner. Climb to upper ledge, then up crack or right corner to top.

Variation, HISSING VULTURE, 5.8. Start 10 feet right under overhang. Follow crack up and left to small inside corner. Continue as above.

39–45 5.7–5.11b. Climbs in the recessed section between Dungeon Wall and Porkchop Buttress. Some of these shorter climbs are more interesting than you might expect (e.g., route 40, a 5.11b face, and route 42, a 5.7 inside corner).

Porkchop Buttress (Diagram 4 W)

Approach: Porkchop Buttress is located 75 feet northeast of Dungeon Wall. The easiest approach is from the Tumbled Rocks Trail. Ascend the bluff 100 feet north of the end of Cottage Grove Road. The first sizable outcropping encountered is Double Chimney. Pass Double Chimney on the north. Porkchop Buttress is above, halfway up the bluff.

Waypoint 81: Porkchop Buttress
   UTM 16T 278328E 4810719N
Base Elevation: 1,141 feet
Top Elevation: 1,211 feet

Routes:

46 5.8. South wall. Most of this wall is guarded by an overhang. Start high up the slope by the base of route 45. Climb right to reach a high ledge, then continue up to the top.

47 THE 100-INCH REACH, 5.11d. Start below and left of large overhang. Climb wall by placing feet on left slab and hands on wall. Move up and right, then pull through overhang.

48 PORK LOIN, 5.7. Southeast crack and face. Climb crack leading to south end of large ledge, then on upper face. Finish by short, wide, diagonal crack near left corner.

49 JACOB'S LADDER, 5.6. Long, inside corner. The steep upper section has a small overhang.

PHAT, 5.7. Start on narrow face just right of inside corner. Avoid using the left or right corner. At ledge 30 feet up join Jacob's Ladder or The Bone (route 50).

Porkchop Buttress

50 THE BONE, 5.5. Start on ledge on right side of smooth, tapered, 20-foot face. Climb the steeply angling inside corner to a moderate overhang. Follow the corner crack to a ledge below the bulging upper section. Move 5 feet right and surmount the bulge to reach the top.

Variation, 5.7. From ledge below bulging upper section stay on corner to top.

51 SWEAT BOX, 5.8. Climb short, thin crack to platform. Continue on corner to loose-looking, overhanging block. Climb directly over block.

Variation, 5.7. A few feet below the block, move left. Finish on upper face.

52 NO EXIT, 5.7. Start in inside corner leading to a sloping platform. Continue up to top overhang, which is passed on the left.

53 5.7. Shallow chimney and crack.

There is a small outcropping (not on diagram) below the southeast side of Porkchop Buttress with a crack climb.

54 WOBBLY BLOCK, 5.5. Crack climb notable because of the wobbly block.

Double Chimney (No Diagram)

Approach: Refer to Approach for Porkchop Buttress.

Routes:

1 THE SHAFT, 5.3. Stem up chimney behind east tower.

2 THE FLUE, 5.2. Narrower chimney of west tower.

3 SMOKE SHELF, 5.8. East side of east tower. Climb a couple of ledges. Stretch far right to northeast corner and continue up.

4 HIGH DRAFT, 5.8. Climb southeast corner for 15 feet. Traverse right to northeast corner and up to top.

Variation, 5.9. Start directly below northeast corner.

5 SMOKESTACK, 5.9. South face of west tower. Start at low point and climb center crack.

Split Tower (see Diagram 7 W, page 255)

Split Tower is an isolated outcropping located between Dutchman Rampart and Turk's Head Ridge.

APPROACH: Refer to Approach for Porkchop Buttress. Walk 150 feet north from the base of Porkchop Buttress or descend about 200 feet from Cleopatra's Needle to reach Split Tower.

Waypoint 82: Split Tower
  UTM 16T 278355E 4810768N
Base Elevation: 1,137 feet
Top Elevation: 1,187 feet

ROUTES:

1 WANING, 5.8. Overhanging south corner.
2 HALF MOON, 5.7. Start on rounded, sloping ledges. Climb jam crack in overhang. Finish on southeast corner.

Split Tower

3 DARK SIDE OF THE MOON, 5.1. Wide chimney that gives Split Tower its name.

4 NEW MOON, 5.8. Rounded corner on right side of wide chimney. Climb to top, staying close to corner.

5 MOON FACE, 5.7. Attractive face and crack route. The first 15 feet are the most difficult.

6–8 5.6–5.7. Short climbs below Split Tower.

Cleo Amphitheater (Diagram 5 W)

APPROACH: From the southern trailhead of the West Bluff Trail, walk until you emerge from the woods at a vantage point that overlooks the lake and Cleo Amphitheater. Cleopatra's Needle is below this vantage point. The most convenient points of descent are above Cleopatra's Needle; these routes may be wet and dirty at times. An alternate access route is in the southwest corner of the amphitheater. Refer to Diagram 5 W.

Waypoint 83: Cleo Amphitheater
  UTM 16T 278303E 4810809N
Base Elevation: 1,294 feet
Top Elevation: 1,370 feet

ROUTES:

1 5.7. Wall below a small tower. Climb ledges for 20 feet, then climb angling crack (crux) to wide ledge at base of tower. Continue on route 4.

2 5.1. Chimney.

3 5.1. Set of ledges at south end of small tower.

4 5.6. From the wide ledge at the base of the tower, step up onto the left end of a sloping shelf. Climb the face above. *Variation*, 5.6. Move right on shelf and climb overhanging jam crack.

5 5.8. Overhanging corner at north end of tower. Start in the little chimney to the right, then hand pendulum onto the corner and up.

6 5.5. Crack.

7 5.8. Short face climb leading to inside corner.

8 5.6. Two overhangs on the southeast side. Each has a choice of climbing left or right of the overhang.

9 5.8. Northeast corner.

10 5.8. Crack 6 feet right of northeast corner. Near top move 3 feet right.

11 5.8. Crack just left of large niche.

12 5.8. Stem up inside niche. Work out onto face directly above, then climb to top.

13 5.4. Short wall with 15-foot block at the top. Climb block on either side.

14 5.4. Start on dirty rock. Finish in one of two short chimneys that are 5 feet apart.

15 5.5. The beginning of this climb is not well defined. Follow a line that crosses two small overhangs higher up.

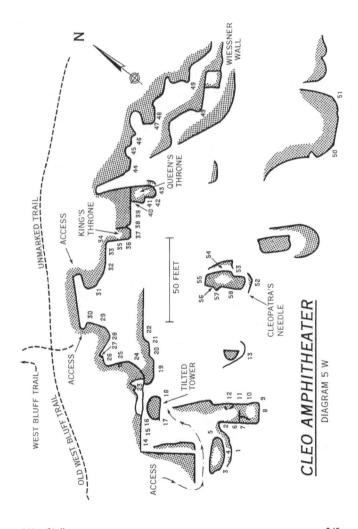

CLEO AMPHITHEATER

DIAGRAM 5 W

16 PINKO, 5.7. Start in crack leading to smooth face. Balance up face on small holds.

17 5.3. South corner of Tilted Tower.

18 TILTED TOWER, 5.9+. Climb left edge of severely overhanging north side of tower.

19 5.7. Climb crack 10 feet to ledge, then move left and continue in crack.

Cleo Amphitheater

Variation, 5.8. From the ledge ascend the rounded right corner.

20   5.4. Inside corner and crack. Finish on left side of pointed overhang.

21   5.4. Crack.

22   5.4. Inside corner.

23   5.8. Start at the north end of the ledge opposite the top of Tilted Tower. Step right to corner for instant exposure. Climb corner to top.
Variation, 5.8–5.10a. Climb upper south face without using corner. Several variations are possible.

24   BARNDOOR, 5.8. Follow crack to top of buttress, highest point along rim of amphitheater.

25   5.5. Narrow chimney.

26   COLOSTOMY, 5.7. Repulsive inside corner.

27   5.3. Wide-angle inside corner. Climb left chimney or right crack.

28   THE PLANK, 5.8. Will you sink or swim when you walk the Plank? Start from route 27 crack. Traverse right just above large ceiling. Move around corner to reach ascent (or sudden descent) crack.
HANG ON, 5.11b. Start 6–8 feet left of Hang Dog (route 29) and climb to overhang. Use a small undercling and reach up high and right to a handhold on the corner. Follow corner to top.

29   HANG DOG, 5.9. Climb to small niche below upper crack at north end of large ceiling. Climb into niche, then move left to corner and up to top.
Variation, 5.8–5.10a. From niche, climb straight to top or slightly right into notch.

30   BETTER WHEN DRY, 5.7. Right side of lichen-covered northeast face. Climb straight up, passing diagonal crack at upper right end.

31   CURVED WALL, 5.8. Start below slightly overhanging corner and climb crack 12 feet to ledge. Continue on wall straight to top.
CURVED WALL LEFT SIDE, 5.7. Start in crack 6 feet left of Curved Wall. Continue up near west end of wall.

32   MICKEY MOUSE, 5.4. Jam crack.

33   MINNIE MOUSE, 5.4. Cracks 6 feet left of Minnie Mum (route 34).

34 MINNIE MUM, 5.2. Crack and inside corner.

35 MISSING LINK, 5.8. Climb is about 5 feet right of Minnie Mum (route 34). The main problem is between the two ledges, which are 12 feet apart.

36 5.5. Set of down-sloping ledges.

37 KING'S THRONE, 5.6. The higher of two promontories that jut into the north half of Cleo Amphitheater. Climb rounded corner on a series of evenly spaced horizontal cracks and ledges.

38 THRONE ROOM, 5.5. Wide crack. At top, climb 15 feet on north side of the highest rock of King's Throne.

39 5.4. Crack.

40 5.3. Inside corner.

41 QUEEN'S THRONE, 5.4. Buttress crowned by 6-foot rock spike. Climb the clean-cut inside corner/crack on comfortable ledges. An old favorite with nice exposure.

42 BETWEEN THE QUEENS, 5.9. Climb on or just left of corner. The middle section is a bit overhanging.

43 QUEEN'S FACE, 5.8. Center of narrow east face of the Queen's Throne Buttress. Do not use the corners.

44 JACK OF SPADES, 5.6. Crack/corner. Climb angling crack partway, then continue on right side of upper corner.

45 UGLY, 5.4–5.5. Wide recess. Finish in left or right inside corner.

46 5.7. Inside corner and face.
Variation, 5.7. Climb lower corner 4 feet left of inside corner.

47 5.7. Climb left corner to top.

48 5.10a. Start at small niche. Climb right corner.

49 5.6. Corner done in two pitches. Climb lower section by left crack or on right side of corner.

50 5.7. Buttress below north end of Cleo Amphitheater. Start climb at south corner or at overhang/crack right of south corner.

51 5.7. Northeast side of buttress. Start on rounded corner and climb straight to top.

Cleopatra's Needle (Diagram 5 W)

APPROACH: Refer to Approach for Cleo Amphitheater. Cleopatra's Needle is the 50-foot-high rock spire in the center of Cleo Amphitheater.

52　53　54

Cleopatra's Needle

Base Elevation: 1,301 feet

ROUTES:

52 SOUTHEAST SIDE, 5.4. The most popular route on Cleopatra's Needle. For aesthetic reasons the climb is usually begun from saddle on northeast side rather than from the lowest point. From saddle, cross to southeast side and climb (in one or two pitches) to base of slender summit pinnacle. Finish with nice face holds on southeast side or traverse to north side just below top.

53 5.4. Inside corner. Same finish as Southeast Side (route 52).

54 NORTH LEDGES, 5.4. Climb ledges. Same finish as Southeast Side (route 52).

55 NORTHWEST SIDE, 5.4. Ascend right side of outward-sloping ledges. Traverse left and up to base of summit pinnacle. Same finish as Southeast Side (route 52). This is the usual *descent route.*

56 5.6. Climb inside corner/crack on left side of Southwest Rib (route 57).

57 SOUTHWEST RIB, 5.7. Climb bottom overhang to reach outside of rib. Follow rib to ledge at base of summit pinnacle. Move left and finish on northwest face of block.

58 5.4. Two cracks right of Southwest Rib (route 57). *Variation,* 5.5. Climb using only right crack.

Turk's Head (Diagram 6 W)

APPROACH: Wiessner Wall links Cleo Amphitheater with Turk's Head. Refer to Approach for Cleo Amphitheater. Near the overlook, follow a faint, unmarked path that gradually descends north for 200 feet. Turn right and follow a gully system down on the north side of Turk's Head.

Waypoint 84: Turk's Head
  UTM 16T 278349E 4810830N
Base Elevation: 1,258 feet

ROUTES:

1 THE WASP, 5.7. Roof at south end of Wiessner Wall. Ascend ledges on inner left wall beneath roof. Traverse right under roof. Step around corner onto east wall. Climb jam crack to Wiessner Ledge.

2 FRITZ, 5.7. Start in moderate crack 15 feet north of roof in The Wasp (route 1). At 15 feet, move 5 feet left and climb thin face crack to Wiessner Ledge.

3 STINGER, 5.8. Climb crack leading to niche, then climb outside and just left of niche to exit crack. Finish at Wiessner Ledge.

4 WIESSNER CHIMNEY, 5.4. Awkward, narrow chimney that will seem harder if you don't find the right combination. Climb chimney to base of slab. Traverse left to north end of Wiessner Ledge.

5 JUST ANOTHER PRETTY FACE, 5.11a. Climb center of face on small holds to base of slab.

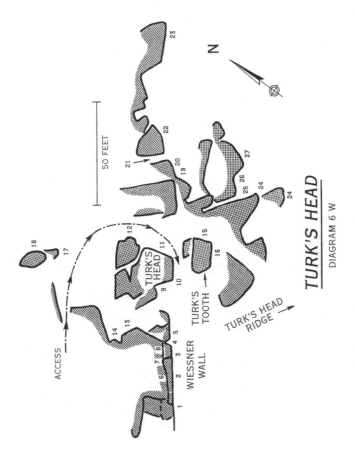

Variation, 5.9. Same start, but move left and climb near edge of face close to Wiessner Chimney (route 4).

6 5.4. From Wiessner Ledge, climb into shallow niche with sloping floor. Continue up chockstone crack.

7 5.2. Wide crack above north end of Wiessner Ledge. There may be loose rock in the crack, but the chief concern is likely to be wasps.

8 WIESSNER FACE, 5.7. Pretty face climb on north part of wall. From north end of Wiessner Ledge, climb onto bulge at top of Wiessner Chimney (route 4). Then climb a set of horizontal cracks and ledges to top.

Variation, 5.7. Start from base of slab near top of Wiessner Chimney (route 4). Climb on or near corner for 15 feet. Continue on Wiessner Face.

9 5.2. Inside corner.

I0 TURK'S HEAD, 5.5. Climb southeast corner to overhang. Finish on south side. Descend on south side, or jump down from short V-chimney on west side.

II BELLY FLOP, 5.6. Northeast ledges and overhang. Climb northeast side of Turk's Head to ledge beneath wide overhang. Reach up in central notch and mantle onto ledge above overhang. Walk around to south side for easiest way to top.

Wiessner Wall and Turk's Head

Variation, 5.6. Surmount overhang by crawling onto shelf at north end. No one has ever looked good doing this.

12 5.7. Rib with overhang. Tackle overhang from either side.

13 5.11b. Center of face.

14 5.2. Adjacent chimneys behind Turk's Head.

15 TURK'S TOOTH, 5.2. Tower just below Turk's Head. Northeast side is a pleasant ledge climb. Descend on west side (the side facing Turk's Head).

16 A POINT OF BALANCE, 5.8. Overhang/chimney. Balance onto the point of a large flake that will allow you to reach the overhang if you're tall enough. Move left and up into hanging chimney that breaches the overhang.

17 5.4. Climb east corner of small tower in two sections. Descend by south crack.

18 5.5. North face of small tower.

19 5.6. Crack/overhang. Climb left-slanting crack for 15 feet, then continue up overhang right of crack.
Variation, 5.7. Same start. At 15 feet, continue up crack. Surprisingly, this turns out to be harder than climbing the overhang.

20 5.7. Same start as route 19. Climb right beneath corner overhang. Reach high and feel for a hold on next ledge. Surmount overhang, continue on wall and ledges above.

21 5.2. Chimney.

22 5.5. Tower. Start on northeast side or near south corner and angle right across southeast face. Mantle left onto a ledge 25 feet up. Traverse right and finish on northeast side.

23 5.7. Climb east corner for 15 feet. Traverse 5 feet left on ledge, then continue up south side. The summit band essentially ends with this buttress.

24 5.7. Corner. Climb uppermost section, obstructed by a pine tree, on north side.

25 GREEN SLIME, 5.10b. A sheer, lichen-encrusted wall with a hanging crack. Climb 10 feet straight up to beginning of crack. At crux, stem right and get a grip using a thumb jam in narrowest part of crack.

26 5.5. Climb face and upper corner, staying a few feet right of chimney.

27 5.8. Face leading to V-chimney. It takes close examination to find holds.

The Blade (Diagram 7 W)

The Blade gets its name from the distinct wedge-shaped corner at the northeast end of the rock outcropping.

Approach: *From below*—Refer to Approach for Prospect Point Towers. From the base of Great Tower, traverse south to The Blade. *From above*—Refer to Approach for Cleo Amphitheater. Follow a faint, unmarked path that gradually descends to the north. This path passes above The Blade approximately 300 feet north of Turk's Head.

Waypoint 85: The Blade
　UTM 16T 278362E 4810935N
Base Elevation: 1,221 feet
Top Elevation: 1,274 feet

The Blade

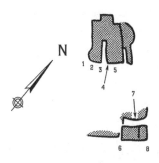

SPLIT TOWER

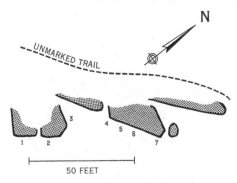

THE BLADE

DIAGRAM 7 W

ROUTES:

1   5.3. Small overhang left of central chimney.

2   5.2. Chimney and adjacent rock.

3   5.7. Crack climbed by layback and jamming.

4   5.4. South corner of main wall.

5   5.6. Climb crack with small pine tree. Continue straight up over top overhang.

6   DEAR ABBEY, 5.8. Climb on small ledges to niche in center of wall. Step up into thin crack. Climb crack to top.

7   THE BLADE, 5.6. Acute-angled northeast corner. Step onto corner from block on north side. Continue on or near corner to top.
Variation, 5.7. Finish in thin crack 5 feet left of corner.

Turk's Head Ridge (No Diagram)

APPROACH: Follow the Tumbled Rocks Trail from its southern trailhead (at the end of Cottage Grove Road) for 350 feet. The lowest outcropping of Turk's Head Ridge is a small tower 200 feet above the trail. The ridge leads to Turk's Tooth (refer to Diagram 6 W).

Fourth Pitch of Turk's Head Ridge

Waypoint 86: Turk's Head Ridge at the First Pitch
UTM 16T 278392E 4810799N
Base Elevation (base of First Pitch): 1,054 feet
Top Elevation (top of Sixth Pitch): 1,258 feet

ROUTES:

First Pitch: A small tower.

1 5.2. Climb wide crack to northeast side of tower. Descend south crack (easiest), southwest corner, or northwest corner.

2 5.9. Northeast side, just left of wide crack.

3 5.5. Southeast corner. Mount block beneath corner overhang. Pass overhang in center of face.

Twenty feet south of the small tower is a short wall with a couple of climbs leading to the Second Pitch platform.

4 5.6. A 20-foot, overhanging, and dirty inside corner.

5 5.8. Narrow face 10 feet left of inside corner. Climb right side on widely spaced ledges.

Second Pitch: A 30-foot wall.

6 5.6. Start from detached platform and climb small ledges on north half of wall.

7 PINCH FINGER, 5.8. Left-angling crack in smooth south part of wall.

Third Pitch: A 15-foot wall.

8 5.2. Climb obvious central crack or chimney on left.

Fourth Pitch: A 40-foot-high, narrow, ridgelike outcrop.

9 5.2. Wide crack starting behind tree on southeast side. Climb crack for 25 feet and finish on southeast ledges.
Variation, 5.4. Same start. About 10 feet up, traverse right to east corner. Climb corner.

10 5.4. Narrow corner on south side separated from main ridge by sloping V-chimney.

11 5.9. Crack in steep north wall. Climb crack through niche. There is a delicate layback move just above the niche. When crack ends, move left to east corner.

Fifth Pitch: A 20-foot step.

12 5.5. Southeast corner.
13 5.4. Climb diagonal crack to northeast corner.
14 5.2. Walk around to south side for other routes.

Sixth Pitch: Scramble up crest of ridge to a platform at base of Turk's Tooth.

15 5.4–5.5. On the south flank of the ridge, below the platform, there is a niche with two cracks radiating upward. The left crack is harder.

Prospect Point Towers (Diagram 8 W)

Prospect Point Towers consists of First Tower, Sun-Top Tower, Great Tower, and Picnic Wall. These towers form a ridge in the middle third of the bluff below Prospect Point.

First Tower (Diagram 8 W)

APPROACH: Walk the Tumbled Rocks Trail to the 150-Foot Boulderfield. This is the first open boulderfield the trail crosses when approaching from the south. This boulderfield (and the 500-Foot Boulderfield to the north) is named for its width. Ascend the south edge of the boulderfield, turning slightly south to reach the base of Prospect Point Towers, or walk the first 250 feet following a faint path in the woods that parallels the south edge of the boulderfield.

Base Elevation: 1,160 feet

ROUTES:
1 5.6. A 25-foot wall below First Tower.
2 5.4. Northeast corner of 15-foot First Tower. The southwest side is the best *descent route*.

Sun-Top Tower (Diagram 8 W)

APPROACH: Refer to Approach for First Tower and Diagram 8 W.

Base Elevation: 1,179 feet

Routes:

3 CAN'T CAN'T, 5.11a. Start near south corner. Climb easily to a ledge at 15 feet, then traverse left to a pointed nose where a chorus-line kick can be employed to achieve a stemming position in the wide inside corner. Work up inside corner. Go left onto nose, or continue straight up.

Sun-Top Tower

4 THE SUCKER, 5.7. Climb short wall with crack leading to ledge at base of V-chimney. Climb chimney to top.

Variation, 5.5. Climb to ledge on south corner. Move right to chimney and continue as in The Sucker.

5 MOON BEAM, 5.11b/c. Climb difficult face between The Sucker (route 4) and Sun-Top (route 6). A long reach makes the climb easier.

6 SUN-TOP, 5.8. Crack/overhang in center of face. Named to commemorate the day a lecherous pine tree snagged the brief garment worn by a female climber. Climb to ledge below overhang. Climb up to reach a good horizontal crack left of overhang. Bring your feet up high while leaning left and reach for a handhold in the exit crack. Then climb to top.

7 MAY FLY, 5.7. Overhang/crack. Start 10 feet right of Sun-Top (route 6) directly below upper small inside corner of route 8. Climb into niche. Continue up and right past overhang to ledge at 20 feet. Then traverse left 6 feet to a crack and follow it to top.

Variation, MAY FLY DIRECT, 5.11d. Same start. From niche, move left to overhanging flake, then up and right to ledge. Finish in upper May Fly crack.

8 5.7. Northeast ridge. Climb sloping ledges to upper small inside corner near top on east side of ridge. Do one hard move to reach platform above.

Great Tower (Diagram 8 W)

APPROACH: Refer to Approach for First Tower and Diagram 8 W.

Waypoint 87: Prospect Point Towers (at Great Tower)
   UTM 16T 278412E 4810981N
Base Elevation: 1,141 feet
Top Elevation: 1,225 feet

ROUTES:
Descent route. From the top of Great Tower, drop down a short wall west of the eastern high point. Contour west until reaching the gully on the south side of the ridge near Picnic Wall.

9 ROCK GARDEN, 5.7. Climb southwest corner with small overhanging section near top.

9   10

Great Tower

10 GARDEN PATH, 5.7. Climb lower overhang and face on sharp holds typical of southern exposures.
Variation, MOON ROCK, 5.8. Same start. Climb up and right to corner. Follow corner to top.

11 THE GREAT CRACK, 5.6. This is the classic climb on Great Tower. It follows the inside corner/crack on the east face just left of the large overhang. The route goes over several ledges that divide it into short sections.

12 STEAK SAUCE, 5.12c. Large overhang with crack. The name relates to the original A1 rating.

13 SMOOTH BUSH, 5.7. Climb corner at north end of overhang. Continue in crack above.

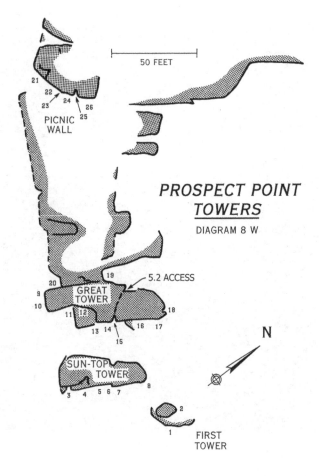

50 FEET

PICNIC WALL

PROSPECT POINT TOWERS

DIAGRAM 8 W

5.2 ACCESS

GREAT TOWER

N

SUN-TOP TOWER

FIRST TOWER

Variation, MOON WALK, 5.10a. Same start. Climb corner to overhang, then hand traverse left to the point of the overhang on holds just above overhang. Pull up and continue to top.

14 5.8. Thin crack in face just south of chimney (route 15).

15 5.4. Chimney.

Climb route 15 or the western 5.2 crack to access the top of the lower large platform at the north end. Refer to Diagram 8 W.

16 CRACKER BARREL, 5.7. Climb flake-edge crack, then straight up short face to large platform. Ledges and short walls lead to top of Great Tower.

17 SLY CORNER, 5.8. Northeast corner. Climb, staying left of corner, to ledge underneath overhang. Move left onto face and up to large platform.

18 5.7. Climb wide crack to ledge under overhang. Step on block beneath overhang and work somewhat right to reach vertical holds that lead to the large platform.

19 5.4. North chimney. Dirty, long, exposed climb.

20 5.2. South chimney. Alpine-like route for ascent or descent.

Picnic Wall (Diagram 8 W)

APPROACH: Refer to Approach for First Tower and Diagram 8 W.

Base Elevation: 1,300 feet
Top Elevation: 1,327 feet

ROUTES:

21 BASKET, 5.6. Climb into niche, then traverse out around right corner. Continue to top.

22 NO PICNIC, 5.9. Here is a climb to stretch you out. Secure a beautiful handhold that is just out of reach from the ground. Reach far up to the right for the second (not the first) little triangular pocket. Continue climbing on widely spaced holds to the overhang, which should now seem easy.

23 TRACK CRACKS, 5.8. Climb the parallel cracks using twin jam holds at the crux 12 feet up. To make two harder climbs out of one, climb each crack separately.

Picnic Wall

24 5.9. Climb face close to right corner.
25 5.5. Chimney. Finish on left corner.
26 5.11b. Boulder problem.

Prospect Point Rampart

Prospect Point Rampart is the summit band in the central portion of the West Bluff. It is bounded on the south by a broad summit boulderfield that creates a break in the contour of the upper bluff directly above Prospect Point Towers. The band continues north for 400 feet, ending 100 feet northeast of the geodetic survey marker. This area features panoramic views of the entire lake.

The main band is described in three sections: Prospect Point Pinnacle to Big Toe, Big Toe to Great Chimney, and Great Chimney to Lost Face. The lower section of the main band is broken by many benches and ledges. Dark Wall is located below the main band near Prospect Point Pinnacle.

Prospect Point Pinnacle to Big Toe (Diagram 9 W)

APPROACH: Follow the West Bluff Trail about 1,000 feet north of Cleo Amphitheater (about 0.5 mile from the southern end of the West Bluff Trail) to a vantage point with a view of the lake. Just south of this spot, one can literally step off the West Bluff Trail down a few steps to a climbers' trail that provides access to the bottom of the climbs and continues north to Lost Face. It takes some route finding, since some paths and ledges are dead ends.

Waypoint 88: Above Prospect Point Pinnacle (on the West Bluff Trail)
    UTM 16T 278285E 4811058N
Waypoint 89: Prospect Point Pinnacle
    UTM 16T 278316E 4811038N
Base Elevation (Prospect Point Pinnacle): 1,384 feet
Top Elevation (Prospect Point Pinnacle): 1,447 feet
Waypoint 90: Big Toe
    UTM 16T 278334E 4811093N
Base Elevation (Big Toe): 1,366 feet
Top Elevation (Big Toe): 1,483 feet

ROUTES:
At the south end there are a number of short routes that offer convenient climbing near the trail.

1   5.8. Corner. Start from the lowest point. Climb corner without using blocks on left.
    5.11d. Narrow face right of corner. Avoid using holds near or on corner.
2   5.6. Awkward crack.

3 5.7. Climb tight crack 4 feet right of corner.
Variation, 5.6. Start in crack a few feet farther right.

4 SON OF A BUSH, 5.4. Inside corner.

5 5.7. Slightly overhanging corner.

6 5.8. Shallow inside corner. Finish in crack.

7 5.9. Climb lower bulging wall to crack. Follow crack to top.

8 HARD SELL, 5.7. Inside corner.

Prospect Point Pinnacle on the Prospect Point Rampart

9   5.10a. Overhang with two cracks above.
10 PROSPECT POINT PINNACLE I, 5.2. This small tower is just off the top of the bluff. Start from saddle between pinnacle and bluff and climb northwest side.
11 PINNACLE ARÊTE, 5.10b. Very sharp south corner.
12 PROSPECT POINT PINNACLE II, 5.8. Start in crack on short wall below pinnacle's southeast side. Climb wall to platform that supports the tower. Continue up southeast side to sloping ledge, then mantle on south side to reach top.

Big Toe, Prospect Point Rampart

Variation, 5.9. Same start. From first ledge (8 feet up), climb thin crack starting at west end of ledge.

13 5.8. Corner of small tower.

14 5.6. Inside corner with crack.

15 CREAMY CAESAR, 5.6. Start at two cracks 3 feet apart. Climb either or both to platform 25 feet up. Ascend ledges and finish on upper wall.

16–17 SECOND-DAY AIR, 5.4. Broken wall with ledges. Mixed climbing and scrambling.

18 5.6. Crack leading to V-niche.

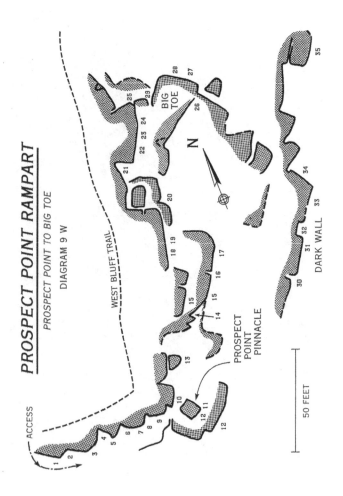

PROSPECT POINT RAMPART

PROSPECT POINT TO BIG TOE

DIAGRAM 9 W

19 5.8. Climb upper wall through two small niches. End with short crack that angles right.

20 5.8. Short, slabby inside corner leading to chimney complex.
TRIPLE BLOCK, 5.10a. Start a few feet right of route 20. Climb three large blocks to top. The crux is on the second block.

21 5.4. V-chimney.

22 5.7. Start up thin crack. Finish a bit left in chimney with overhanging capstones.

23 WIDULE 7, 5.9. Start with a bucket hold on the first ledge 4 feet north of route 22. Mount the ledge and continue straight to the top.

24 5.9. Overhanging section of lower wall. Start in short crack. At 6 feet, step right onto ledge. Continue in the flaring crack using a jam hold.

25 THE HEEL, 5.11a. Climb northeast corner with an interesting heel hook.

26 BIG TOE, 5.2. Start behind cobra head–shaped tower. Climb near east corner of Big Toe to large sloping platform.

27 5.9. Crack on northeast side of Big Toe.

28 5.7. Flake route 5 feet right of route 27.
Variation, 5.8. Climb first 8 feet directly.

29 5.2. Short chimney leading to top of Big Toe.

Dark Wall (Diagram 9 W)

APPROACH: Refer to Approach for Prospect Point Pinnacle to Big Toe and Diagram 9 W. Dark Wall is directly below the southern end of Prospect Point Rampart.

Waypoint 91: Dark Wall
   UTM 16T 278351E 4811045N
Base Elevation: 1,331 feet

ROUTES:

30 5.2. Chimney.
MISSING CRACK, 5.7. Tight crack 8 feet right of route 30.

31 5.7. Wall with ledge halfway up. Climb to south end of ledge, then up left to top.

32 5.3. Wide recess. Climb right or left inside corner.

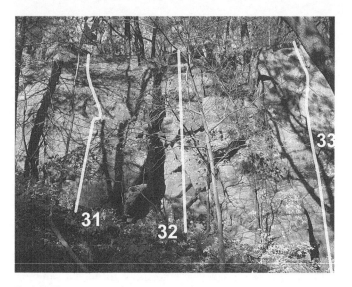

Dark Wall

33 SOUL FOOD, 5.9. Slightly overhanging face. Climb to ledge at 10 feet, then up thin crack to top.
SAM, 5.10a. Northeast corner of slightly overhanging face.
34 5.6. Two cracks on northeast-facing wall.
35 5.7. Face of tower at north end of Dark Wall.

Big Toe to Great Chimney (Diagram 10 W)

APPROACH: Refer to Approach for Prospect Point Pinnacle to Big Toe. The central portion of Prospect Point Rampart is best reached from the West Bluff Trail. Great Chimney is located 50 feet south of a geodetic survey marker. There is a park service road, a stretcher, and an emergency call box located near the survey marker. Access to the base of the climbs is by the climbers' trail that starts at the south end of the rampart. It is also possible to descend the Great Chimney (route 54), which involves a few 5.3 moves. Another access gully is located 75 feet north of the geodetic survey marker. Refer to Diagram 11 W.

Waypoint 92: Emergency Call Box
UTM 16T 278315E 4811144N
Waypoint 93: Great Chimney
UTM 16T 278329E 4811112N

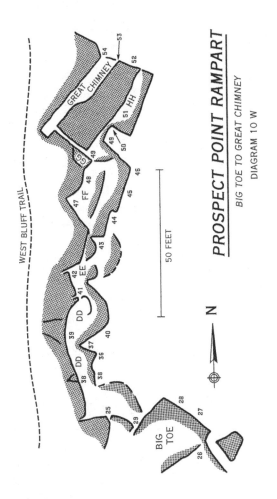

PROSPECT POINT RAMPART

BIG TOE TO GREAT CHIMNEY

DIAGRAM 10 W

Base Elevation: 1,384 feet
Top Elevation: 1,490 feet

ROUTES:

Some of these routes are on the lower half of the cliff. Others are on the upper half. Use various combinations to form complete ascents. Ledges separating lower and upper routes are labeled DD to HH on Diagram 10 W.

36 5.10b. Start below pointed nose located 20 feet up. Climb to top of nose, then up crack to ledge DD.

Variation, 5.9. Climb 10 feet on rib below slab. Step left and up delicate, lichen-covered rock to ledge level with top of pointed nose.

37 5.6. Chimney on north side of pointed nose.

38 GRAND ILLUSION, 5.9. Crack/overhang. Climb left-slanting crack beginning 15 feet up as a tight finger crack toward notch in upper wall. Don't go into notch. Traverse left beneath overhang and climb crack in overhang to top. *Variation,* 5.9. Start at lowest point of wall and climb small rib/corner. At 15 feet move left a few feet, then diagonally up and right to the crack. Continue as above.

39 5.2. Climb a couple of steps leading to a recessed section in the upper wall. This is more or less an escape route from ledge DD to the top.

40 5.4. Start in chimney (route 37). Cross north to first large ledge, then into a small inside corner. Scramble up to ledge EE.

41 5.8. Crack and notch just north of corner on upper wall. Reach the crack from ledge EE or by traversing north on ledge DD.

42 5.5. Inside corner with chimney above north end of ledge EE.

43 5.4. Climb in V-chimney, then continue to the right and up slabby rock to ledge FF.

44 5.7. Inside corner and cracks on 30-foot lower wall.

45 ICARUS, 5.11d. Climb face with wide stems and long reaches to ledge FF.

46 5.4. Start on corner and climb right to a 20-foot crack. Pass 6-foot arrowhead flake and step onto ledge above. Go left around corner and scramble to ledge FF.

47 5.4. Inside corner above south end of ledge FF. *Variation,* 5.8. Climb overhanging crack just left of inside corner.

48 5.7. From north end of ledge FF, climb short wall to small platform (ledge GG) 15 feet below top. Finish on south wall.

49 DOUBLE JEOPARDY, 5.6. This chimney provides a continuous ascent of the entire wall. Start in south inside corner of rectangular recessed section. Climb chimney past a couple of overhanging chockstones to ledge GG, then to top.

Son of Great Chimney (Diagram 10 W, route 52). Climber: Alex Andrews. Photo: Sven Olof Swartling.

50 STUCK KNEE, 5.7. Start in north inside corner of recessed section. Climb 15 feet to first ledge, then up a crack to base of a narrow chimney. Climb chimney (crux) to ledge. Finish in 12-foot inside corner or on easy ledges to left.

51 BIVOUAC LEDGE, 5.12b, a.k.a. DANCE OF THE GHOST PSAMEAD. Climb onto the point of a boulder resting on ledge HH. Climb wall above following a crack past overhang to bivouac ledge, then up wider crack at north end of ledge.

52 SON OF GREAT CHIMNEY, 5.11a. A hideous promontory, suggestive of The End on the East Bluff. From ledge HH, cross over to northeast corner of promontory. Go around corner, then up north wall to cramped ledge. Continue up overhanging crack (crux) a few feet to handholds at same level as bivouac ledge (to which escape is possible). Traverse right and grasp a welcome rock prong on northwest corner. Climb corner to top.
SON OF GREAT CHIMNEY DIRECT, 5.12a. Same start. Instead of traverse to northwest corner, climb shallow dihedral in center of upper face.

53 MATCH THE SNATCH, 5.12a/b. Start on face near left corner 15 feet above base of Great Chimney. Climb up and left to corner. Pass overhang, then move up right for the snatch. Finish on Son of Great Chimney (route 52).

54 GREAT CHIMNEY, 5.3. Frequently used access route. There is a steep part at the bottom that is tricky.

Great Chimney to Lost Face (Diagram 11 W)

APPROACH: Refer to Approach for Big Toe to Great Chimney.

Waypoint 94: Lost Face
   UTM 16T 278339E 4811160N
Base Elevation (Lost Face): 1,370 feet
Top Elevation (Lost Face): 1,481 feet

ROUTES:
55 COUP D'ÉTAT, 5.11b. Start in zigzagging crack just left of Handle with Care (route 56). Continue straight up textured rock in thin crack.

56 HANDLE WITH CARE, 5.5. Climb flaky crack to platform. Continue in short chimney to top.

57 5.8. Start on face near chimney (route 58). Move left to ledge and follow crack to platform.

58 5.6. Narrow chimney. Stay outside chimney for better climbing.

59 5.6. Crack.

60 THE GOOD, THE BAD, AND THE JACKED, 5.12c. Start 3 feet right of corner on left edge of huge block. Climb past fixed pin and enjoy a dynamic move at top.

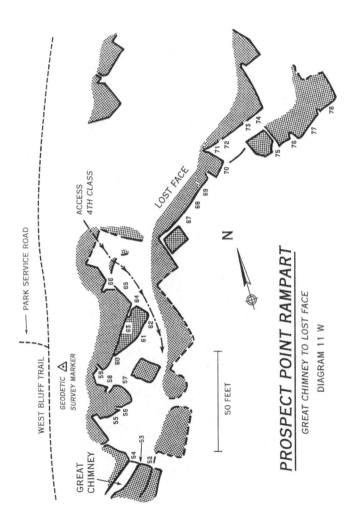

PROSPECT POINT RAMPART

GREAT CHIMNEY TO LOST FACE

DIAGRAM 11 W

61 CRACKER JACK, 5.8. Climb obvious 30-foot crack to top of huge block, then 10 feet (crux) to next ledge. Continue more easily to top.

62 MILKING THE BULL, 5.12c. Face with thin cracks and overhang at top.

Lost Face

Lost Face Overhang II (Diagram 11 W, route 67). Climber: Marcus Hall. Photo: Sven Olof Swartling.

63 WILD WEST HOMO, 5.11a. Overhanging face 10–15 feet right of The Good, The Bad, and The Jacked (route 60).

64 5.4. Narrow chimney.

65 WHIPPING BOY, 5.10c. Climb cracks.

66 5.4. Inside corner with crack.

67 LOST FACE, 5.6. The longest climb on the West Bluff. Start on slanting ledge. Climb crack system that leads fairly directly to niche in center of face. Climb inside corner of niche, then ledges. End at large ledge on south side of summit boulder.

Variation, LOST FACE OVERHANG I, 5.8. Before reaching niche, traverse left and climb right side of overhang 6 feet south of niche. Continue to large ledge.

Variation, LOST FACE OVERHANG II, 5.8. Before reaching niche, traverse left and climb overhang using crack 12 feet south of niche. Continue straight up to large ledge.

NOAH VAIL, 5.8. Start near north end of large block left of Lost Face. Climb face, then continue on Lost Face Overhang II.

CLOUT BUSTER, 5.6. Start behind large block left of Lost Face. Climb inside corner to top of block. Continue straight up or move right to face.

68 5.7. Thin crack that splits 5 feet up. The left crack joins Lost Face (route 67). The right crack ends at walk off halfway up north edge of face.

69 IBEX, 5.11a. Smooth section of face between crack (route 68) and north edge. Ends on narrow bulge 40 feet up.

70 DELICATE MOVES, 5.8. Separate steep slab with delicate moves, especially on the upper part near the north edge.

71 5.4. Chimney.

72 5.8. Start in niche. Climb overhang and crack.

73 5.7. Crack at north end of small overhang.

74 5.2. Crack used as an access route.

75–78 5.5–5.7. Short chimneys and faces.

Reclining Tower (Diagram 12 W)

APPROACH: Reclining Tower is located north of Prospect Point Rampart. Follow the West Bluff Trail 175 feet north of the geodetic survey marker to an access gully on the south side. There is a longer access north of Reclining Tower.

Waypoint 95: Access above Reclining Tower (on the West Bluff Trail)

UTM 16T 278324E 4811170N

Waypoint 96: Reclining Tower

UTM 16T 278363E 4811202N

Base Elevation: 1,372 feet

Top Elevation: 1,444 feet

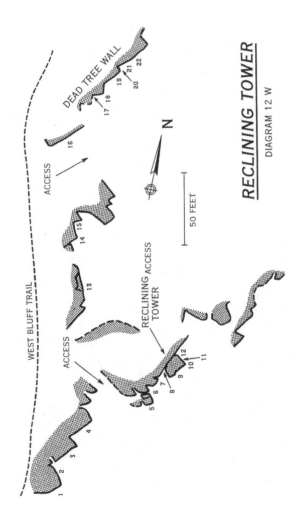

RECLINING TOWER

DIAGRAM 12 W

ROUTES:

1 5.2. Broken ledges.
2 5.6. Start under overhang, then continue in crack.
3 5.7. Climb just south of corner.
4 X-RATED, 5.10a. Start near northeast corner. Climb 8 feet up and left to flake under overhang. Move right toward corner, reach up for small projection, and retable. Continue on corner to top.

Reclining Tower

5 5.7. Climb east corner to base of small tower. Balance up left onto south corner. Climb corner to top of tower, then step over gap and climb short wall above.

6 5.7. Climb crack and V-chimney for 25 feet to ledge on right. Retable to next ledge. Continue up and right to third ledge, then to top.

7 TWO FLAKES, 5.6. Climb north edge of flakes, then join route 6.
DON'T TOUCH THE PINE, 5.9. Climb crack 4 feet right of Two Flakes. Halfway up, at small overhang, move slightly left and continue to top.

8 5.4. Chimney on south side of Reclining Tower. At one point you can squeeze behind the tower and reach the north side (route 12).

9 PINE TREE CRACK, 5.8. Start in inside corner. Climb crack and overhang 15 feet to large platform with pine tree. Continue on arête (5.6) to top of tower.

10 RECLINING TOWER ARÊTE, 5.11d. Climb lower difficult corner to large platform at 20 feet. Continue on arête (5.6) to top of tower.
Variation, 5.6. Start on route 12. At 20 feet, traverse left to large platform. Continue on arête (5.6) to top of tower.

11 SOLAR WIND, 5.11c. Climb short face to large platform just left of route 12.

12 5.6. Climb inside corner and deep, awkward crack on north side to top of tower.

Dead Tree Wall (Diagram 12 W)

Approach: Follow the West Bluff Trail 425 feet north of the geodetic survey marker (250 feet north of Reclining Tower) to Dead Tree Wall. An access gully is south of the formation.

Waypoint 97: Access above Dead Tree Wall (on the West Bluff Trail)
  UTM 16T 278310E 4811241N
Waypoint 98: Dead Tree Wall
  UTM 16T 278350E 4811254N
Base Elevation: 1,425 feet
Top Elevation: 1,472 feet

ROUTES:

13 TOUCH OF CLASS, 5.9. Climb face with two ledges.

14 GRASSY LEDGE, 5.7. Climb lower corner and upper wide cracks.

15 WALTZING MARY, 5.7. Start in inside corner. At 15 feet, move left, passing overhang on left. Continue in crack above.

Variation, 5.5. Follow inside corner to top.

16 5.6. Short face climb.

17 5.6. Inside corner.

18 AMAZING GRACE, 5.9. Climb onto detached block below first overhang. Pass overhang on right with a nice balance move. Pass upper overhang on left.

Variation, 5.12a. Climb upper overhang directly.

19 DEFEAT OF THE BOYS, 5.11c. Climb the shallow dihedral and tight seam 4–6 feet left of Dead Tree Climb (route 20).

20 DEAD TREE CLIMB, 5.8. Start in inside corner. Continue in wide crack that used to be home to a tree. The overhang below the wide crack is the crux.

21 THE CMC LIVES, 5.11c. Face and overhang between Dead Tree Climb (route 20) and Tardis (route 22).

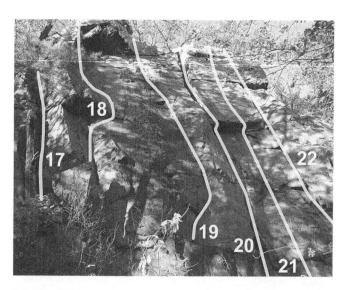

Dead Tree Wall

22 TARDIS, 5.10b. Thin crack 10 feet north of Dead Tree Climb (route 20).

Variation, 5.9. Start farther right (north). At 12 feet traverse left into crack system.

Cave Rocks Rampart (Diagram 13 W)

Cave Rocks Rampart descends northeast from Reclining Tower. The rampart is low for much of its length. The cave is about halfway down the bluff at the northeast end.

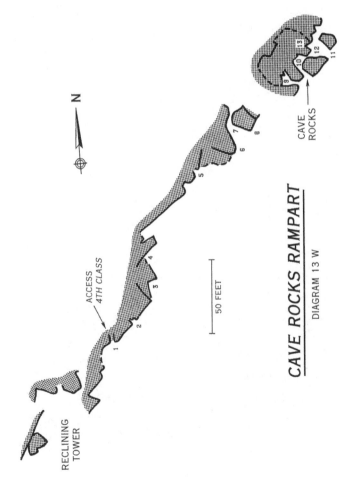

APPROACH: Refer to Approach for Reclining Tower and Diagram 13 W. Descend northeast from the lower (north) end of Reclining Tower.

Waypoint 99: Cave Rocks Rampart
  UTM 16T 278411E 4811269N
Base Elevation: 1,233 feet
Top Elevation: 1,254 feet

Cave Rocks Rampart. Photo: Pete Mayer.

Routes:

1 5.0. Access gully.

2 5.7. Broken wall with overhangs. There is some loose rock.

3 5.8. Corner.

4 5.4. Crack.

5 5.5. Climb short chimney to notch containing a tree. Continue on left or right side of notch.

6 THE CLAMSHELL, 5.6. Climb corner crack on south side of large chimney (route 7) to a pair of sharp-edged blocks that cover the chimney. Continue behind upper block or crawl between the two. Four feet below top of upper block, step over (south) to platform. Finish on wall above.

7 5.2. Large chimney.

8 5.5. Climb on south side of corner for 15 feet. Move right around corner and climb to top.

9 SOUTH ENCLOSURE, 5.7. Climb inside enclosure by stemming or laybacking.

10 NORTH ENCLOSURE, 5.6. Climb inside enclosure facing north. Layback using left-hand crack.

11–13 5.3–5.6. Short climbs.

Hangman Towers

Hangman Towers includes scattered rocks and towers above the Slant Boulderfield 100–500 feet north of Dead Tree Wall. The Hangman, Twin Ridge, Knobby Pillar, Birdbath Tower, The Beast, Go-Go Tower, and Shark's Tooth are all located on the upper half of the bluff within this general area.

The Hangman (No Diagram)

Approach: The Hangman is roughly midlevel on the bluff 100 feet above the Turtle. Refer to West Bluff Approaches, Tumbled Rocks Trail.

Waypoint 100: The Hangman
   UTM 16T 278448E 4811323N
Base Elevation: 1,172 feet
Top Elevation: 1,205 feet

Hangman Towers

ROUTES:
1 THE HANGMAN, 5.7. Deep inside corner and crack with
   overhang. Where the crack runs through the overhang it
   appears possible to hang by one's head. To avoid this possibility, use an incredibly dirty chockstone.
2 5.6. Southeast side of The Hangman (route 1). The climb
   starts from a block.

Twin Ridge (No Diagram)

APPROACH: *From above*—From Dead Tree Wall, follow the West Bluff Trail about 300 feet north. Twin Ridge is located 100–150 feet below. Twin Ridge is not visible from the trail. *From below*—From The Hangman, walk up and slightly south for 150 feet to the base of Twin Ridge. The north ridge starts

South Twin Ridge

at a lower level and is separated from the south ridge by a narrow gully.

Waypoint 101: Twin Ridge (at the base of the North Ridge)
   UTM 16T 278394E 4811327N
Base Elevation: 1,298 feet
Top Elevation: 1,348 feet

ROUTES:

1 NORTH TWIN RIDGE, 5.4. Climb as four or five short pitches, starting with two towers and a short wall that lead to a back-sloping platform called the Lunch Spot about 100 feet below the trail. Many variations are possible.

2 SOUTH TWIN RIDGE, 5.6. The base of the south ridge is a pair of detached blocks. Chimney up behind lower block (a tricky start) to base of imposing section. Continue on south side of corner.

3 NOWHERE LEDGE, 5.10a. Step onto diagonal ledge below imposing upper section of east face of south ridge. Move right on ledge and climb near northeast corner to platform above.
   Variation, 5.10a. Start lower, below northeast corner.

4 ONCE IS ENOUGH, 5.9. North side of south ridge. Climb cul-de-sac chimney into a hanging inside corner. Continue up corner to top.

5 SHARP EDGE, 5.8. Climb crack 3 feet right of Once Is Enough (route 4) to overhanging block. Pass block on right.

The low wall 25 feet west of the Lunch Spot has several nice climbs in the 5.5–5.8 range.

Knobby Pillar and Bird Bath Tower (No Diagram)

APPROACH: Knobby Pillar is a narrow tower located 50 feet southwest of the Lunch Spot on the North Twin Ridge. The top of the pillar is visible from the trail. Bird Bath Tower is a 25-foot tower located 60 feet south of the upper part of South Twin Ridge. Many variations exist besides the two routes listed below.

Waypoint 102: Bird Bath Tower
   UTM 16T 278367E 4811322N
Base Elevation: 1,369 feet

1   KNOBBY PILLAR, 5.4–5.8. Start at south corner or climb more difficult northeast overhang and corner.

2   BIRD BATH TOWER, 5.8. Climb the northeast side using the seemingly innocuous ledge halfway up.

Bird Bath Tower

The Beast (No Diagram)

APPROACH: From the base of the South Twin Ridge, walk south 100 feet, crossing a low rock ridge with a southeast-facing wall. The Beast is the 15-foot block sitting on top of a pedestal.

Waypoint 103: The Beast
UTM 16T 278376E 4811309N
Base Elevation: 1,343 feet
Top Elevation: 1,380 feet

ROUTES:

1 5.4. Climb obvious inside corner on east side of pedestal, then northeast corner of block.

The Beast

On a compact group of towers 40 feet south of The Beast there are three routes in the 5.5–5.7 range.

The low, southeast-facing wall just north of The Beast has a couple of interesting climbs.

Go-Go Tower (No Diagram)

APPROACH: Go-Go Tower is located 70 feet north of the Lunch Spot on North Twin Ridge. The top of the tower is visible from the trail.

Go-Go Tower

Waypoint 104: Go-Go Tower
   UTM 16T 278384E 4811359N
Base Elevation: 1,348 feet

ROUTES:
 1 5.7. Southeast face.
 2 GO-GO, 5.7. Southeast corner with interesting layback and dynamic moves.
 3 GOING, GOING, GONE, 5.9. Overhanging ledges on east side.
    Variation, 5.9. Between the second and third ledge, climb the northeast corner.

A small outcropping 75 feet above Go-Go Tower, 30 feet below the West Bluff Trail, has a couple of nice routes on the overhanging east face (5.9–5.11). A few easier routes can be found on either side of the overhanging face.

Shark's Tooth (No Diagram)

APPROACH: From Go-Go Tower, follow a faint path angling down and north to a band of rocks 80 feet long. Shark's Tooth is about a third of the way down the bluff, 200 feet north of Twin Ridge.

Waypoint 105: Shark's Tooth
   UTM 16T 278419E 4811378N
Base Elevation: 1,254 feet
·Top Elevation: 1,277 feet

ROUTES:
 1 SHARK'S TOOTH, 5.7. Tower at the upper (south) end of band. Climb V-chimney that starts above first ledge. Avoid little platform on north side of chimney.
 2 5.8. Northeast corner. Avoid ledge on left.
 3 THE PORPOISE, 5.4. Narrow, fin-shaped structure at lower (north) end of the band. It is easily climbed on the ridge, which is more solid than it appears.
 4 5.7. North side of the Porpoise. Climb center of face. The difficulty depends on how resolutely one stays on the face.

Shark's Tooth

5 5.8. The center section of the band consists of two shapeless buttresses. Climb south buttress on south corner or southeast face.

6 NERVES, 5.7. Southeast corner of north buttress.

Tree Tower (Diagram 14 W)

Tree Tower is located well north of Hangman Towers below the crest of the bluff, about 80 feet off the trail. It is quite easy to miss because of intervening trees. There is a small pine tree growing near its top.

Approach: *From the north*—The easiest and shortest approach is to follow the West Bluff Trail south about 2,400 feet from the northern trailhead. *From the south*—Tree Tower is located about 425 feet north of Go-Go Tower. This is about two-thirds of the way to the north end of the lake, 200 feet north of a small boulderfield that reaches almost to the West Bluff Trail. The access gully is a little south of Tree Tower.

Tree Tower

Waypoint 106: Above Tree Tower (on the West Bluff Trail)
    UTM 16T 278366E 4811496N
Waypoint 107: Tree Tower
    UTM 16T 278393E 4811495N
Base Elevation: 1,328 feet
Top Elevation: 1,384 feet

ROUTES:

1 TREE TOWER, 5.7. The traditional route on the tower. Start near lowest point. Climb ledges on east ridge to inside corner on northeast side. Climb this interesting inside corner with a peculiar rock splinter. Descend by route 3.

2 5.2. Southeast side broken by favorable vertical holds.

3 5.2. Flake on south side used as *descent route*.

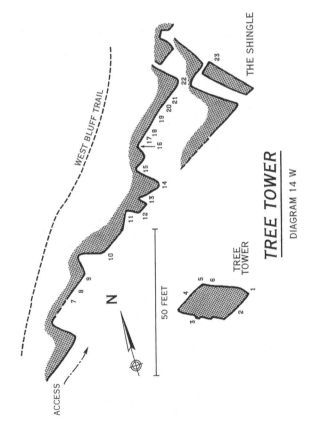

TREE TOWER

DIAGRAM 14 W

4 BOWLER'S GRIP, 5.8. Northwest side using (if possible) two finger holes below upper horizontal crack.

5 5.8. Start just left of the obtuse north corner. Climb diagonally up and left to ledge with block. Continue up short crack to ledge with pine tree.

6 TOON TOWN, 5.11c/d. Climb lower face a few feet left of obtuse corner to ledge. Continue straight up face without using block. This route crosses route 5 near the start.

7 5.8. Climb just left of small overhang.

8 5.8. Climb directly up small overhang.

9 5.7. Corner adjacent to recess.

10 5.4. Ledges adjacent to corner on north side of recess.

11–16 5.2–5.6. Chimneys and corners.

17 5.6. Layback crack.

18 FLYING INDIAN, 5.7. Climb crack using mostly finger and toe jams. Routes 17 and 18 are only a couple of feet apart. They are most interesting if kept separate.

19 SERENDIPITY, 5.11b/c. Face with thin holds and high steps.

20 TROUBLE, 5.9. Face with thin crack. Avoid moving right near top.

21 NO TROUBLE, 5.8. Climb thin crack past small overhang.

22 KOALA BEAR, 5.11a. Shinny up corner using holds on both sides.

23 THE SHINGLE, 5.10a. Narrow vertical formation below the main wall. Climb northwest corner adjacent to gap.

Cake Walk (No Diagram)

APPROACH: Cake Walk is a 30-foot summit wall located 150 feet south of Tree Tower above a small boulderfield. Refer to Approach for Tree Tower.

Waypoint 108: Cake Walk
  UTM 16T 278377E 4811470N
Base Elevation: 1,361 feet

ROUTES:

1 DER SCHNOZZEL, 5.8. Start just right of sharp corner. Step up onto corner, then climb from ledge to ledge until you reach the rock divot on right side. Continue in crack above divot. Please use the divot carefully and replace it for the next climber.

Cake Walk

2 CAKE WALK, 5.9. Start 4 feet left (south) of sharp corner, Der Schnozzel (route 1). Climb face to tight crack, then move up and left and follow offset crack to top.

3–5 5.4–5.6. Inside corner and face climbs on wall 20–40 feet south of Cake Walk (route 2).

Tyrolean Tower (No Diagram)

Tyrolean Tower is located 175 feet north of Tree Tower, 100 feet below a small, elevated vantage point along the crest of the bluff. It is barely visible from this point.

Approach: *From the north*—The easiest and shortest approach is from the north. Refer to Approach for Tree Tower. Tyrolean Tower is 325 feet south of the obvious vantage point. *From the south*—There is a short rise in the West Bluff Trail when approaching from the south that is distinguishable because the trail in this area has begun its slow descent to the north. The steep access gully is south of Tyrolean Tower.

Waypoint 109: Above Tyrolean Tower (on the West Bluff Trail)
    UTM 16T 278387E 4811559N

Waypoint 110: Tyrolean Tower
   UTM 16T 278412E 4811539N
Base Elevation: 1,307 feet

ROUTES:
I 5.3. Easy chimney on south side leading to gap behind
   20-foot summit block.

Tyrolean Tower

WEST BLUFF CLIMBS

2 5.10b. Face just right of chimney (route 1) also leading to gap behind summit block.

3 5.6. Start 15 feet right of chimney (route 1). Climb crack up and left into gap behind summit block.
Variation, 5.6. Climb partway up crack, then traverse right and climb to north platform level with gap behind summit block.

4 THE GAP, 5.8. Start in gap on southwest side of summit block. Climb thin crack for 5 feet, then move right to south corner and follow corner to top.
Variation, 5.9. Continue straight up above thin crack.

5 TYROLEAN TOWER, 5.10d. Start at base of tower. Climb southeast rounded corner and overhang to top.

6 FREE AT LAST, 5.9. From base of tower, climb lower inside corner, then right corner to ledge. Move left a few feet and continue up crack to north platform. Finish on north wall of summit block. There is no easy way off the tower.

The wall immediately southwest of Tyrolean Tower has three nice routes.

7 RIGHT EDGE, 5.7. Climb broken rock near right edge of wall to ledge. Move right a few feet and continue on upper southeast corner.

8 LONE PINE DIAGONAL, 5.8. Climb diagonal crack 8 feet left of Right Edge (route 7). Continue following crack when it becomes vertical about two-thirds of the way up.

9 LAST CRACK, 5.10c. Thin crack on left side of wall.

Pearly Gate (No Diagram)

Pearly Gate is a summit buttress 500 feet north of Tyrolean Tower with a distinctive inside corner. It is not visible from the West Bluff Trail.

APPROACH: *From the north*—Refer to Approach for By Gully. Pearly Gate is 200 feet south of By Gully. *From the south*—After the small, elevated vantage point above Tyrolean Tower the trail passes a second, larger, obvious vantage point. Continue an additional 150 feet north and look for a narrow, descending cleft that leads 25 feet east to the top of Pearly Gate.

Waypoint 111: Pearly Gate
UTM 16T 278429E 4811642N

Base Elevation: 1,295 feet
Top Elevation: 1,350 feet

ROUTES:

1 5.11a. North side of buttress. Start in crack and continue up north face to top.

2 5.7. Same start as route 1. Climb crack up and left to corner. Move left around corner and finish on east face with creaking flake.

Pearly Gate

WEST BLUFF CLIMBS

3 PEARLY GATE, 5.9. Climb obvious inside corner on east side of buttress.

4 ARM POWER, 5.11d. South corner. Start just left of corner. Climb face and overhang straight up to top.

5 5.7. South side of buttress. Climb left-angling crack. Pass overhang on left.

The buttress immediately to the south has a few easier climbs.

There is another outcropping 150 feet south of Pearly Gate at a lower level.

6 INCH WORM, 5.8. Climb shallow inside corner on southeast side past north end of overhang.

By Gully (No Diagram)

Approach: About 0.25 mile from the north end of the West Bluff Trail the trail dips and crosses the head of a large dirt gully. By Gully is on the north side of the gully, about 100 feet down. It consists of two buttresses.

Waypoint 112: By Gully
  UTM 16T 278462E 4811738N
Base Elevation: 1,232 feet
Top Elevation: 1,275 feet

Routes:
1 5.6. South corner and cracks of south buttress adjacent to gully. Start at slightly overhanging crack right of corner. Climb crack and then corner to top.

2 PEE-WEE'S INNOCENT, 5.12a. Climb center of overhanging southeast face of south buttress.

3 ROCK DIVOT, 5.9. North-facing wall of south buttress. Climb thin crack just right (west) of corner. A small rock divot hides one of the good holds.
  Variation, 5.9. Climb corner left of crack.

4 USE YOUR FEET, 5.8. North-facing wall of south buttress. Climb into obvious niche, then continue in cracks leading right or left of nose.

5 MOSS BE GONE, 5.9. Thin crack located 4 feet right of niche noted in Use Your Feet (route 4).

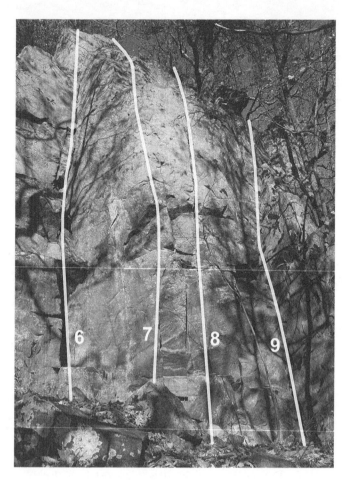

By Gully

6 5.6. South side of north buttress. Climb inside corner with crack.

7 NOT YET, 5.10b. Southeast corner of north buttress. Climb as close to corner as possible.

8 ARE WE HAVING FUN YET, 5.10d. Slightly overhanging southeast face of north buttress. Start directly below crack in upper part of face. Finish in upper crack.

9 5.4. Inside corner a couple of feet right (north) of Are We Having Fun Yet (route 8).

Hollywood and Vines (Diagram 15 W)

This summit band is located directly above the north shore of the lake and extends 400 feet along the West Bluff Trail. It is named for two towers below a recessed section in the northern part of the band. The eastern vine-covered tower is Hollywood; the other tower is Vines. Broken summit rocks continue north for 150 feet.

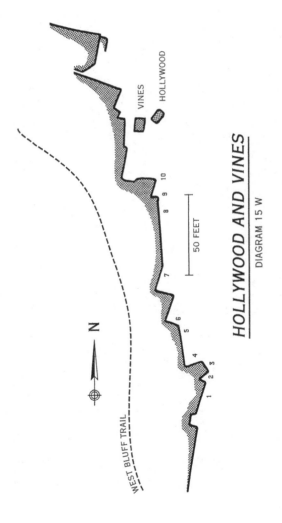

HOLLYWOOD AND VINES

DIAGRAM 15 W

Approach: Follow the West Bluff Trail south 850 feet from its north end to an access at the south end of Hollywood and Vines.

Waypoint 113: Hollywood and Vines
   UTM 16T 278491E 4811892N
Base Elevation: 1,237 feet
Top Elevation: 1,261 feet

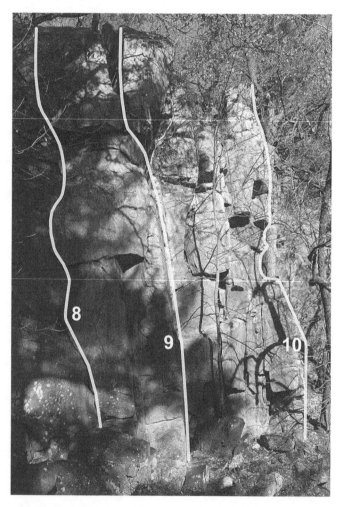

Hollywood and Vines

ROUTES:

1   5.7–5.9. Several variations are possible on this short face. It is harder on the left (south) side.

2   5.6. V-chimney with wide crack. Climb on left side of V or in right crack, first as a chimney, then on the outside when crack narrows and finally splits.

3   5.7. Start just left of corner and climb straight to top. *Variation*, 5.8. Same start, but finish in layback crack on right (north) side.

4   NEVER AGAIN, 5.8/9. This rating varies, depending on your fist size. Climb blocks leading to wider crack. Jam your way up crack.

5   5.10b. Climb lower and upper smooth faces directly. *Variation*, 5.8. Start on north side, then traverse around east corner to ledge. Finish on smooth upper face.

6   5.10a. Climb, staying on north side of corner.

7   5.7. There is a large oak tree, growing at an unnatural angle across the wall, that blocks the start of this climb as well as a couple of potential routes. Start by walking 4 feet up the trunk, then step on the wall/crack, or start at the base of the tree and traverse right to the crack.

8   5.6. Wall with three large flakes. Climb following flakes.

9   5.8. Climb corner accentuated by a reddish rib or prominence to an overhanging crack that, luckily, contains a chockstone (albeit a loose one).

10   5.8. Climb corner, using projecting rock finger at 20 feet for foothold. Then follow overhanging crack to top.

The Bottom (No Diagram)

APPROACH: The Bottom is a wall 30 feet high and 40 feet wide in a hidden spot east and below the south end of Hollywood and Vines. Refer to Approach for Hollywood and Vines. From the south end of Hollywood and Vines, walk east about 100 feet and follow a short ridge that extends downward (east) about 100 feet until it ends abruptly at The Bottom.

Waypoint 114: The Bottom
UTM 16T 278513E 4811831N
Base Elevation: 1,153 feet
Top Elevation: 1,187 feet

1 5.10a. Face and overhang 4 feet left of Left Cheek (route 2).
2 LEFT CHEEK, 5.8. South half of wall. Climb slight rib and crack with small overhang near top.
3 THE HEART, 5.10a. Climb face 4–5 feet right of Left Cheek (route 2). End at small notch.
4 5.4. Climb center crack. At ledge, step right and continue to top.

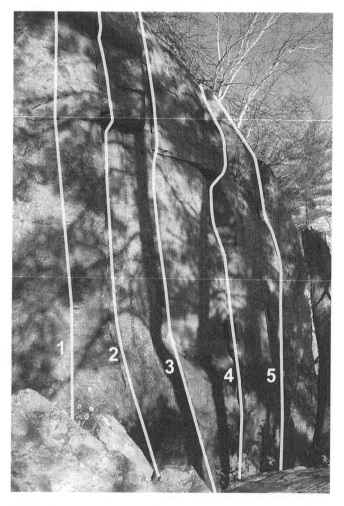

The Bottom

5 RIGHT CHEEK, 5.10a. North half of wall. Start 8 feet left of north corner. This is a fuzzy route on down-sloping ledges.

North Slope (Diagram 16 W)

APPROACH: North Slope is the last rock band along the West Bluff Trail, located 375 feet south of the north end of the West Bluff Trail. The elevation of the bluff as you proceed north decreases rather rapidly. The trail follows some slabs along the edge of the bluff.

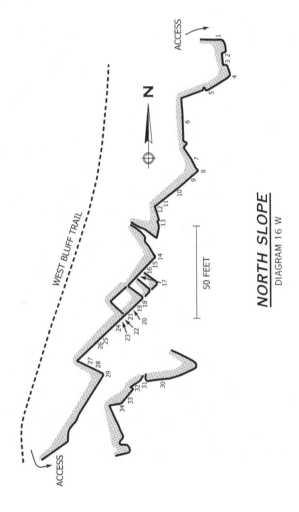

NORTH SLOPE
DIAGRAM 16 W

Waypoint 115: North Slope
  ·UTM 16T 278508E 4812035N
Base Elevation: 1,161 feet
Top Elevation: 1,212 feet

ROUTES:

1 FARTHEST NORTH, 5.5. North side of buttress near corner.
2 FERNIE, 5.8. Overhanging inside corner/crack.
3 5.8. Overhanging inside corner/crack.

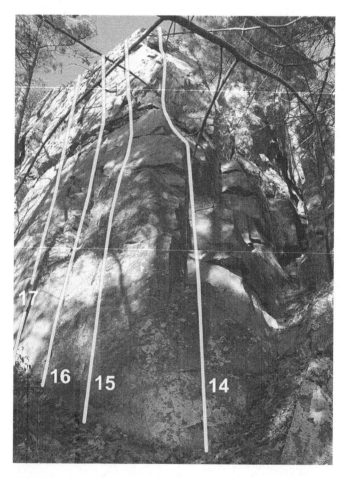

North Slope

4 5.7. East corner. Start from block and climb corner.
Variation, 5.6. Same start, but climb just right of corner.

5 DIVERGENT CRACK, 5.10a. Start on wall directly below crack in upper part of face. Continue in crack, which curves right near top. Avoid use of left corner.

6 5.7. Start in crack and climb past overhanging blocks. Finish in upper niche.

Routes 7–9 end below the top.

7 5.4. Crack.

8 5.6. Climb, staying close to leaning corner.

9 5.3. Wide diagonal crack 3–4 feet left of corner.

10 5.7. Start on first ledge. Climb toward crack in middle of upper face.

11 5.6. Start below small overhang 6–8 feet right of inside corner (route 12). Climb up and slightly left to top.

12 5.4. Dirty, blocky, inside corner.

13 5.7. Climb layback crack in inside corner. Continue on corner.

14 OIL SLICK, 5.7. Climb slightly overhanging ledges on or near corner.

15 5.7. Face between Oil Slick (route 14) and route 16. Join Oil Slick near top.

16 5.6. Crack 7 feet left of corner.

17 5.10a. Start 6 feet left of crack (route 16). Climb lower face without use of big holds on left. Several variations are possible above overhang.

Routes 18–20 end on platform below top.

18 SORE TOES, 5.7. Crack 3 feet left of corner.

19 5.5. Climb deeper crack with block.

20 5.6. Face with thin cracks.

21 5.5. Start in crack below high point of wall. Finish on shattered rock above.

22 5.5. Wide crack/chimney.

23 5.9. Face with thin/tight crack 1–2 feet left of route 22. Avoid use of wide crack (route 22).

24 5.3. Crack leading to large alcove.

25 5.6. Crack leading to inside corner.

26 5.6. Start 6 feet left of route 25. Climb to ledge, then in upper shallow inside corner.

27 5.7. Overhanging broken rock 4 feet left of overhanging wide crack.

28 5.6. Tight, slightly overhanging crack in open book.

29 FRACTURED, 5.8. Climb nose. Overhanging at the start. An easier start is 4 feet left of nose.

30 5.5. Face and ledges. Start at lowest point between wall and boulder.

31 5.4. Wide crack. Climb by stemming outside the crack.

32 5.4. Inside corner and crack.

33 DOWN SOUTH, 5.9. Narrow face with vertical cracks.

34 5.6. Climb crack and flakes 7 feet left of Down South (route 33).

The rocks farther south offer little interest to climbers.

SOUTH BLUFF CLIMBS

SOUTH BLUFF

One of the most rewarding features of the South Bluff is the superb view of the lake and of the East and West Bluffs. The area is rarely visited.

The climbs are concentrated on a cluster of small towers located in the boulderfield near the top of the bluff. The three main towers can be seen from the South Shore picnic area as well as from the East and West Bluffs. The short climbs should not be overlooked, as they offer a full day of climbing. The tallest tower is approximately 30 feet high.

At the base of the bluff below the towers there is a small abandoned quarry cut. In the winter, after a wet summer, natural springs in the quarry freeze, forming short ice walls.

South Bluff Towers (Diagram 1 S)

APPROACH: From the South Shore picnic area entrance road, walk east through the woods, parallel to the railroad track, to the small quarry cut. Turn south and climb the steep talus

South Bluff Towers

and tree-covered slope to the upper boulderfield. The towers are at the top of the boulderfield.

Waypoint 116: South Bluff quarry cut
  UTM 16T 279999E 4809508N
Waypoint 117: South Bluff Towers
  UTM 16T 279950E 4809297N
Base Elevation: 1,406 feet
Top Elevation: 1,433 feet

ROUTES:
I 5.7. Start climb below crack in upper part of face. Finish in small notch at top.

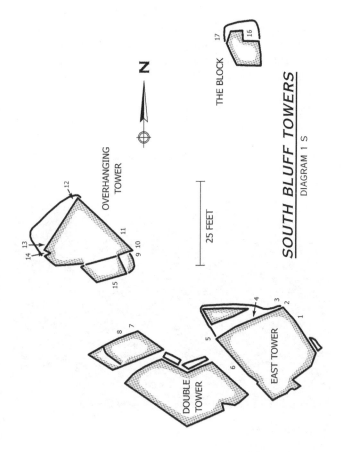

SOUTH BLUFF TOWERS
DIAGRAM 1 S

2 5.8. Climb, staying on corner to top.

3 MOSS MANTLE, 5.8. Climb just right of corner.

4 5.7. Start from ledge behind east end of block. Climb crack and corner.

5 5.7. Corner. Use only holds on or near corner. Several variations are possible.

6 5.4. Crack.

7 5.6. Start 4 feet right of corner below obvious layback crack. Climb straight to top.

8 WHEN DRY, 5.7. Climb lichen-covered wall to ledge and easy finish.

9 5.4. Climb just left of corner on nice ledges.

10 5.6. Start from ledge and climb right of corner. Joins route 9 near top.

11 5.11b. Thin crack in overhanging face.

12 5.9. Start from ledge 6–8 feet right of corner. As soon as possible traverse to corner and follow to top.

13 5.7. Face just left of corner.

14 5.3. V-chimney.

15 5.5–5.6. Face with several variations.

16 5.8. Climb small slab at base. Continue in jam crack. Move right at top.

17 5.6. Climb small slab at base. Follow jam crack to top.

BIBLIOGRAPHY

Armstrong, Patricia K. "Cryptogram Communities on Quartzite of Devil's Lake, Wisconsin." M.S. thesis, University of Chicago, 1968.

———. "Devil's Lake, Geological Showplace of the Midwest." *Earth Science* (May–June 1966): 112–15.

Attig, John W., Lee Clayton, Kenneth I. Lange, and Louis J. Maher. *The Ice Age Geology of Devil's Lake State Park.* Education Series 35. Madison: Geological and Natural History Survey, 1990.

Black, Robert F. "Geomorphology of Devil's Lake Area, Wisconsin." *Wisconsin Academy of Sciences, Arts and Letters* 56 (1967–68): 117–48.

———. "Ice-Wedge Casts of Wisconsin." *Wisconsin Academy of Sciences, Arts and Letters* 54 (1965): 187–222.

———. "Potholes and Associated Gravel of Devil's Lake State Park." *Wisconsin Academy of Sciences, Arts and Letters* 53 (1964): 165–75.

Curtis, John T. *The Vegetation of Wisconsin.* Madison: University of Wisconsin Press, 1959.

Dalziel, I. W. D., R. H. Dott, Jr., R. F. Black, and J. H. Zimmerman. *Geology of the Baraboo District, Wisconsin.* Information Circular 14. Madison: Geological and Natural History Survey, 1970.

Danzinger, Hillel M., and Kris Fulsaas, eds. *Mountaineering: Freedom of the Hills.* 7th ed. Seattle: Mountaineers Books, 2003.

Farris, Mike. *Rock Climbing Minnesota and Wisconsin.* Helena, MT: Falcon Publishing, 2000.

Fassett, Norman C. *Spring Flora of Wisconsin.* Madison: University of Wisconsin Press, 1931.

Fralick, Jack. "Rock Climbing in the Chicago Area: An Historical Guide." Manuscript, Chicago, 1941. 90 pp.

Hermacinski, Leo. *Extremist's Guide to Devil's Lake New Climbs.* Privately printed, 1985.

———. "Extremist's Guide to Devil's Lake New Climbs." Updated manuscript, 1992. 21 pp.

Knower, Jay. "Climbing Devil's Lake Wisconsin." Mountain Project. http://www.mountainproject.com/v/wisconsin/devils_lake/105729927 (last accessed February 21, 2007).

Lange, Kenneth I. *Ancient Rocks and Vanished Glaciers: A Natural History of Devil's Lake State Park, Wisconsin.* Stevens Point, WI: Worzalla Publishing Co., 1989.

Lange, Kenneth I., and Ralph T. Tuttle. *A Lake Where Spirits Live: A Human History of the Midwest's Most Popular Park.* Baraboo, WI: Baraboo Printing, 1975.

Plumley, William J. "Rock Climbing in the Chicago Area." Manuscript, Chicago, 1941. 55 pp.

Primak, William. *Guidebook to the Local Practice Climbing Areas of the Chicago Mountaineering Club, Devil's Lake Section.* Chicago: Chicago Mountaineering Club, 1965.

Smith, David, and Roger Zimmerman. *Climbers and Hikers Guide to Devil's Lake.* Madison: Wisconsin Hoofers, 1970.

GPS WAYPOINTS

Latitude and Longitude

East Bluff Climbs

Sandstone Bluff

1 Parking for Old Sandstone Area	N 43°24.713′ W 089°41.247′
2 Old Sandstone Area	N 43°24.809′ W 089°41.166′
3 On road below New Sandstone Area	N 43°24.631′ W 089°40.773′
4 New Sandstone Area	N 43°24.694′ W 089°40.799′

East of the Quarry Rocks

5 On road below Siamese Buttress	N 43°24.701′ W 089°41.570′
6 Siamese Buttress	N 43°24.777′ W 089°41.553′
7 Prayer Wall	N 43°24.777′ W 089°41.598′
8 Rattlesnake Ridge	N 43°24.775′ W 089°41.618′
9 Bandshell Ridge	N 43°24.771′ W 089°41.675′
10 Mousehole Buttress	N 43°24.761′ W 089°41.720′
11 Condor Corner	N 43°24.784′ W 089°41.742′
12 Bastille Rock	N 43°24.765′ W 089°41.751′
13 On road below Aladdin's Castle	N 43°24.681′ W 089°41.793′
14 Aladdin's Castle	N 43°24.776′ W 089°41.842′
15 U-Haul Overhangs	N 43°24.753′ W 089°41.822′
16 On Ice Age Trail/Upland Trail above September Wall	N 43°24.822′ W 089°42.044′
17 September Wall	N 43°24.789′ W 089°42.031′
18 February Wall	N 43°24.845′ W 089°41.874′

West of the Quarry Rocks

19 On road below Crashing Rock Wall	N 43°24.662′ W 089°42.330′
20 Crashing Rock Wall	N 43°24.732′ W 089°42.307′
21 Lost Temple Rock	N 43°24.729′ W 089°42.290′
22 Farewell to Arms	N 43°24.743′ W 089°42.318′
23 Pitchfork Tower	N 43°24.747′ W 089°42.318′
24 Red Nose Wall	N 43°24.766′ W 089°42.303′
25 Vulture Lookout	N 43°24.774′ W 089°42.253′
26 Hidden Buttress	N 43°24.717′ W 089°42.390′
27 Juniper Wall	N 43°24.730′ W 089°42.372′
28 White Wall	N 43°24.737′ W 089°42.414′
29 Poison Ivy Wall	N 43°24.742′ W 089°42.380′

| 30 | Bird-Foot Buttress | N 43°24.756′ W 089°42.392′ |
| 31 | West Post | N 43°24.768′ W 089°42.478′ |

The Guillotine

32	CCC Parking Area	N 43°24.660′ W 089°42.645′
33	No Sweat	N 43°24.768′ W 089°42.701′
34	Guillotine Wall	N 43°24.785′ W 089°42.709′
35	The Guillotine	N 43°24.791′ W 089°42.702′

East Rampart

36	The Monster	N 43°24.800′ W 089°42.724′
37	D'Arcy's Buttress	N 43°24.813′ W 089°42.734′
38	Pedestal Buttress	N 43°24.809′ W 089°42.763′
39	Gill's Buttress and Brinton's Buttress	N 43°24.807′ W 089°42.776′
40	Two Pines Buttress	N 43°24.819′ W 089°42.797′
41	Many Pines Buttress	N 43°24.821′ W 089°42.818′
42	Bill's Buttress	N 43°24.807′ W 089°42.848′
43	Bottom of Leaning Tower Gully	N 43°24.811′ W 089°42.902′
44	Rainy Wednesday Tower	N 43°24.812′ W 089°42.866′
45	Four Brothers	N 43°24.792′ W 089°42.889′
46	Leaning Tower	N 43°24.822′ W 089°42.908′
47	Pseudo Hawk's Nest	N 43°24.803′ W 089°42.905′
48	Hawk's Nest	N 43°24.807′ W 089°42.942′

Doorway Rocks

49	Top of gully east of Major Mass	N 43°24.853′ W 089°43.183′
50	Major Mass, Upper Band	N 43°24.849′ W 089°43.202′
51	Major Mass, Lower Band	N 43°24.826′ W 089°43.185′
52	Minor Mass	N 43°24.831′ W 089°43.150′
53	Red Rocks	N 43°24.833′ W 089°43.093′
54	Access gully above Ramsay's Pinnacle	N 43°24.885′ W 089°43.271′
55	Ramsay's Pinnacle	N 43°24.856′ W 089°43.235′

Balanced Rock Areas

56	Balanced Rock Wall	N 43°24.848′ W 089°43.513′
57	Liederkranz	N 43°24.856′ W 089°43.479′
58	Hole-In-The-Wall	N 43°24.854′ W 089°43.419′
59	Top of The Slab	N 43°24.844′ W 089°43.334′
60	The Effie	N 43°24.848′ W 089°43.332′

Railroad Tracks Areas

61	Railroad Amphitheater	N 43°25.087′ W 089°43.634′
62	Birthday Rocks	N 43°25.022′ W 089°43.614′
63	Horse Rampart	N 43°25.000′ W 089°43.567′
64	Squirrel's Nest Tower	N 43°24.930′ W 089°43.542′

North End of the East Bluff

65	Elephant Rocks	N 43°25.533′ W 089°43.515′
66	Tomahawk Rocks	N 43°25.497′ W 089°43.493′
67	Monolith Blocks	N 43°25.367′ W 089°43.465′

Steinke Basin Rocks

68	Cibola Wall	N 43°25.397′ W 089°42.919′
69	Triple Tower Wall	N 43°25.573′ W 089°43.083′
70	Steinke Wall	N 43°25.626′ W 089°43.124′
71	Storm Wrack Wall	N 43°25.762′ W 089°43.366′

West Bluff Climbs

72	Old West Bluff Trailhead	N 43°24.824′ W 089°44.363′
73	Stettner Rocks	N 43°24.873′ W 089°44.376′
74	Lincoln's Chair	N 43°24.937′ W 089°44.340′
75	Climbers' Trail to Misery Rocks	N 43°25.008′ W 089°44.451′
76	On Cottage Grove Road below Misery Gully	N 43°24.958′ W 089°44.269′
77	Misery Rocks	N 43°24.986′ W 089°44.341′
78	The Pantry	N 43°24.970′ W 089°44.319′
79	The Frigate	N 43°24.998′ W 089°44.323′
80	Dungeon Wall	N 43°24.997′ W 089°44.306′
81	Porkchop Buttress	N 43°24.995′ W 089°44.288′
82	Split Tower	N 43°25.022′ W 089°44.269′
83	Cleo Amphitheater	N 43°25.043′ W 089°44.309′
84	Turk's Head	N 43°25.055′ W 089°44.275′
85	The Blade	N 43°25.112′ W 089°44.268′
86	Turk's Head Ridge at the First Pitch	N 43°25.039′ W 089°44.243′
87	Prospect Point Towers	N 43°25.138′ W 089°44.232′
88	Above Prospect Point Pinnacle	N 43°25.177′ W 089°44.328′
89	Prospect Point Pinnacle	N 43°25.167′ W 089°44.305′
90	Big Toe	N 43°25.197′ W 089°44.293′
91	Dark Wall	N 43°25.171′ W 089°44.279′
92	Emergency Call Box	N 43°25.224′ W 089°44.308′
93	Great Chimney	N 43°25.207′ W 089°44.297′
94	Lost Face	N 43°25.233′ W 089°44.291′
95	Access above Reclining Tower	N 43°25.238′ W 089°44.302′
96	Reclining Tower	N 43°25.256′ W 089°44.274′
97	Access above Dead Tree Wall	N 43°25.276′ W 089°44.314′
98	Dead Tree Wall	N 43°25.284′ W 089°44.285′
99	Cave Rocks Rampart	N 43°25.293′ W 089°44.240′
100	The Hangman	N 43°25.323′ W 089°44.214′
101	Twin Ridge	N 43°25.324′ W 089°44.254′
102	Bird Bath Tower	N 43°25.321′ W 089°44.274′
103	The Beast	N 43°25.314′ W 089°44.267′
104	Go-Go Tower	N 43°25.341′ W 089°44.262′

105	Shark's Tooth	N 43°25.352′ W 089°44.237′
106	Above Tree Tower	N 43°25.415′ W 089°44.279′
107	Tree Tower	N 43°25.415′ W 089°44.259′
108	Cake Walk	N 43°25.401′ W 089°44.270′
109	Above Tyrolean Tower	N 43°25.449′ W 089°44.265′
110	Tyrolean Tower	N 43°25.439′ W 089°44.246′
111	Pearly Gate	N 43°25.495′ W 089°44.236′
112	By Gully	N 43°25.547′ W 089°44.214′
113	Hollywood and Vines	N 43°25.631′ W 089°44.196′
114	The Bottom	N 43°25.598′ W 089°44.178′
115	North Slope	N 43°25.708′ W 089°44.187′

South Bluff Climbs

| 116 | South Bluff quarry cut | N 43°24.371′ W 089°43.022′ |
| 117 | South Bluff Towers | N 43°24.256′ W 089°43.053′ |

Universal Transverse Mercator (UTM)

East Bluff Climbs

Sandstone Bluff

1	Parking for Old Sandstone Area	UTM 16T 282415E 4810064N
2	Old Sandstone Area	UTM 16T 282530E 4810238N
3	On road below New Sandstone Area	UTM 16T 283049E 4809891N
4	New Sandstone Area	UTM 16T 283018E 4810009N

East of the Quarry Rocks

5	On road below Siamese Buttress	UTM 16T 281978E 4810055N
6	Siamese Buttress	UTM 16T 282006E 4810195N
7	Prayer Wall	UTM 16T 281945E 4810197N
8	Rattlesnake Ridge	UTM 16T 281918E 4810195N
9	Bandshell Ridge	UTM 16T 281841E 4810190N
10	Mousehole Buttress	UTM 16T 281779E 4810173N
11	Condor Corner	UTM 16T 281751E 4810217N
12	Bastille Rock	UTM 16T 281738E 4810182N
13	On road below Aladdin's Castle	UTM 16T 281676E 4810028N
14	Aladdin's Castle	UTM 16T 281616E 4810206N
15	U-Haul Overhangs	UTM 16T 281641E 4810163N
16	On Ice Age Trail/Upland Trail above September Wall	UTM 16T 281346E 4810300N
17	September Wall	UTM 16T 281361E 4810239N
18	February Wall	UTM 16T 281576E 4810335N

West of the Quarry Rocks

19	On road below Crashing Rock Wall	UTM 16T 280950E 4810017N
20	Crashing Rock Wall	UTM 16T 280985E 4810145N
21	Lost Temple Rock	UTM 16T 281008E 4810139N
22	Farewell to Arms	UTM 16T 280971E 4810166N

23 Pitchfork Tower	UTM 16T 280971E 4810173N
24 Red Nose Wall	UTM 16T 280993E 4810208N
25 Vulture Lookout	UTM 16T 281061E 4810220N
26 Hidden Buttress	UTM 16T 280872E 4810121N
27 Juniper Wall	UTM 16T 280898E 4810144N
28 White Wall	UTM 16T 280841E 4810159N
29 Poison Ivy Wall	UTM 16T 280887E 4810167N
30 Bird-Foot Buttress	UTM 16T 280872E 4810193N
31 West Post	UTM 16T 280757E 4810219N

The Guillotine

32 CCC Parking Area	UTM 16T 280525E 4810027N
33 No Sweat	UTM 16T 280456E 4810229N
34 Guillotine Wall	UTM 16T 280446E 4810261N
35 The Guillotine	UTM 16T 280456E 4810272N

East Rampart

36 The Monster	UTM 16T 280427E 4810289N
37 D'Arcy's Buttress	UTM 16T 280414E 4810314N
38 Pedestal Buttress	UTM 16T 280375E 4810308N
39 Gill's Buttress and Brinton's Buttress	UTM 16T 280357E 4810305N
40 Two Pines Buttress	UTM 16T 280329E 4810328N
41 Many Pines Buttress	UTM 16T 280301E 4810332N
42 Bill's Buttress	UTM 16T 280260E 4810308N
43 Bottom of Leaning Tower Gully	UTM 16T 280187E 4810317N
44 Rainy Wednesday Tower	UTM 16T 280236E 4810318N
45 Four Brothers	UTM 16T 280204E 4810282N
46 Leaning Tower	UTM 16T 280180E 4810338N
47 Pseudo Hawk's Nest	UTM 16T 280183E 4810303N
48 Hawk's Nest	UTM 16T 280133E 4810312N

Doorway Rocks

49 Top of gully east of Major Mass	UTM 16T 279811E 4810408N
50 Major Mass, Upper Band	UTM 16T 279785E 4810401N
51 Major Mass, Lower Band	UTM 16T 279806E 4810358N
52 Minor Mass	UTM 16T 279854E 4810365N
53 Red Rocks	UTM 16T 279931E 4810367N
54 Access gully above Ramsay's Pinnacle	UTM 16T 279694E 4810471N
55 Ramsay's Pinnacle	UTM 16T 279741E 4810415N

Balanced Rock Areas

56 Balanced Rock Wall	UTM 16T 279365E 4810413N
57 Liederkranz	UTM 16T 279411E 4810426N
58 Hole-In-The-Wall	UTM 16T 279492E 4810420N
59 Top of The Slab	UTM 16T 279606E 4810398N
60 The Effie	UTM 16T 279609E 4810405N

Railroad Tracks Areas

61	Railroad Amphitheater	UTM 16T 279216E 4810861N
62	Birthday Rocks	UTM 16T 279239E 4810739N
63	Horse Rampart	UTM 16T 279301E 4810697N
64	Squirrel's Nest Tower	UTM 16T 279331E 4810566N

North End of the East Bluff

65	Elephant Rocks	UTM 16T 279404E 4811681N
66	Tomahawk Rocks	UTM 16T 279431E 4811613N
67	Monolith Blocks	UTM 16T 279461E 4811371N

Steinke Basin Rocks

68	Cibola Wall	UTM 16T 280200E 4811403N
69	Triple Tower Wall	UTM 16T 279989E 4811736N
70	Steinke Wall	UTM 16T 279937E 4811836N
71	Storm Wrack Wall	UTM 16T 279619E 4812098N

West Bluff Climbs

72	Old West Bluff Trailhead	UTM 16T 278217E 4810406N
73	Stettner Rocks	UTM 16T 278202E 4810497N
74	Lincoln's Chair	UTM 16T 278254E 4810614N
75	Climbers' Trail to Misery Rocks	UTM 16T 278109E 4810751N
76	On Cottage Grove Road below Misery Gully	UTM 16T 278352E 4810650N
77	Misery Rocks	UTM 16T 278256E 4810705N
78	The Pantry	UTM 16T 278285E 4810674N
79	The Frigate	UTM 16T 278281E 4810726N
80	Dungeon Wall	UTM 16T 278304E 4810724N
81	Porkchop Buttress	UTM 16T 278328E 4810719N
82	Split Tower	UTM 16T 278355E 4810768N
83	Cleo Amphitheater	UTM 16T 278303E 4810809N
84	Turk's Head	UTM 16T 278349E 4810830N
85	The Blade	UTM 16T 278362E 4810935N
86	Turk's Head Ridge at the First Pitch	UTM 16T 278392E 4810799N
87	Prospect Point Towers	UTM 16T 278412E 4810981N
88	Above Prospect Point Pinnacle	UTM 16T 278285E 4811058N
89	Prospect Point Pinnacle	UTM 16T 278316E 4811038N
90	Big Toe	UTM 16T 278334E 4811093N
91	Dark Wall	UTM 16T 278351E 4811045N
92	Emergency Call Box	UTM 16T 278315E 4811144N
93	Great Chimney	UTM 16T 278329E 4811112N
94	Lost Face	UTM 16T 278339E 4811160N
95	Access above Reclining Tower	UTM 16T 278324E 4811170N
96	Reclining Tower	UTM 16T 278363E 4811202N
97	Access above Dead Tree Wall	UTM 16T 278310E 4811241N
98	Dead Tree Wall	UTM 16T 278350E 4811254N

99	Cave Rocks Rampart	UTM 16T 278411E 4811269N
100	The Hangman	UTM 16T 278448E 4811323N
101	Twin Ridge	UTM 16T 278394E 4811327N
102	Bird Bath Tower	UTM 16T 278367E 4811322N
103	The Beast	UTM 16T 278376E 4811309N
104	Go-Go Tower	UTM 16T 278384E 4811359N
105	Shark's Tooth	UTM 16T 278419E 4811378N
106	Above Tree Tower	UTM 16T 278366E 4811496N
107	Tree Tower	UTM 16T 278393E 4811495N
108	Cake Walk	UTM 16T 278377E 4811470N
109	Above Tyrolean Tower	UTM 16T 278387E 4811559N
110	Tyrolean Tower	UTM 16T 278412E 4811539N
111	Pearly Gate	UTM 16T 278429E 4811642N
112	By Gully	UTM 16T 278462E 4811738N
113	Hollywood and Vines	UTM 16T 278491E 4811892N
114	The Bottom	UTM 16T 278513E 4811831N
115	North Slope	UTM 16T 278508E 4812035N

South Bluff Climbs

| 116 | South Bluff quarry cut | UTM 16T 279999E 4809508N |
| 117 | South Bluff Towers | UTM 16T 279950E 4809297N |

INDEX OF CLIMBS AND AREAS

NOTE: *Climbing ratings appear in italics and precede page numbers.*